AGRICULTURAL PRACTICES AND CROP DISEASE CONTROL

ENV BOOKS SERIES

AGRICULTURAL PRACTICES AND CROP DISEASE CONTROL

Editors

Dr. Alka Chauhan

Society for Environment, Health, Awareness of Nutrition & Toxicology (SEHAT)
1775, Sohan Ganj, Near Clock Tower
Delhi - 110 007 (INDIA)

Dr. Anubhuti Sharma

Senior Scientist in Directorate of Rapeseed-Mustard Research (ICAR Institute)
Sewar, Bhuratpur
Rajasthan
(INDIA)

Series Editor

Dr. Pawan Kumar 'Bharti'

Vice President
Society for Environment, Health, Awareness of Nutrition & Toxicology (SEHAT)
1775, Sohan Ganj, Near Clock Tower
Delhi - 110 007
(INDIA)
E-mail: gurupawanbharti@gmail.com

DPH

DISCOVERY PUBLISHING HOUSE PVT. LTD.
INDIA

Published by:

Namit Wasan

DISCOVERY PUBLISHING HOUSE PVT. LTD.

4383/4B, Ansari Road, Darya Ganj
New Delhi-110 002 (India)
Phone : +91-11-23279245, 43596064-65
Fax : +91-11-23253475
E-mail : discoverypublishinghouse@gmail.com
namitwasan9@gmail.com
sales@discoverypublishinggroup.com
website: www.discoverypublishinggroup.com

***First Edition:* 2017**

ISBN: 978-93-5056-859-0

Agricultural Practices and Crop Disease Control

Printed at:
Infinity Imaging Systems
Delhi

ENV Books Series, (India)

Calls lengthy and error free chapters for further volumes of books on various environmental issues. (Send your manuscripts to envbooks@gmail.com)

Founding Editor (Editor-in-Chief)

Dr. Pawan Kumar 'Bharti'

Society for Environment, Health, Awareness of Nutrition & Toxicology (SEHAT-India)
1775, Sohanganj, Near Clock Tower, Delhi-7, (India)
E-mail:*gurupawanbharti@rediffmail.com*

Other Titles by Editor-in-Chief:

1. **Advances in Biotechnology and Ecological Sciences**
   Bharti, P.K., Chauhan, A. and Ray, J. (eds.)
   (ISBN: 978-93-5056-358-8).
2. **Advances in Agriculture and Ecology**
   Bharti, P.K.; Chauhan, A. and Ezeaku Peter Ikemefuna (eds.)
   (ISBN: 978-93-5056-362-5).
3. **Agriculture and Environmental Biotechnology**
   Bharti, P.K. and Chauhan, A. (eds.)
   (ISBN: 978-93-5056-479-0).
4. **Agriculture Development and Sustainable Environment**
   Ray, J. and Bharti, P.K. (eds.)
   (ISBN: 978-93-5056-759-3).
5. **Agriculture Ecology and Environment**
   Bharti, P.K. and Olubukola O. Babalola (eds.)
   (ISBN: 978-93-5056-480-6).
6. **Agriculture Ecology, Sustainable Development and Agribusiness Management**
   Mehta Piyush; Sharma Pankaj; and 'Bharti' P.K. (eds.)
   (ISBN: 978-93-5056-851-4).
7. **Agriculture, Environment and Nano-science**
   Bharti, Pawan K. (ed.)
   (ISBN: 978-93-5056-760-5).

8. **Agro-biodiversity:** ***Conservation & Sustainable Development***
Sharma, Pankaj; Singh, Narayan; and Bharti, P.K. (eds.)
(ISBN: 978-93-505-782-1).

9. **Agro-forestry and Climate Change**
Bharti, Pawan K. and Singh, Narayan (eds.)
(ISBN: 978-93-5056-514-8).

10. **Agro-forestry and Sustainable Agriculture**
Sharma, Pankaj; Bharti, P.K. (eds.)
(ISBN: 978-93-5056-786-9).

11. **Aquaculture and Fisheries Environment**
Gupta, S.K. and Pawan K. Bharti (eds.)
(ISBN: 978-93-5056-408-0).

12. **Aquatic Biodiversity and Pollution**
Bharti, P.K.; Chauhan, A. and Kaoud, H.A.H. (eds.)
(ISBN: 978-93-5056-359-5).

13. **Aquatic Ecology and Biotechnology**
Bharti, P.K. and Zaki, M.S.A. (eds.)
(ISBN: 978-93-5056-451-6).

14. **Aquatic Environment and Toxicology**
Bharti, Pawan K. (ed.)
(ISBN: 978-93-5056-236-9).

15. **Biodiversity, Biotechnology and Environmental Conservation**
Bharti, P.K. and Bhandari, G. (eds.)
(ISBN: 978-93-5056-750-0).

16. **Biodiversity of Aquatic Ecosystem:** ***Significance, Threat and Conservation*** **(2013)**
Bharti, P.K. and Kaoud, H.A.H. (eds.)
(ISBN: 978-93-5056-297-0).

17. **Biological Diversity and Ecology**
Arya, M.K.; Bharti, P.K. and Ritesh Joshi (eds.)
(ISBN: 978-93-5056-785-2).

18. **Bioremediation and Microbial Biotechnology**
Gupta, Sandeep; and Bharti, P.K. (eds.)
(ISBN: 978-93-5056-783-8).

19. **Biotechnological Approaches & Water Ecosystem**
Zaki, M.S.A.; and Bharti, P.K. (eds.)
(ISBN: 978-93-5056-779-1).

20. **Biotechnology, Agro-ecology and Environment**
Chauhan, Avnish and Bharti, P.K. (eds.)
(ISBN: 978-93-5056-757-9).

21. **Clean Technologies and Environmental Protection**
Chauhan, A.; Sharma, S. and Bharti, P.K. (eds.)
(ISBN: 978-93-5056-731-9).

22. **Climate Change and Agriculture**
Bharti, P.K. and Chauhan, Avnish (eds.)
(ISBN: 978-93-5056-148-5).

23. **Climate Change and Biodiversity**
Bharti, P.K. and Chauhan, Avnish (eds.)
(ISBN: 978-93-5056-360-1).

24. **Climate Change, Disaster Management and Environment**
Chauhan, Alka; Bharti, P.K. (eds.)
(ISBN: 978-93-5056-784-5).

25. **Conservation and Cultivation of Medicinal Plants**
Bharti, P.K. and Singh Narayan (eds.)
(ISBN: 978-93-5056-740-1).

26. **Crop Productivity and Plant Disease Management**
Chauhan, Alka; Bharti, P.K. and Sadana, Deepti (eds.)
(ISBN: 978-93-5056-791-3).

27. **Eco-toxicology and Eco-technology**
Bharti, P.K. and Zaki, M. (eds.)
(ISBN: 978-93-5056-313-7).

28. **Environmental Biotechnology and Application**
Bharti, P.K. and Chauhan, Avnish (eds.)
(ISBN: 978-93-5056-262-8).

29. **Environmental Conservation and Biotechnology**
Chauhan, A. and P.K. Bharti (eds.)
(ISBN: 978-93-5056-512-4).

30. **Environmental Health and Problems**
Bharti, P.K. and Gajananda, Kh. (eds.)
(ISBN: 978-93-5056-263-5).

31. **Environmental Pollution and Biodiversity**
Bharti, P.K.; Chauhan, Avnish and Kumar, P. (eds.)
(ISBN: 978-93-5056-149-2).

32. **Farming Techniques and Crop Production**
Chauhan Alka; Sharma Anubhuti; Ray Jaswant and 'Bharti' P.K. (eds.)
(ISBN: 978-93-5056-855-2).

33. **Fisheries and Toxicology**
Zaki, M.S.A.; Bharti, P.K. and Chauhan, A. (eds.)
(ISBN: 978-93-5056-452-3).

34. **Fish Habitat and Aquaculture**
Bharti, P.K.; Gupta Kr. Sanjay (eds.)
(ISBN: 978-93-5056-744-9).

35. **Food Processing, Management and Nanotechnology**
Chauhan, Avnish; Bharti, P.K. (eds.)
(ISBN: 978-93-5056-796-8).

36. **Freshwater Ecosystem and Xenobiotics**
Bharti, P.K.; Zaki, M. and Chauhan, A. (eds.)
(ISBN: 978-93-5056-299-4).

37. **Limnology and Aquatic Science**
Sharma, S. and Bharti, P.K. (eds.)
(ISBN: 978-93-5056-735-7).

38. **Medicinal Plants: *Distribution, Utilization & Significance***
Sharma, P.; Bharti, P.K. and Narayan Singh (eds.)
(ISBN: 978-93-5056-734-0).

39. **Microbial Applications and Environment**
Bharti, Pawan K. (ed.)
(ISBN: 978-93-5056-515-5).

40. **Microbial Ecology and Habitat**
Bharti, Pawan K. (ed.)
(ISBN: 978-93-5056-514-8).

41. **Microbial Environment and Bioremediation**
Chauhan Alka; K. Rathoure Ashok; and K Maheshwari Raaz (eds.)
(ISBN: 978-93-5056-856-9).

42. **Natural Ecosystem and Climate Change**
Bharti, P.K., and Kh. Gajananda (ed.)
(ISBN: 978-93-5056-745-6).

43. **Pest Management and Agro-Techniques**
Biswas, Asim; Bharti, P.K., Chauhan, Avnish (eds.)
(ISBN: 978-93-5056-794-4).

44. **Prakriti me Aushadhi (*in Hindi*)**
Singh, J.R.; Bharti, P.K. and Bharti, B.
(ISBN: 978-93-5056-200-0).

45. **Seed Technology, Plant Growth and Cropping System**
Tyagi, P.K. and Bharti, P.K. (eds.)
(ISBN: 978-93-5056-738-8).

46. **Seed Treatment, Plant Heath and Agro-technology**
Chauhan, A. and Bharti, P.K. (eds.)
(ISBN: 978-93-5056-810-1).

47. **Soil Characteristics and Agro-ecology**
Avnish Chauhan and Bharti, P.K. (eds.)
(ISBN: 978-93-5056-758-6).

48. **Soil Contamination and Conservation**
Ezeaku, P.I. and Bharti, P.K. (eds.)
(ISBN: 978-93-5056-737-1).

49. **Soil Quality and Contamination**
Bharti, P.K. and Chauhan, Avnish (eds.)
(ISBN: 978-93-5056-361-8).

50. **Sustainable Aquaculture Management**
Gupta, S.K.; Bharti, P.K (eds.)
(ISBN: 978-93-5056-797-5).

51. **Waste Disposal and Management**
Bharti, P.K.; Tabassum, B. and Bajaj, P. (eds.)
(ISBN: 978-93-5056-729-6).

52. **Waste Generation and Utilization**
Bajaj Priya; Tabassum, B., and Bharti, P.K. (eds.)
(ISBN: 978-93-5056-792-0).

53. **Waste Management and Environmental Health**
Tabassum, B., Bajaj Priya, and Bharti, P.K. (eds.)
(ISBN: 978-93-5056-777-7).

54. **Water Resources and Agriculture**
Bharti, P.K. and Ezeaku Peter Ikemefuna (eds.)
(ISBN: 978-93-5056-481-3).

55. **Waste Resources Management:** *Monitoring & Assessment*
Gupta, Sandeep and Bharti, P.K. (eds.)
(ISBN: 978-93-5056-799-9).

Preface

Certain cultural practices are invaluable in reducing plant disease losses. A control programme is enhanced whenever one can utilise as many methods of control as possible. New strains of an organism may develop that will attack resistant varieties or become tolerant to certain pesticides when these practices are used alone. Combining practices reduces the risk of failure.

Rotation with unrelated crops is probably the most utilised cultural practice for disease control. This helps keep populations of pathogens from building up to damaging numbers. One should not expect rotation to eliminate disease development, but it certainly aids in reducing damage from most diseases.

Fertilizer usage may have some bearing on development of certain diseases. It differs with each crop and each disease but, in general, nitrogen out of balance with other nutrients enhances foliage disease development and predisposes some plants to other diseases. Potash, on the other hand, helps reduce disease development when it is in balance with other elements.

Deep burial of crop residue helps control certain diseases by placing the organism contained in the residue at a depth where there is an oxygen deficiency. This reduces the population of the disease-causing organism and permits the crop to escape much of the damage.

Planting on a raised bed is helpful in preventing certain diseases such as: Southern blight and certain of the wilt diseases. This practice is advisable when growing leguminous crops such as: peanuts, soybeans, and guar, and when growing vegetable crops in tight, poorly drained soils.

Burning of crop residue has been discouraged because of destruction of valuable organic matter and creation of an air pollution problem. The fact remains, however, that it is a highly effective means of eradicating some disease-causing organisms associated with crop residue.

Time of seeding has an important bearing on disease prevention in many cases. Delayed planting of wheat will help escape the chances of wheat streak mosaic virus. Early spring planting of cotton may effectively help escape cotton root rot.

Removal of undesirable plants that might serve as a host reservoir for virus diseases that attack cultivated crops aid in preventing infection. Infected rhizomes of Johnsongrass are the primary overwintering host for the maize dwarf mosaic virus that attacks grain sorghum, forage sorghum, and corn. Wild Solanaceae weeds, such as: jimsonweed, horsenettel and silverleaf nightshade harbor viruses that attack potato and tomato.

Volunteer plants from a harvested crop are often means of carrying a disease organism from one crop season to the next. Rusts of cereal crops and spinach constitute an example of this type disease dissemination.

Roguing (removal) of diseased plants as they appear is often an effective method in helping reduce the spread of a destructive disease. Virus diseases of stone fruits and bacterial wilt of cucurbits are examples where roguing is worthy of consideration.

These cultural control practices have been found to be economically feasible in reducing disease losses. Growers should properly identify the diseases that limit production and then use a variety of controls in combination.

Disease development is dependent on the interaction between the pathogen, its host (crop plant) and the environment. In agriculture the key components are crop, cultivar, soil, plant nutrition, cropping pattern, agronomic practices, weather factors and disease presence. Changes to one component can have positive or negative repercussions on the others ultimately affecting overall crop production. The objective for organic farmers is to manage the components of the farm system to favour crop plants over disease organisms. To achieve this organic growers apply a diverse approach to suppressing disease incidence. This approach relies, above all, on the creation of diverse farm habitats, cultural practices and host resistance. This paper details the cycle of infection of diseases and considers the specific mechanisms and processes present that serve to control diseases in organic crops.

In general, disease is seen to arise when crop plants are growing under 'stress' and therefore emphasis must be given to preventing crop stress, principally through appropriate care for the soil in which the crop is grown. A number of practices used in agriculture can heighten the crops susceptibility to disease. For example artificial fertilisers can cause nutrient imbalances either by luxury uptake and storage or by blocking uptake and release of other nutrients. Disease increases have also been seen after soil sterilisation or heavy irrigation where the effect is to partially clean or sterilise the soil (Huber and Watson 1970).

The present book updates the subject content of agricultural practices, modern, techniques, crop pest, impact of climate, plant diseases, control of diseases and few interrelated issues.

The book will be helpful for the researchers, academia working in the field of agricultural practices, modern, techniques, crop pest, impact of climate, plant diseases and control of diseases.

– Editors

(envbooks@gmail.com)

Contents

Page 1-19

AGRICULTURAL PRACTICES AND CROP DISEASE CONTROL
***Edited by*: Dr. Alka Chauhan and Dr. Anubhuti Sharma**
***Edition* : 2017**
ISBN : 978-93-5056-859-0
***Published by*: Discovery Publishing House Pvt. Ltd., New Delhi (India)**

1

Impact of Organic Agriculture on Agro-ecosystem Health

Raashee Abhilashi[1]
Sudha Sambyal Malik[2*]
Pooja Solanki[2]

INTRODUCTION

Growing awareness of health and environmental issues associated with the intensive use of chemical inputs has led to the interest in alternate forms of agriculture in the world. Organic agriculture is one among the broad spectrum of production methods that are supportive for environment. This is accomplished by using where possible agronomic, biological and mechanical methods, as opposed to using synthetic materials to fulfill any specific function within the system. A form of agriculture which is mainly based on the use of organic fertilizers, natural pesticides, natural feed for cattle and poultry, and indigenous varieties of crops is an organic farming. According to the Codex Alimentarious, a joint body of FAO and WHO - "organic agriculture is a holistic food production management systems, which promotes and enhances agro-ecosystem health, including: biodiversity, biological cycles and soil biological activity. It emphasizes the use of management practices in preference to the use of off-farm inputs, taking into account that regional conditions require locally adapted systems. According to the International Federation of Organic Agriculture Movements (IFOAM)". Organic agriculture is a production system that sustains the health of soils, ecosystems and people.

1. Department of Biology and Environmental Sciences, CSKHPKV, Palampur, HP. India.
2. Department of Environment Sciences, M.D. University, Rohtak, Haryana, India.

Organic agriculture is now practiced in more than 130 countries with a total area of 30.4 million hectares in 0.7 million number of organic farm. This constitutes about 0.65 per cent of the total agriculture land of the world (Willer *et al.* 2008). In India, about 528,171 hectare area is under organic farming with 44,926 numbers of certified organic farms (Ramesh *et al.* 2010). The chemical fertilizers and pesticides are causing ill effects on soil, water and air deteriorating the agro-ecosystem health. Now it has become essential to devise methods and practices of farming respectful of ecological principles.). Fertilizers have played a prominent role in increasing food grain production of the country in the past and are going to be crucial input in future as well.

Heavy use of agrochemicals since the 'green revolution' of the 1960s boosted food productivity at the cost of environment and society. It killed the beneficial soil organisms and destroyed their natural fertility, impaired the power of 'biological resistance' in crops making them more susceptible to pests and diseases. Chemically grown foods have adversely affected human health. The scientific community all over the world is desperately looking for an economically viable, socially safe and environmentally sustainable alternative to the agrochemicals.

The Green revolution technology, particularly in India, led to many fold increase in food grains production, but has made demands on water, fertilizer and farm power. The effect of intensive cropping has resulted in deteriorating soil tilth and decreased organic matter content high level of chemical inputs is increasing pollution hazard and result further degradation of soil health, the increased use of agro-chemical is polluting water and atmosphere and thus effect on crop production, and animal and reflect on human health. However, due to intensification of agriculture the soils are being rapidly depleted of their fertility and are now showing signs of fatigue. The inadequate and imbalanced use coupled with neglect of organic manure has caused deficiency of primary and secondary micronutrients in many parts of the country. The falling organic matter levels in the soils are adversely affecting the physical, chemical and biological soil properties deteriorating the health of agro-ecosystem.

The agro-ecosystem health refers to the capacity of soil to function in a desired manner such as: to produce healthy crops with no health hazards to animals and humans, resist erosion and minimize environmental impacts (Parr *et al.* 1992). The required capacity of the agro-ecosystem may be maintained by precise monitoring of changes in soil fertility and crop productivity in relation to proper nutrient management for sustainable production through the long term study. Present paper reviews the effect of organic farming on the agro-ecosystem health.

Effects of Organic and Inorganic Nutrients on Crop Productivity

Kundu *et al.* (1994) studied the effect of crop waste on production in a rice-wheat crop sequence under rainfed conditions on sandy loam soils of West Bengal and recorded the highest paddy grain yields in the treatment receiving crop waste at 3 t/ha coupled with either 25 per cent or 50 per cent of the recommended dose of mineral fertilizer than the treatment receiving organic crop waste alone. 20 to 50 per cent nitrogen through farm yard manure or green manure (*Sebania aculeate*) with 50-70 per cent fertilizers to rice gave either equal or more yield compared with 100 per cent NPK fertilizers alone on a sodic soil.. The integrated sources made the continuous availability of nutrients from both organic and inorganic sources (Malik *et al.* 2014). The slightly higher grain yield of rice was reported in the strip receiving 10 t FYM and the highest NPK rates compared with the control in a field experiment at Ludhiana, Punjab by Brar *et al.* (1995). The significant increase in grain yield has also been reported by Tiwari *et al.* (1999) due to an addition of crop residues and biogas slurry.

Lacko-Bartosava *et al.* (1999) studied the effect of ecological and integrated arable farming systems on crop productivity and soil fertility. Ecological farming system showed slightly better physical and chemical soil parameters and higher quality of soil organic matter. The highest values of COX, Nbiol, daily soil respiration and nitrification were measured in the ecological system. Differences of crop yields between the systems were greater under minimum cultivation than under conventional tillage. Compared to the integrated system, the ecological system reflected the rotational effect on the winter wheat yield more clearly. The pre-crop effect of leguminous crops on yield was higher for winter wheat in the ecological system.

Krishnakumar *et al.* (2005) conducted an experiment during July 2003-October 2004 in Tamil Nadu, India, to determine the effect of organic farming with various sources of organic manures (farmyard manure (FYM), Sesbania rostrata, Azolla, neem cake (NC), on soil fertility, and yield and quality of ADT 36 rice. Soil used in the study was classified as an Entic Haplustert. Application of FYM+NC at the rate of 90 kg N/ha., gave the highest straw yield in the kharif and rabi season (6520 and 6020 kg/ha, respectively).

Vennila C. and Jayanthi C. (2007) conducted an experiment at Tamil Naidu Agriculture University, Coimbatore to study integrated nitrogen management for wet seeded rice and daincha dual cropping system and found that integrated use of organic and chemical fertilizers enhanced the growth and yield attributing characters.

Ramesh *et al.* (2010) conducted the study in Tamil Nadu, India, to determine the effect of organic farming with various sources of organic manures (farmyard manure (FYM), Sesbania rostrata, Azolla, neem cake (NC), composted coirpith, and their combinations) on soil fertility, yield and quality of ADT 36 rice. Soil used in the study was classified as an Entic Haplustert. Application of FYM+NC at the rate of 90 kg N/ha showed significantly reduced bulk density and increased hydraulic conductivity, water holding capacity and per cent pore space during kharif and rabi. The population of bacteria, fungi and actinomycetes in the soil were also higher in the same treatment. FYM+NC at the rate of 90 kg N/ha gave significantly higher grain yield (5675 and 5175 kg/ha) during the kharif and rabi season respectively.

Impact of Organic Farming on Physical Properties of the Soil

Acharya *et al.* (1988) while studying the effect of organic and inorganic fertilizers on physical properties and the bulk density of soil reported decrease in bulk density due to an addition of FYM for 10-11 years while the application of inorganic inputs increased the same. Similarly, Anderson *et al.* (1990) reported that annual addition of manure for hundred years decreased the bulk density by an average of 0.12 g cm^{-3} compared to unfertilized treatments.

Zebarth *et al.* (1993) reported that annual applications of organic wastes for as long as 4 years increased soil water retention of coarse textured soils. Schjonning *et al.* (1994) reported favorable effects of graded doses of NPK fertilizers and organic matter in lowering the bulk density of soil in a long term experiment on rice-wheat-cowpea system.

Sheeba and Chellamuthu (1996) reported that an application of N and P increased the water holding capacity as against N alone and was reported to increase further with depth over a long period of time.

Sharma *et al.* (2001) indicated that the bulk density of soils decreased with the integrated use of organic and inorganic fertilizers for twelve years on an Inceptisols with rice-wheat cropping sequence. A trial conducted an ongoing long term experiment by Kaushal (2002) revealed that with the application of recommended dose of NPK along with FYM decreased bulk density to the lowest in soil over control. Similarly, Bhattacharya *et al.* (2004) studied the dynamics of soil characteristics in an ongoing long-term fertility experiment at Uttaranchal and reported that the bulk density was minimum with the application of NPK and FYM treatment.

An experiment conducted to study the effect of Vermicompost on physical properties of soil under chilli-spinach system by Hangarge *et al.* (2004) revealed that application of Vermicompost with soil conditioner improved physical condition by reducing bulk density, increased porosity, water holding capacity and infiltration rate.

Selvi *et al.* (2005) studied the effect of in-organics alone and in combination with organics and reported that the continuous application of balanced fertilizers along with organics significantly reduced the bulk density in soil and increased hydraulic conductivity, porosity and water holding capacity than NPK alone.

Table 1.1: Comparison of physical, chemical, biological properties of soil and crop yield among three different farming systems

Parameters	Organic Treatment	Inorganic Treatment	Integrated Treatment	References
Physical properties				
Water holding capacity (%)	59.865	57.03	59.365	Malik *et al*. 2014
Field capacity (%)	27.755	26.55	29.14	
Bulk density mg/cm	1.36	1.445	1.415	
Permanent wilting point (%)	17.055	17.505	19.085	
Chemical properties				
pH	5.65	5.55	5.95	Malik *et al*. 2014
Organic carbon (g/Kg)	1.4	0.995	1.03	
Available N_2 kg/ha	250.88	191.055	353.805	
Total N_2 kg/ha	1213.42	1369.445	1387.405	
Available P kg/ha	29.065	25.12	49.17	
Total P kg/ha	103.745	73.15	124.79	
Available K kg/ha	199.82	181.45	287.61	
Total K kg/ha	252.255	265.315	353.54	
Cation exchange capacity (c mol(p+)/kg)	13.4	10.495	12.88	
Bacterial properties				
Bacterial count ($\times 10^6$ cfu/gm of soil)	6.495	2.675	5.87	Malik *et al*. 2014
Fungal population ($\times 10^4$ cfu/gm of soil)	4.85	3.85	4.53	
Actinmycetes population ($\times 10^3$ cells/gm of soil)	56.83	39.83	37.66	
Microbial respiration µg/gm/hr	12.98	6.315	10.33	
Dehydrogenase activity µg TPF/gm/hr	2.855	1.44	1.7	
Phosphatase activity µg/gm/hr	2.865	2.28	4.15	
Urease activity µg urea/gm dry soil/min	3.02	2.26	5.44	
Microbial biomass carbon µg/gm	335.77	141.265	203.75	
Grain yield (tonnes/ha)	2.13	1.33	2.16	Malik *et al*. 2014
Straw yield (tonnes/ha)	4.33	3.7	4.86	

Pathak *et al.* (2005) conducted a long term field experiment at Ranchi, Jharkhand and studied the cumulative effect of organic and inorganic sources of nutrients on water holding capacity and reported that there is significant improvement in water holding capacity of the soil. Krishnakumar *et al.* (2005) conducted an experiment to determine the effect of organic farming with various sources of organic manures (farmyard manure (FYM), Sesbania rostrata, Azolla, Neem Cake (NC), composted coirpith, and their combinations) on soil fertility, and yield and quality of ADT 36 rice. Soil used in the study was classified as an Entic Haplustert. Application of FYM+NC at the rate of 90 kg N/ha showed significantly reduced bulk density and increased hydraulic conductivity, water holding capacity and per cent pore space.

Pathak *et al.* (2005) when working on the cumulative effect of organic and inorganic sources of nutrients on bulk density at Ranchi reported a significant improvement in bulk density of the soil in long-term field experiment. Similarly, Verma (2006) conducted a trial in the ongoing long-term experiment initiated in 1972 at CSKHPKV, Palampur and studied the integrated effect of organic and inorganic fertilizers on bulk density and found that with the application of recommended dose of NPK along with FYM resulted in an increase in bulk density and saturated hydraulic conductivity in soil over control. Rajesh *et al.* (2008) while studying the effect of organic farming with various sources of organic manures and their combinations on soil physical fertility reported that the substitution of recommended dose of 90 kg N ha-1 by 90 kg N ha-1 through FYM+Neem cake has improved the soil physical fertility as measured by bulk density (1.24 Mg m-3), water holding capacity (51.2%), hydraulic conductivity (6.3 cm h-1) and pore space (56.9%).

Impact of Organic Farming on Chemical Properties of Soil

Prasad *et al.* (1997) studied the changes in different forms of P in an acid alfisol due to long-term manuring and fertilization and found that total P status of soil increased from 605 to 1020mg/kg soil with thw increase in NPK level from 50-150 per cent of the recommended dose. Lamani *et al.* (2000) compared the effects of organics and green manuring on the organic carbon content of soil and reported that addition of organics and green manuring improved the organic carbon content of the soil over the control. Highest organic carbon content (0.79%) was recorded in the plots treated with poultry manure.

Dinesh *et al.* (2000) while studying the effect of green manuring on phosphorus transformation from rock phosphate in which soil was incubated with Gliricidia along with graded levels of phosphorus reported higher phosphorus concentration through out the incubation period compared to no green manure incubated soil. The increase has partly been ascribed to the release of phosphorus during mineralization of added green manure. An increase in organic carbon due to manuring in rice-wheat cropping sequence has also been reported by Gupta *et al.* (2000). Trehan (2000) conducted an incubation experiment over a period of one year to find gross and net mineralization of nitrogen from cattle slurry and found extensive mineralization and immobilization of nitrogen in slurry embedded soil.

Gami *et al.* (2001) also observed the build up of total P in plots receiving FYM compared to NPK treatments. Similarly, improvement in the available N, P and K content of soil due to the application of NPK fertilizers in potato has also been recorded by Singh and Lal (2001) in the soils of Meghalaya. Patil and Bhilare (2001) also reported significant improvement in the content of available N, P and K with the use of vermicompost prepared from press mud at Rahuri (Maharashtra).

Kanwar *et al.* (2002) found that organic carbon contents were higher in the plots which received organic manures (Vermicompost or FYM) alone than the plots which received NPK fertilizers only. Rajkhowa *et al.* (2003) investigated the effect of conjoint use of vermicompost and inorganic fertilizers on nutrient build up in the soils of Assam and found that soil organic carbon, available N, P and K status improved significantly with the application of Vermicompost alone or in combination with fertilizers. Tolanur and Badanur (2003) conducted a field experiment to study the effect of integrated use of organic manure, green manure and fertilizer nitrogen on nutrient status of soil and productivity of sorghum-chickpea cropping system and observed that organic carbon content of soil was higher as compared to soil received inorganic fertilizers alone and control.

Singh B.S. (2005) studied the effect of green manuring and nitrogen yield and uptake of micro nutrient by rice in which a field experiment was conducted to study the effect of different green manures with and without different levels of fertilizer nitrogen and observed a significant increase in nitrogen levels. Varalakshmi *et al.* (2005) conducted an experiment at farmer's field on Alfisol and studied the effect of integrated nutrient management and reported that with the application of 100 per cent NPK + 7.5 t FYM ha^{-1}, available nitrogen content has significantly improved.

Varalakshmi *et al.* (2005) conducted an experiment at farmer's field on Alfisol and studied the effect of organic and inorganic sources of nutrients and reported that with the application of 100 per cent NPK + 7.5 t FYM ha^{-1}, the phosphorus, organic carbon and potassium contents of the soil have significantly improved.

A significant increase in soil pH with the use of inorganic and organic manure was also reported by Laxaminarayana (2006) who conducted an experiment at ICAR Mizoram Centre, Kolasib for three consecutive seasons during 1998-2000 on a typic Hapludult. He reported a significant increase in potassium content, available nitrogen and organic carbon. Kaushal (2006) also conducted a trial in medium textured soils and studied the cumulative effect of organic and inorganic fertilizers on available potassium and found that with the application of recommended dose of NPK along with FYM resulted in highest available potassium content in soil over control. Similarly, Verma (2006) conducted a trial in the ongoing long-term experiment initiated in 1972 at CSKHPKV, Palampur and studied the integrated effect of organic and inorganic fertilizers on soil organic carbon and found that with the application of recommended dose of NPK along with FYM resulted in significant increase in soil organic carbon content in soil over control.

Sharma *et al.* (2006) conducted a field experiment on okra-onion sequence to study the influence of combined use of organic manure and chemical fertilizers on the available nutrient status in the silt clay loam soil of Palampur (Himachal Pradesh) and concluded that the highest available NPK contents (303.1, 28.1 and 345.3 kg ha^{-1} respectively) were observed in case of the treatment comprising of 10 t Vermicompost ha^{-1} to okra and 25 Vermicompost ha^{-1} to onion along with 100 per cent NPK to these crops. The study further revealed that the extent of increase in the contents of available N, P and K was much higher in case of Vermicompost treatment than FYM application when applied at the same rate. Korwar *et al.* (2006) conducted a field experiment to study the influence of organics and in-organics on the soil quality in semi-arid tropics in Aonla at Hyderabad (Andhra Pradesh) and noted highest increase in organic carbon (0.90 %) and K_2O (359 kg ha^{-1}) with the application of Vermicompost alone @ 15 kg per plant while increase in P_2O_5 (33.29 kg ha^{-1}) was found with the application of 50 per cent inorganic fertilizers along with 50 per cent Vermicompost over the inorganic fertilizer alone.

Bajpai *et al.* (2006) conducted a long term experiment to develop suitable integrated nutrient supply system and reported an increase in the available phosphorus and nitrogen contents of the soil with an incorporation of organic sources . Kaushal (2006) conducted a trial in medium textured soils and studied the cumulative effect of organic and inorganic fertilizers on available nitrogen and phosphorus and found that with the application of recommended dose of NPK along with FYM resulted in highest available nitrogen and phosphorus contents in soil over control. Similarly, Verma (2006) while studying the integrated effect of organic and inorganic fertilizers on the available nitrogen found a significant increase in the available nitrogen content in soil over control with the application of recommended dose of NPK along with FYM.

Alok *et al.* (2007) studied comparative efficacy of compost and Vermicompost on physico-chemical characteristics of salt affected soils of U.P. All the characteristics of soil exhibited positive correlation with increasing composting material. From their study conducted on sandy loam soils of Lucknow (Uttar Pradesh), Singh *et al.* (2007) concluded that the application of organic manures to sugarcane crop enhanced the soil fertility markedly. The highest significant increase in organic carbon, total N, available P, soil microbial biomass carbon and soil microbial biomass nitrogen was recorded with the application of 10 t Vermicompost ha^{-1}.

Sarwar *et al.* (2008) also reported an increase in organic matter content of the soil with an application of compost. Jaun *et al.* (2008) studied that long-term effect of combined application of organic and mineral fertilizers on soil enzymatic activities and reported that with the application of combined use of organic and inorganic sources of nutrients resulted in an increase in total phosphorus over the application of inorganic sources of nutrients. Similarly, Bedi and Dubey (2009) studied the long-term effect of organic and inorganic fertilizers on nutrient build-up and their relationship with microbial properties in a rice-wheat cropping sequence and reported high total phosphorus content in soil over control with the application of organic and inorganic sources of nutrients.

Walia *et al.* (2010) conducted an experiment at the Research Farm, Department of Agronomy, Punjab Agricultural University, Ludhiana and studied the long-term effect of integrated use of organic and inorganic sources of nutrients on soil available potassium, pH, available nitrogen and organic carbon contents and reported that there is significant increase in their contents with the application of recommended dose of inorganic fertilizers along with FYM. Adeniyan *et al.* (2011) while evaluating the organic manures reported that cane rat droppings improved soil chemical properties the best. Plant dry matter yield increased with application of NPK fertilizer compared with compost, poultry manure and cane rat droppings in both the soils. In acid soil, application of NPK fertilizer gave the highest dry matter yield of 4.77 g/plant while in nutrient depleted soil; application of NPK fertilizer gave the highest dry matter yield of 5.58 g/plant.

Impact of Organic Farming on Biological Properties of Soil

Soil is a habitat for vast, complex and interactive community of soil microorganisms whose population and activities largely determine the chemical and physical properties of soil and growth of the plants. There is a continuous interaction among the soil-plant and microbes in rhizosphere. The interaction may be neutral, harmful or beneficial and accordingly influence the plant and soil health.

Soil is considered as biological entity *i.e.,* a living tissue (Quastel. 1946) with complex biochemical reactions and these reaction are catalyzed by different types of enzymes. The chemical factors play a crucial role in the survival of microorganisms in different ecological niches of soil, Chapman (1965). Each of the organic and mineral fractions in soil has a special influence on specific enzyme activity, Mclaren (1975) and Schimidt and Laskowski (1961). Fungi are dominant in acidic soils while bacteria and actinomycetes show their abundance in neutral to alkaline soils, Alexander (1977).

The amount of microbial biomass although comprise a small portion of soil organic matter, yet reflects the total organic matter content within the living microbial component. The total amount of microbial C and N in soil is generally greater in soils of cooler and wetter regions compared to warmer and dried regions, Allison (1973) and Spain *et al.* (1983). Microbial biomass was found comprised of 2-3 per cent of soil carbon, Jenkinsion and Ladd (1981). Coleman *et al.* (1983) reported that microbial biomass acts as a catalyst for the conversion of plant nutrient from stable organic forms over longer period. Microbial biomass constitutes the active fraction of soil organic matter, Paul and Varoney (1984).

The effect of organic residues (sugarcane trash and mustard straw) along with 60 and 120 kg ha $^{-1}$ nitrogen application was studied on the soil of Palampur by Dev (1987) and he observed that micro floral population of actinomycetes, bacteria and fungi increased significantly over control. But the increased levels of inorganic N application decreased all micro-floral population. He further observed that *Eupatarium adenopforum* @ 2.5 and 5 tonnes ha $^{-1}$ with 60 kg N ha $^{-1}$ significantly improve the microfloral population over inorganic N application alone during both seasons. But inorganic N @ 120 kg ha $^{-1}$ was at par with control. The application of Eupatorium *adenopforum* @ 2.5 tonnes ha $^{-1}$ alone, *Eupatarium adenopforum* @ 5.0 tonnes ha $^{-1}$ with and without 60 kg N recorded the population of actinomycetes significantly higer than that observed in control.

Sharma *et al.* (1987) conducted a six year field experiment to study the use of organics in rice-wheat cropping sequence and found that FYM and crop residues with graded nitrogen significantly increased microbial population. Tarafdar *et al.* Phosphatase activity has been found to be a good indicator of the organic matter, Hattori (1988). (1989) studied the phosphatase activities under rainfed conditions and found that combined application of FYM and N was more effective than N alone. Das and Mukharjee (1990) studied the effects of wheat straw and neem cake application to an alluvial soil on the soil microbial population and observed that the total bacterial and non symbiotic nitrogen fixing bacterial population increased with the increased levels of wheat straw application, than the neem cake addition. Whereas, Badiyala *et al.* (1990) studied the effect of fertilizers and management practices on micro flora in an Alfisol and found that with increase in the rates of fertilizer, the bacterial population significantly increased but that of fungi was not affected.

Hickisch and Muller - (1990) studied the effect of various fertilizers regimes NPK, (N, P, K, FYM, no fertilizers) on soil microorganisms, CO_2 output, soil structure and carbon content in a long-term experiment and found that FYM with fertilizers increased the number of bacteria and fungi as compared to control. The measure of the size of the soil microbial biomass is of importance in the studies of nutrient cycling in soils and has been used as an ecological marker by Smith and Paul (1990). Naumova and Barsukov (1991) studied the amounts of turnover rates of microbial biomass carbon and nitrogen in a dernopodzolic soil after 45 years of cropping and found that NPK plots contained 10-30 per cent and manured treatments 1.5 times more microbial biomass as compared to control. Goyal *et al.* (1992) studied the effect of continuous inorganic fertilization and organic amendments on the organic matter microbial biomass relationship and found that soil microbial biomass carbon and nitrogen increased with the balanced fertilization.

Kale *et al.* (1992) evaluated the effect of conjunctive use of vermicompost and chemical fertilizers on microbiological activity such as: total microbes, N fixers, actinomycetes and spore formers and the results demonstrated that the population of these microbes except for actinomycetes increased significantly with the combined use of vermicompost and chemical fertilizers over the control. The bacteria and actinomycetes have significantly positive relationship with crop yield and available nutrient status in the plot receiving organic and inorganic fertilizers while fungal is negatively correlated to FYM addition.

The soil P status plays a significant role in influencing the microbial growth. Microbial biomass and their count increase with increasing application of organic manure (FYM and others) and both the parameters are more in treatment receiving inorganic N along with FYM over a period of time due to better root growth, Kukreja *et al.* (1991), Goyal *et al.* (1992) and Sri Ramachandera Sekhran *et al.* (1995).

Hayano *et al.* (1995) studied the behaviour of selected micro flora (Bacteria, actinomycetes and Fungi) in rice wheat cropping sequence for two years in Japan under rice-straw compost manured rhizosphere soil and reported that the population of bacteria, actinomycetes and fungi did not change by the application of rice straw compost. Where as Saha *et al.* (1995) studied the effect of decomposition of organic matter namely barseem straw, bagasse, rice straw, *Cassia sophera, Cestrum diurum* and *Ipomea cornea* on activities on microorganisms and availability of nitrogen, phosphorus and sulphur in soil and reported that decomposition of organic matter in general not only increase the microbial population but also enriched the soil by increasing available plant nutrients to a greater extent. Singram and Kamlakumari (1995) observed that higher rates of NPK fertilization enhanced the activities of soil enzymes but the effect was more pronounced with FYM in combination with NPK fertilizers.

Biological oxidation of organic compound in soil is generally dehydrogenation. Soil enzyme activities are believed to indicate the extent of specific processes and also act as an indicator of soil fertility.

Walia *et al.* (1995) also observed the increase in microbial population in rice incorporated soils of Punjab. Murata *et al.* Murata *et al.* (1997) found that microbial biomass carbon and nitrogen increased with organic matter application. (1997) also found that microbial biomass carbon and nitrogen increased with the organic material application. Milev and Naukova, (1997) conducted a field experiments on spring pea in Bulgeria with 5 fertilization levels and reported that the application of nitrogen fertilization alone increased the NPK removal as compared to bacterial fertilization. Patil and Varade (1998) studied the effect of application of NPK fertilizers to a sorghum-wheat cropping sequence on a vertisol in field experiment in Maharashtra and reported that population of fungi, bacteria and actinomycetes were affected significantly with increasing rates of fertilizers. Singh *et al.* (1999) observed that microbial biomass C, N and P was highest in straw treatment and lowest on control soil. While studying the effect of inorganic fertilizer and fertilizer - manure combination on soil physico-chemical properties and dynamics of microbial biomass, Santhy *et al.* (1999) reported the highest microbial biomass under the integrated usage of farmyard manure.

Biological oxidation of organic compound in soil is generally dehydrogenation. Soil enzyme activities are believed to indicate the extent of specific processes and also act as an indicator of soil fertility. Simek *et al.* (1999) studied the effect of organic and inorganic fertilizers on soil chemical properties, estimates of soil microbial community size and activity of enzymes and found that dehydrogenase activity was lower in soils that had received the largest amount of inorganic fertilizers alone as compared to the combined application of inorganic fertilized soils.

Dinesh *et al.* (2000) also observed that soil amended with organic manures consistently registered greater enzyme activities as compared to the unamended soils. Similarly, Sharma *et al.* (2000) also found that microbial population enhanced significantly due to crop residue and FYM incorporation along with chemical fertilizers as compared to chemical fertilizers alone. Manna and Ganguly (2001) also observed that low activity of phosphatase and dehydrogenase in the inorganic fertilizers applied treatments and control than combined application of FYM and fertilizer under soybean-wheat-fallow cropping system. Sri Ramchandra Sekharan (2002) studied the effect of different levels of fertilizers on dehydrogenase activity under maize-cowpea crop rotation and found that the application of FYM along with recommended dose of fertilizers registered the highest dehydrogenase activity as compared to the inorganic fertilizers and control.

Srinivas *et al.* (2002) studied the effect of organic manure on soil dehydrogense activity in submerged vertisol rice soils and observed that the addition of organic manures caused significant differences in dehydrogenase activity. They further observed amongst the organic manures, FYM at 10 tonne ha^{-1} gave the highest activities of dehydrogenase. Lai *et al.* (2002) also reported high phosphatase activity in manure + N treatment than the control under rice wheat cropping system. While studying the influence of incorporated organic manure on the enzymatic and biological activities and on the growth of the rice and barley in pot experiment, Liang *et al.* (2003) found that the incorporation of organic manure into the soil significantly increased.

Batra L. (2004) conducted an experiment at Central Soil Salinity Research Institute, Karnal, Haryana and reported that Alkali soil showed minimum dehydrogenase activity, whereas it was almost at par for saline and normal soils. In vertisols of Maharashtra, significantly higher count of bacteria and fungi (Bacteria 92.66 × 10^6 cells per g of soil and Fungi 20.33 × 10^4 cells per g of the soil) was recorded in vermicompost treated plots as compared to untreated plots by Hangarge *et al.* (2004).

Krishnakumar *et al.* (2005) conducted an experiment in Tamil Nadu, India, to determine the effect of organic farming with various sources of organic manures (farmyard manure (FYM), Sesbania rostrata, Azolla, neem cake (NC), composted coirpith, and their combinations) on soil fertility, and yield and quality of ADT 36 rice. Soil used in the study was classified as an Entic Haplustert. Application of FYM+NC at the rate of 90 kg N/ha. The population of bacteria, fungi and actinomycetes in the soil were also higher in the same treatment. FYM+NC at the rate of 90 kg N/ha gave significantly higher grain yield (5675 and 5175 kg/ha during the kharif and rabi season, respectively).

Roy and Singh BP. (2006) conducted a greenhouse experiment during *Kharif* and *rabi* at New Delhi and reported an increase in soil urease activity with the application of N fertilizer and crop residue. Kadlag *et al.* (2007) studied the influence of different sources of phosphorus in combination with different levels of FYM on urease activity and found that there is an increase in urease activity after the application of FYM along with single super phosphate over the application of single super phosphate. Jaun *et al.* (2008) when working on long term effect of combined application of organic and mineral fertilizers on soil enzymatic activities reported an increase in urease activities with the application of combined use of organic and mineral fertilizers over the application of inorganic sources of nutrients. Higher urease activity was observed in integrated use of both organic and inorganic fertilizers. The higher urease activity in integrated treatment may be attributed to the application of organic source and inorganic source together which maintain the continuity of conversion of nutrients from organic to inorganic form because it acts on C-N bond other than linear peptide bond (Malik *et al.* 2014).

Bedi and Dubey (2009) studied the long-term effect of organic and inorganic fertilizers on nutrient build-up and their relationship with microbial properties in a rice-wheat cropping sequence and reported that with the application of organic and inorganic sources of nutrients resulted in high dehydrogenase and high phosphatase activity over control. The treatments which received the combined application of organics and inorganics (T3 to T6) gave higher phosphatase activity than others. It may attributed the addition of organic and inorganic sources which maintain the continuity of addition of nutrients, so the substrate of phosphorus *i.e.,* monoesters or diesters are continuously available and cause phosphatase activity (Malik *et al.* 2014). Similar results were also obtained by Liang *et al.* (2003) in some soils from China. Lower values in complete organic treatments receiving chopped crop residues may be ascribed to narrow C: N ratio which resulted in slow mineralization from organic forms to di and mono esters.

Microbial biomass accounts for the total carbon content contributed by living organisms in soil. Bedi *et al.* (2009) reported that microbial biomass carbon was more in wheat straw-treated treatment followed by FYM and green manure treated treatments respectively. Bio-fertilizer based integrated nutrient management package treatment showed the highest content of soil microbial biomass carbon, which was at par with the treatment of 50 per cent recommended dose of fertilizers plus 50 per cent N through FYM, Gogoi *et al.* (2010). Similarly Malik *et al.* 2014 reported that microbial biomass carbon was maximum in organic treatments as compared to inorganic treatment. It is *firstly* due to increase in microbial population and *secondly* due to the formation of root exudates, mucigel, sloughed off cells and underground roots of previous cut crops, which also play an important role in increasing biomass carbon (Malik *et al.* 2014).

REFERENCES

Acharya C.L., Bishnoi S.K. and Yaduvanshin H.S. (1988). Effect of Long-term Application of Fertilizers, and Organic and Inorganic amendments under Continuous Cropping on Soil Physical and Chemical Properties in an alfisol. *Indian Journal of Agricultural Sciences* 58(3): 509-516.

Adeniyan O.N., Ojo A.O., Akinbonde O.A. and Adediran J.A. (2011). Comparative Study of different Organic Manures and NPK Fertilizer for Improvement of Soil Chemical Properties and Dry Matter Yield of Maize in two different Soils. *Journal of Soil Science and Environmental Management* 2 (1): 9-13.

Alexander M. (1977). *Introduction to Soil Microbiology*. John Willey and Sons. New York, USA.

Allison FE. (1973). Soil Organic Matter and its Role in Crop Production. *Elsevier, Amsterdam.*

Alok Bhardwaj, Richa Singh, Agarwal AK and Surendra Singh. (2007). Comparitive Efficacy of Compost and Vermicompost on Physico-chemical Characterstics of Salt Affected Soils. *Flora and Fauna, Jhansi* 13(2):335-339.

Badiyala S.D., Awasthi R.P. and Gupta R.D. (1990). Effect of Fertilizers and Management Practices on Microflora in Alfisols Growing Citrus. *Journal of the Indian Society of Soil Sciences* 38(3):537-540.

Bajpai R.K., Chitale S., Upadhyay S.K. and Urkurkar J.S. (2006). Long-term Studies on Soil Physic-chemical Properties and Productivity of Rice-wheat System as Influenced by Integrated Nutrient Management in Inceptisol of Chhatisgarh. *Journal of the Indian Society* 54(1): 24-29.

Batra L. (2004). Dehydrogenase Activity of Normal, Saline and Alkali Soils under different Agricultural Management Systems. *Journal of Indian Society of Soil Science. Volume*: 52(2):160-163.

Bedi P. and Dubey YP. (2009). Long-term Influence of Organic and Inorganic Fertilizers on Nutrient Build-up and their Relationship with Microbial Properties under a Rice-wheat Cropping Sequence in an Acid Alfisol. *Biomedical and Life Sciences* 57(3): 297-306.

Bedi P. Dubey Y.P. and Naveen D. (2009). Microbial Properties under Rice-wheat Cropping Sequence in an Acid Alfisol. *Journal of Indian Society of Soil Science* 57(3):373-377.

Bhattacharya P., Chakkabarti K., Chakkabarti A. and Bhattacharya B. (2004). Laboratory Incubation Studies to Observe the Effect of Municipal Solid Waste Compost Addition (Organic matter) (@ 0 and 20t/ha) on Microbial Carbon, glucose Induces Soil Respiration, urease and phosphatase Activities of three Soils of West Bengal. *Journal of Indian Society of Soil Science* 49(1): 98-104.

Chapman HD. (1965). Chemical Factor of the Soil as they Affect Microorganisms. *In: Ecology of Soil Borne Plant Pathogens-prelude to Biological Control. John Murray, London.* pp. 120-139.

Coleman D.C., Beid CPP and Cole CV. (1983). Biological Strategies of Nutrient Cycling in Soil System. *Advances in Ecological Research.* Academic Press, New York 1-55.

Das AC and Mukherjee D. (1990). Microbiological Changes during Decomposition of Wheat Straw and Neem cake in Soil. *Environment and Ecology* 8(2):1012-1015.

Dev SP. (1987). Recycling of Crop and Plant Wastes in Improving Crop Yields, N-use Efficiency and Soil Properties. *Ph.D Thesis.* CSKHPKV, Palampur.

Dinesh R., Dubey R.P., Ganeshmurthy AN and Prasad GS. (2000). Organic Manuring in Rice Based Cropping System: Effects of Soil Microbial Biomass and Selected Enzyme Activities. *Current Science* 79(1): 1716-1720.

Gami S.K., Ladha J.K., Pathak H., Shah M.P., Pasuquin E., Pandey S.P., Hobbs P.R., Joshy D. and Mishra R. (2001). Long-term Changes in Yield and Soil Fertility in a Twenty Year Rice-wheat Experiment in Nepal. *Biology an Fertility of Soils* 34(7): 73-78.

Gogoi B., Barua N.G. and Baruah T.C. (2010). Effect of Integrated Supply of Nutrients on Soil Microbial Biomass Carbon in an Inceptisol of Asa=sam. *Journal of Indian Society of Soil Science* 58(2): 241-244.

Goyal S., Mishra M.M. Hooda I.S., Singh R., Beri V., Chaudhary M.R., Sidhu P.S., Pashricha N.S. and Bajwa MS. (1992). Build up of Microbial Biomass with Continuous use of Inorganic Fertilizer and Organic Amendments. *Proceedings of the International Symposium on Nutrient Management for Sustained Productivity* 2(2):149-151.

Gupta R.K., Arora B.R., Sharma K.N. and Aluwalia S.K. (2000). Influence of Biogas Slurry and FYM Application on Changes in Soil Fertility under Rice-wheat Cropping Sequence. *Journal of Indian Society of Soil Science* 48(3):500-505.

Hangarge D.S., Raut R.S., Hawate G.R., Gaikwad G.K. and Dixit R.S. (2004). Influence of coirpith Compost and Vermicompost Application on the Microbial Population in Vertisols. *Journal of Soils and Crops* 14(2): 447-449.

Hangarge D.S., Raut R.S., Hawate G.R., Gaikwad G.K. and Dixit R.S. (2004). Influence of Coirpith Compost and Vermicompost Application on the Microbial Population in Vertisols. *Journal of Soils and Crops* 14(2): 447-449.

Hattori H. (1998). Microbial Activities in Soil Amended with Sewage Sludge. *Soil Science and Plant Nutrition* 34(4): 221-232.

Hayano K., Watanabe K. and Asakawa S. (1995). Behaviour of Selected Microbial Populations and their Activity in Rice and Wheat rhizosphere Soils in Long-term Experimental Paddy Fields with or without Organic Matter application in South-West Japan. *Bulletin of the Kyushu National Agricultural Experiment Station* 28(1):139-155.

Hickisch B. and Muller G (Jr.) (1990). Effect of Fertilization on Microorganisms in a Long-term Field Experiment. *Agrokemia-es-Talatan* 39(2): 415-418.

Jaun L., Bingqiang Z., Xiuying L., Ruibo J. and Hwatbing S. (2008). Effects of Long-term Combined Application of Organic and Mineral Fertilizers on Microbial Biomass, Soil Enzyme Activities and Soil Fertility. *Agricultural Sciences in China* 7(3): 336-343.

Jenkison D.S. and Ladd J.N. (1981). Microbial Biomass in Soil Measurements and Turnover. *Soil Biochemistry* 5(2): 415-563.

Kadlag A.D., Jadhav A.B. and Vyavahare MT. (2007). Soil Urease and Acid phosphate Enzyme Activity as Influenced by rock phosphate. *Asian Journal of Soil Science* 2(2):6-12.

Kale R.D., Mallesh B.C., Bano Kand Bagyaraj DJ. (1992). Influence of Vermicompost Application on the Available Macronutrients and Selected Microbial Populations in a Paddy Field *Soil Biology and Biochemistry* 24(12):1317-1320.

Kanwar K. and Paliyal SS and Nandal TR. (2002). Integrated Nutrient Management in Cauliflower (Pusa Snow Ball K-1). *Research on Crops* 3(3): 579-583.

Kaushal V. (2006). Dyanamics of the Organic Pool of the Nutrients as Influenced by Long-term use of Chemical Fertilizers and Amendments in a Acid Alfisols. *PhD. Thesis,* Department of Soil Science, Csk Himachal Pradesh Krishi Vishwavidyalaya, Palampur, India , pp. 67-68.

Korwar G.R., Pratibha G., Ravi V. and Palanikumar D. (2006). Influence of Organics and Inorganics on Growth, Yield of anola (Emblica officinalis) and Soil Quality in Semi-arid Tropics. *The Indian Journal of Agricultural Sciences* 76(8):457-461.

Krishankumar S. and Jawahar D. (2005). Coir pith Compost. *Kisan World* 28(6): p. 65.

Kukreja K., Mishra M.M., Dhankar S.S., Kapoor K.K. and Gupta AP. (1991). Effect of Long Manorial Application on Microbial Biomass. *Journal of Indian Society of Soil Science* 39(4):685-688.

Kundu A.L., Ghosh R.K. and Mondal T.K. (1994). Effect of Crop Waste on Production in a Rice-wheat Crop Sequence under Rainfed Condition in Gangetic Plains of West Bengal. *Advances in Plant Sciences* 7(1): 228:234.

Lacko-Bartosava M., Szombathova N. and Zaujec A. (1999). Effect of Ecological and Integrated arble Farming Systems on Crop Productivity and Soil Fertility. In: Oleson JE, Eltun R., goodings MJ (eds.), Procs. Int. *Workshop on Designing and Testing Crop Rotations for Organic Farming. Tjele DARCOF* pp. 297-304.

Lai C.M., Liu K.L., Jeng GI and Helen W. (2002). Effects of Fertilization Management on Soil Enzyme Activities Related to the C, N, P ands cycles in soils. Paper No. 1382. 17th World Congress of Soil Science 14th-21st August , 2002, Bangkok, Thailand Symposia.

Lamani C.S., Pallad Y.B. and Shenoy H. (2000). Effect of Nitrogen level and Decomposition Hasteners on Organic Carbon Content of Soil Cropped with Hybrid Maize. *Current Research University of Agricultural Sciences Bangalore* 29(7/8):112-113. *Legume Research* 26(1): 63-65.

Laxminarayana K. (2006). Effect of Integrated use of Nutrients and Organic Manures on Soil Properties, Yield and Nutrient Uptake of Rice in Ultisols of Muzoram. *Journal of the Indian Society of Soil Science* 54(1): 120-123.

Liang Y.C., Yang Y.F., Yang C.G., Shen Q.R., Zhou JM and Yang LZ. (2003). Soil Enzymatic Activity and Growth of Rice and Barley as Influenced by Organic Manure in an Anthropogenic Soil. *Geoderma* 115(3):149-160.

Sudha Sambyal Malik1*, Ramesh C Chauhan1, J.S. Laura2, Tanvi Kapoor1, Raashee Abhilashi1, and Natasha Sharma. (2014). Influence of Organic and Synthetic Fertilizers on Soil Physical Properties. *Int. J. Curr. Microbiol. App. Sci.* 3(8) 802-810.

Sudha Sambyal Malik and Ramesh C. Chauhan. (2014). Impact of Organic Farming in Enhancing the Soil Microbial Pool. Climate Change and Biodiversity. Vol. 1. pp. 186-196.

Sudha Sambyal Malik and Ramesh C. Chauhan. (2014). *Journal of International Academic Research for Multidisciplinary* 2(7). pp. 349-360.

Mclaren AD. (1975). Soil as a System of Humus and Clay Immobilized Enzymes. *Chemistry Science* 8(4): 97-99.

Milev G. and Naukova M. (1997). Removal of nitrofen phosphorus and potassium along with the Over Ground Field pea Depending Upon Fertilization. *Poschvznania agrokhimigia-i-Ekalogiya Bulgaria Soil Science. Agrochemistry* 32(3): 32-35.

Murata T., Tanaka H., Sakagami K., Asaka D. and Hanada R. (1997). The Influence on Microbial Biomass, Available Soil N and Nuptial Sugar Composition Induced by Wheat Straw and Manure Application. *Japanese Journal of Soil Science and Plant Nutrition* 68(2): 249-256.

Naumova N.B. and barsukov PA. (1991). Influence of Long-term Fertilization on Microbial Biomass Content and Dyanamics in dernopodzolic Soils. *Izvestiya Sibiviskogo Otedenleniya Akademi Nauk Sibirski biolgicheski-i-zhurnal* 3(1): 59-97.

Parr J.F., Papendick R.I., Hornick S.B. and Meyer R.E. (1992). Soil Quality: Attributes and Relationship to Alternative and Sustainable Agriculture. *American Journal of Alternative Agriculture* 7(1): 2-3.

Pathak S.K., Singh S.B., Jha N. and Sharma R.P. (2005). Effect of Nutrient Management on Nutrient Uptake and Changes in Soil Fertility in Maize (Zea mays)-wheat (Triticum aestivum) Cropping System. *Indian Journal of Agronmy* 50(4):269-273.

Patil V.S. and Bhilare R.L. (2001). Effect of Vermicompost Prepared from different Organic Sources on Growth and Yield of Wheat. *Journal of Maharashtra Agricultural Universities* 25(3): 305-306.

Paul E.A. and Varoney R.P. (1984). Field Interpretation of Microbial Activity Measurements. In: Current Perspectives in Microbial Ecology (Eds Klug MJ and Reddy CA) pp. 509-514. *American Society for Microbiology*, Washington.

Prasad J., Mathur BS and Srivastava NC. (1997). Changes in different Forms of phosphorus in An Acid Alfisol due to Long-term Manuring and Fertilization. *Jounal of the Indian Society of Soil Sciences* 45(2): 190-192.

Quastel JH. (1946). Soil Metabolism. The Royal Institute of Chemistry of Great Britain and Ireland, London.

Rajesh B., Yeom TIJ, Esakkiraj S., Kumar N and Logakanthi. (2008). Biomanagement of sogo-slude using an Earthworm. *Journal of Environmental Biology* 29(2):143-146.

Rajkhowa D.J., Saikia M and Rajkhowa KM. (2003). Effect of Vermicompost and Level of Fertilizer on Green Gram. *Legume Research* 26(1): 63-65.

Ramesh P., Panwar N.R., Singh A.B., Ramana S., Yadav S.K., Shrivastava R., and Subba R.A. (2010). Status of Organic Ferming in India. *Current Science* 98(9): 1190-1194.

Roy D.K. and Singh BP. (2006). Effect of Level and Time of Nitrogen Application with and without Vermicompost on Yield, Yield Attributes and Qualitu of Malt Barley (*Hordeum vulgare*). *Indian Journal of Agronomy.* 51(1):40-42.

Saha N., Das A.C. and Mukherjee D. (1995). Effects of Decomposition of Organic Matter on the Activities of Microorganisms and Availability of Nitrogen, phosphorus and Sulphur in Soil. *Journal of the Indian Society of Soil Science* 43(1): 210-215.

Santhy P., Velusamy M.S., Murugappan B. and Selvi D. (1999). Effect of Organic Fertilizers and Fertilizer Manure Combination on Soil physic-chemical Properties and Dynamics of Microbial Biomass in an Iceptisol. *Journal of the Indian Society of Soil Science* 47(1):479-482.

Sarwar G., Schmeisky H., Hussain N., Muhammad S., Ibrahim M. and Safdar E. (2008). Improvement of Soil Physical and Chemical Properties with Compost Application in Rice-wheat Cropping System. *Pakistan Juornal of Botany* 40(1): 275-282.

Schjonning P., Christenson B.T. and Carstensen B. (1994). Physical and Chmical Properties of Sandy Loam Receiving Animal Manure, Mineral Fertilizers or no Fertilizers for 90 Years. *European Journal of Soil Science* 45(2): 257-268.

Selvi D., Santhy P. and Dhakshinamoorthy. (2005). Effect of Inorganics alone and in Combination with FYM on Physical Properties and Productivity of Vertic Haplustepts under Long-term Fertilization. *Journal of Indian Society of Soil Science* 553(3):302-307.

Sharma H.L., Singh C.M. and Modgal S.C. (1987). Use of Organics in Rice-wheat Crop Sequence. *Indian Journal of Agricultural Sciences* 57(2):163-168.

Sharma M.P., Bali S.B. and Gupta D.K. (2000). Crop Yield and Properties of Inceptisol as Influenced by Residue Management Under Rice - Wheat Cropping Sequence. *Journal of the Indian Society of Soil Science* 48(1): 506-509.

Sharma P.K. Bhushan L. (2001). Physical Characterization of Soil Amended with Organic Residues in A Rice-Wheat Cropping System using A Single Value Physical Index. *Soil and Tilage Research* 60(2): 143-152.

Sharma R.P., Datt N., Chander G and Sharma, A. (2006). Influence of Conjoint use of Vermicompost and Chemical Fertilizers on Productivity, Nutrient uptake and Available Nutrient Status in okra (*Abelmoschus esculentus*) - Onion (*Allium cepa*) sequence. In Balanced Fertilization for Sustainable Crop Production edited by Sharma S.P., Sharma S.K. and Verma T.S. CSK Himachal Pradesh Krishi Vishwavidyalaya, Palampur, HP. p. 151-152.

Sheeba S. and Chellamuthu S. (1999). Long-term Influence of Organic an Inorganic Fertilization on the Macro Nutrients Status of Inceptisols. *Journal of Indian Society of Soil Science* 47(3): 803-804.

Simek M., Hopkins D.W., Kalcik J., Picek T., Santruckova H., Stana J. and Traunik K. (1999). Biological and Chemical Properties of arable Soils as Affected by Long-term Organic and Inorganic Fertilizer Applications. *Biology and Fertility of Soils* 29(1):300-308.

Singaram P. and Kamalakumari K. (1995). Long-term Effect of FYM and Fertilizers on Enzyme Dynamics of Soil. *Journal of the Indian Society of Soil Science* 43(2): 378-381.

Singh BS. (2005). Effect of Green Manuring and Nitrogen on Yoeld and Uptake of Micro Nutrient by Rice. *Journal of Soils and Crop.* 2(3) p. 183.

Singh S.K. and Lal SS. (2001). Nutrient Management in Potato-vegetable Sequence under Rainfed Conditions of Meghalaya. *Journal of Indian Potato Association* 28(1): 38-39.

Spain A.V., Isbell RF and Probert ME. (1983). Soil Organic Matter. IN: Soils: An Australian View Point. CSIRO, Melbourne/Academic Press, London p. 551-563.

Srinivas D., Saroja R. and Raman S. (2002). Effect of Organic Manures on Soil dehydrogenase Activity in Submerged Vertisol Planted Rice. *Journal of Maharashtra Agricultural University* 27(2):247-250.

Tarafdar J.C., Pal H.P. and Jana A.K. (1989). Phosphatase and dehydrogenase Activity under Rainfed Condition as Affected by Manures and Chemical Fertilizers on Corchorus sp. *Jute Development Journal* 9(1): 36-39.

Tiwari V.N., Tiwri K.N. and Upadhyay R.M. (1999). Effect of Crop Residues and Biogas Slurry Incorporation in Wheat on Yield and Fertility. *Journal of Indian Society of Soil Science* 47 (3): 515-520.

Tolanur SI and Badanur VP. (2003). Effect of Integrated use of Organic Manure, Green Manure and Fertilizer Nitrogen on Sustaining Productivity of *Rabi* sorghum-chickpea System and Fertility of A Vertisol. *Journal of the Indian Society of Soil Science* 51(1).

V Hangarge D.S., Raut R.S., More S.D., Birajdar R.R. and Pholane L.P. (2002). Effect of Vermicompost and Soil Conditioner on some Physical Properties of Soil under chilli-spinach System. *Journal of Soils and Crops* 12(1): 41-45.

Varalakshmi B.R., Srinivasamurthy C.A. and Bhaskar S. (2005). Effect of Integrated use of Organic Manures and Inorganic Fertilizers on Organic Carbon, available N.,P. and K. in Sustaining Productivity of Groundnut-finger Millet Cropping Scheme. *Journal of Indian Society of Soil Science* 53(3):325-318.

Vennila C. and Jayanthi C. (2007). Residual Effect of Integrated Nitrogen Management of Wet Seeded rice + daincha dual cropping System on Yield and Nutrient Uptake of Greengram. *Agricultural Science Digest* 27(4).

Verma S. (2006). Physical Characterization of An Acid alfisol Under Maize-wheat Cropping. *Ph.D. Thesis,* Department of Soil Science, CSK Himachal Pradesh Krishi Vishavidhyalaya, Palampur, India. pp. 67-68.

Walia M.K., Walia S.S. and Dhaliwal. (2010). Long-term Effect of Integrated Nutrient Management of Properties of Typic Ustochrept After 23 Cycles of an Irrigated Rice (*Oryza sativa* L.)-wheat (*Triticum aestivum* L.) System. *Journal of Sustainable Agriculture* 34(7):724-774.

Willer H., Yussefi-Menzler M and Sorensen N. (2008). The World of Organic Agriculture: Statistics and Emerging Trends 2008. Current Statistics. pp. 23-46.

Zebarth B.J., Neilsen G.H., Hogue E. and Neilsen D. (1993). Influence of Organic Waste Amendments on Selected Soil Physical and Chemical Properties. *Canadian Journal of Soil Science* 79(2): 501-504.

AGRICULTURAL PRACTICES AND CROP DISEASE CONTROL
Edited by : **Dr. Alka Chauhan** and **Dr. Anubhuti Sharma**
Edition : 2017
ISBN : 978-93-5056-859-0
Published by : Discovery Publishing House Pvt. Ltd., New Delhi (India)

2

Salient Features of Fertilizer Control Order with Special to Indian Legislation for Protecting and Restoring Environment

Prasann Kumar

ABSTRACT

Fertilizer has played and will continue to play a pivotal role in increasing agricultural production in the country. According to FAO, 50 per cent of increase in food grain production is attributed to fertilizer alone. To ensure the availability of right quality and adequate quantity of fertilizers, at right time and at fair price, to the farmers in all parts of the country, the central government promulgated the following order in exercise of the power conferred under section 3 of the E.C.A., to regulate manufacture, quality, sale, distribution, price, and movement etc., of fertilizer. Initially, the F.C.O., was issued on 23.4.1957 and came into force w.e.f. 15.5.1957. Since then, a lot of changes in fertilizer technology, production and distribution system took place. Finally, the revised FCO called FCO, 1985 was issued on 25.9.1985 which came into force with immediate effects. The Directive Principles of State Policy of the Indian Constitution provide the State's commitment to protect the environment. A series of separate legislations occurring in different time and space depicts an integrated understanding of the causes of environmental degradation and destruction and its remedial measures. The constitutional provisions made the way to formulate regulatory environmental protection law such as: The Factories Act, 1948; The Water (Prevention and Control Pollution) Act, 1974; The Water (Prevention and Control of Pollution)

Department of Plant Physiology, Institute of Agricultural Sciences, Banaras Hindu University, Varanasi, 221 005, India.

Cess Act 1977; The Air (Prevention and Control of Pollution) Act 1981; The Environment (protection) Act 1986; The Public Liability Insurance Act 1991; The National Environment Tribunal Act 1995; The Forest (Conservation) Act 1980; The Wildlife (Protection) Act 1972; and The Biological Diversity Act 2002. These legislations have been formulated to ensure the protection of the environment with an aim of sustainable development.

In this paper, I will cover both i.e., fertilizer control order as well as rules related to environment and its protection.

Keywords: Agriculture, Biotic, Control, Diffuse, Ensure, Fertilizer, Quality.

INTRODUCTION

The main objective of the FCO is to protect the interest of the farmers as well as that of genuine traders/manufactures from the exploitation by unscrupulous elements. These are achieved by ensuring the availability of fertilizers of right quality and at right time by regulating their quality, price, distribution, sale etc. In a nutshell, FCO consists of 39 clauses and can be divided mainly into following chapters: - 1. Short titles and commencement (cl.1); 2. Definitions (cl.2); 3. Price control (Cl.3-5); 4. Control on distribution of fertilizers by manufacturers/importers (Cl.6); 5. Authorization of registration for dealers (Cl.7-1); 6. Manufacture of mixture of fertilizer, organic fertilizers and biofertilizers (Cl.12-18); 7. Restriction on manufacture, import, sale etc., of fertilizers (Cl. 19-25); 8. Enforcement authorities (Cl. 26-28); 9. Analysis of fertilizer samples (Cl. 29-30); 10. Miscellaneous (Cl. 31-39).

Details of clauses are as under:

Clause 1: Clause 1 stipulates that this order may be called as the fertilizer control order, 1985.

Clause - 2: This clause deals with the definition of various terms used in the FCO, 1985. Such as: grade, importer/pool handling agency, retail dealer, wholesale dealer, industrial dealer, notified authority, registering authority.

Clause - 3, 4 and 5: The central Government is empowered to fix the prices of fertilizer through notification in official Gazette. The central governments also fix different prices for different areas or for different classes of consumers, of the same fertilizer, if the circumstances so require. The state government tares empowered vides order GSR No. 59(E) dated 10.2.1984 to fix the maximum prices for mixture of fertilizers.

Clause - 6: The central Government is empowered to direct the manufactures/ importers, through notification of officials Gazette, to see the specified quality of fertilizer produced by him in the specified states and within specified period.

Clause - 7-11 and 22: For authorization every person including: manufacturer, importer, pool handling agency, wholesale and retail dealer shall make a memorandum of intimation to the notified authority in form A1, in duplicate along with CS in form "O" and prescribed fee under clause 36, the notified authority shall issue an acknowledgement of receipt in form "A2" and it shall be deemed to be an authorization letter granted to the concerned person as authorized dealer for wholesale or retail.

Clause - 12 to 18: No person shall carry on the business of preparing any mixture of fertilizer, special mixture of fertilizer, Bio Fertilizers or organic fertilizers except under and in accordance with the term and conditions of a certificate of manufacture (CM) granted to him under clause 15/16. The grades of various mixtures of fertilizers are notified by central government and state government. The power to notify the grades of mixture of liquid fertilizers and 100 per cent water soluble mixture of fertilizer rests with the central government only. Any notified mixture of fertilizers or special mixture of fertilizer can be prepared only after obtaining a vital CM in form "F or G "respectively from registering authority (RA).

Clause - 19: No person shall himself of any other person on his behalf manufacture/import for sale, offer for sale, stock or exhibit for sale or distributed any fertilizer which is not of prescribed slandered.

Clause - 20: Notwithstanding anything contained in this order, the central government and order, published in the official gazette, fix separate specifications in respect of imported fertilizers.

Clause - 21: Every manufacturers/importers and pool handling agencies have to comply with certain requirements in regard to packing and marking etc. Some of the requirements are as follows:

(i) every container in which any fertilizer is packed shall be conspicuously super scribed the word 'Fertilizer';

(ii) on the container of the imported fertilizers, which a manufacturers is also a pool handling agency or an importer, the word "p" or "I" as the case my be, shall be written against the name of manufacturer.

Clause - 23: In FCO special provision has been made for disposal of non standard fertilizer. The bags of non standards fertilizers are to be marked with the word 'Non-standard' and "x" in red colour.

Clause - 24: Every manufacturing organization, importer and pool handling agency shall appoint in that organization and in consultation with the central government, an officer, who shall be responsible for compliance with the provisions of this order.

Clause - 25: The sale/use of fertilizers for the purposes other than agriculture *i.e.,* industrial purposes is prohibited, except with the permission of the central Government. However, no prior permission is required for industrial use, if the fertilizer is purchased from the 'Industrial dealer' possessing a valid CR issued by controller of fertilizer, in accordance with the provision of clauses 9-11 of FCO.

Clause - 26-27: Under clause 26, the state Government may, by notification in the official gazette, appoint such number of persons, as it thinks necessary, to be registering authorities for the purpose of this order and ay, in any such notification define the limits of local area within which each registering authority shall exercise his jurisdiction.

Clause - 28: It includes power of fertilizers inspectors.

(*a*) to call for information about manufacture and disposal of fertilizer;

(*b*) to Draw sample of fertilizers;

(*c*) to enter upon and search any premises where fertilizer are manufactured, stocked or sold;

(*d*) to seize and detain any fertilizer, books of accounts or documents relating to manufacture, storage, sale etc., of fertilizer in respect of which he has reasons to believe that the contravention of order has been or is being or is about to be committed;

(*e*) to stop, search any person or any vehicle or any receptacle used or intended to be used for the export of fertilizers from one state to another.

Clause - 29: A fertilizer sample, drawn by an inspector, shall be analyzed in accordance with the instruction contained in schedule ii in the central fertilizer quality control and training institute, Faridabad or regional fertilizer control laboratories at NAVI Mumbai, Chennai and kalyani or in any other laboratory notified for this purpose by the TATA governments. In order to ensure accurate analysis of fertilizer samples, every laboratory notified under this clause should posses' minimum equipment and other laboratory facilities as may be specified from to time by the controller of fertilizer.

Clause - 30: Time limit for analysis and communication of result.

1. sample drawn by Fertilizer inspector shall be dispatched along with memorandum in form K to the laboratory for analysis within a period of 7 days from the date of its drywall;
2. laboratory shall analyses the sample and forward the analysis report in form L within 30 days from the date of receipt of sample in the laboratory;
3. the authority to whom the analysis report is sent, shall communicate the result of the analysis to the dealer/manufactures/importer from whom sample was drawn within 15 days from the date of receipts of analysis report.

Clause - 31: Authorization letter 9AL)/certificate of Manufacture (CM) or any other certificate granted under FCO can be suspended or cancelled/ debarred by the AL/CM for the following reasons:

(a) if certificate was obtained by misrepresentation;

(b) if any provision of FCO, 1985 or any terms and condition of such certificate/authorization letter has been violated.

Clause - 32: Ay person aggrieved by the analysis report of CFQC AND TI/RFCLs may appeal o the controller of fertilizer-is for referee analysis of such sample within a period of 30 days from the date of receipt of analysis report.

Clause - 33: Notified authority/registration authority may grant duplicate copies of authorization letter or certificate of manufacture/certificate of registration etc.

Clause - 34: Notified Authority/registration authority may issue amendment of authorization letter or certificate of manufacture/certificate of registration etc.

Clause - 35: The controller of fertilizer may direct the dealers, manufacturers/ importer and pool handling agencies to maintain such books of accounts, records etc., relating to their business in form N and submit to such authority, returns and statement in such from and containing such information relating to their business and within such time as may be specified in that order.

For import of fertilizer, every importer shall inform the director of agriculture of the state in which he intends to discharge the imported fertilizer, under intimation to the central Government, before the import is made or within a period of 15 days after an indent for import is placed it detailed information.

Clause - 36: Fees for grant/renewal/duplicate etc. of different certificate authorization (excepting for industrial dealership) under FCO, 1985 are to be fixed the state Government. In respect of CR for industrial dealer, it is prescribed by central Government.

Clause - 37: Service of order and directions.

Clause - 38: This provide for setting up of the advisory committee both at central government and state government level. The central fertilizer committee of 11 member under the chairmanship of agriculture commissioner, in different matters relating to FCO919850, such as: Amendments in fco, Pecification of fertilizer/Incluson of new fertilizer, laboratory facilities for testing etc. Similarly, there is the state fertilizer committee, consisting of 5 members including chairman, renders advice to the state governments regarding the specification of various grade/ formulation of mixture of fertilizer etc. to be manufactured and sold in the state.

Clause - 39: The control order, 1957 is repealed except as respects things done or omitted to be done under the said order the commencement of this order. In nutshell FCO is consisting of 39 clauses, 22 forms and 4 schedules.

The planet earth is the abode of man, an intelligent creature of nature. It also houses plants, animals, insects, birds, and other living beings. There are also billions of objects formed by five basic elements-water, air, soil, sky and fire. Man influences and is influenced by all these living and non-living creations of nature. The totality of all such objects is usually referred to as his environment. Human rights are inextricably linked with environmental rights. Thus, every Indian should know the broad outlines of different legislations meant for the purpose. The Constitution of India overtly makes environmental conservation a duty. The provisions for environmental protection in the constitution were made within four years of Stockholm Conference, in 1976, through the 42nd amendment as follow:

- *Article 48-A of the Constitution Provides*: "The state shall endeavour to protect and improve the environment and to safeguard forests and wildlife of the country".
- *Article 51 A (g) Provides*: "It shall be the duty of every citizen of India to protect and improve the natural environment including forests, lakes, rivers and wildlife and to have compassion for living creatures."

Thus our constitution includes environmental protection and conservation as one of our fundamental duties. Mrs. Indira Gandhi, the Prime Minister of India, was the only visiting head of State to attend the Conference on 'Human Environment' at Stockholm, from 5th June to 12th June 1972. Government of India actively participated in the conference and Mrs. Gandhi presented a thought provoking paper on poverty and environment and strongly voiced concerns. Several measures were taken in India for Environmental Protection before the conference but there was no general legislation on holistic manner to protect the environment. The existing laws dealt directly or indirectly with several environmental issues like forest conservation, wild life conservation, etc., but no general comprehensive law existed to deal with pollution prevention, control and abatement. India has witnessed >50 fold increase in Industrial sector by 1970s and the increasing tendency of industrialization and urbanization led to discharge of high volumes of effluents and municipal sewage to water bodies causing environmental pollution and health hazards. Indian surface water in rivers (all 14 major rivers), ponds and lakes is unfit for human consumption. WHO data show that 21 per cent of all communicable disease in India are water related. Over exploitation, enhanced pumping, intrusion of saline water in coastal areas, discharge of toxic effluents on land and in water bodies have led to decline in water table and contamination of groundwater resources. The Indian ground water Board has identified 231 blocks, where ground water depletion has reached critical level.

The Factories Act, 1949 (Amendment 1949)

The Factories Act, 1948 is a post-independence state that shows explicit concern for the environment. The Act contains a comprehensive list of 29 categories of industries involving hazardous processes (First Schedule of the Act). Section 2 (c, b) of the Act defines 'hazardous process' as any process or activity in relation to an industry specified in the first schedule, where unless special care is taken, raw materials used therein or the intermediate or finished products, byproducts, wastes or effluents thereof.

Chapter IV-A : Provisions relating to hazardous processes.

Section-41A : Constitution of site appraisal committees.

Section-41B : Compulsory disclosure of information by the occupier.

Section-41C : Responsibility of an occupier for workers' medical checkup.

Section-41D : Inquiry committee for the occurrence of an accident.

Section-41E : Emergency standard.

Section-41F : Permissible limits of exposure of chemical/toxic substance.

Section-41G : Workers' right to warn about imminent danger.

Constitutional Provisions

Article 21 opines "No person shall be deprived of his life or personal liberty except according to procedure established by law". The Supreme Court interpreted this Article to include right of having a living environment congenial to human existence, while disposing the Vellore Tannery case in 1996. So pollution due to different industrial activities can be interpreted by the Supreme Court as violation of Article 21. Under Article 39A (42nd amendment) (equal justice and free legal aid), PIL was introduced. Article 47 status that "the state is to ensure as its primary duty of:

A Raising standard of living of its people.

B To increase the level of nutrition of the people and to bring improvement in public health.

In 42nd amendment of the Constitution, two articles (Article 48A and 51A-g) having direct bearing on environmental were incorporated in 1976. The Article 48A states that "the state shall endeavor and to safeguard the forests and wildlife of the country." The article 51A (g) states that "it is the duty of citizen to protect and improve rivers and wildlife and to have compassion for all living creatures". In addition, Article 372 and PIL (Public Interest Litigations) are legal instruments to initiate proactive actions towards the environment.

The Water (Prevention and Control of Pollution) Act, 1974, (Amendment 1978 and 1988)

A committee was set up in 1962 to draw a draft enactment to prevent water pollution. The report was circulated to the state governments and considered by the Central Council of Local Self-Government (CCLF). A draft bill was prepared and considered in the joint session of CCLF and 5th conference of the sate ministry on Town and Country planning held in 1965.

Finally the water (Prevention and Control of Pollution) bill was passed by both the Houses of Parliament under Article 252(1) of the Constitution and received the assent of the President on 23rd March, 1974. The Water Act, 1974 represents one of India's first attempts to deal comprehensively with an environment issue. The act was amended in 1988 to conform closely to provisions of the Environment (Protection) Act, 1986. This act is meant for the prevention, control and abatement of water pollution and maintaining or restoring the wholesomeness of water. It applies to streams, inland water, subterranean water and sea or tidal water. Its primary objective was to established pollution control boards and assigning them the necessary powers and functions. Central Pollution Control Board (CPCB) was established in September, 1974. Standards for the discharge of the effluents or the quality of receiving waters are not specified in the Act itself. Instead, the act enables the CPCB and the State Board to prescribe these standards. The Water Act regulates water pollution through a system of 'command and control'. This Act provides for a permit system or consent procedure to abate, prevent and control pollution. A person must obtain consent from the State Board before taking steps to establish any industry, operation or process, any treatment or disposal system or any extension or addition to such a system.

The Water Act, 1974

Section-2	: Definitions.
Section-3 and 4	: Setting up of CPCB and SPCB.
Section-16	: Functions of the CPCB.
Sections-17	: Functions of the SPCB.
Sections-19	: Power to restrict the application of the Water Act to certain areas.
Section-23	: Power of entry and search.
Section-24	: Prohibitions on use of streams or wells for disposal of polluting matter.
Section-25	: Application for Consent.
Section-26	: Refusal of Consent.
Section-28	: Review by an appellant authority.
Section-30	: Notice.
Section-31	: Furnishing information.
Section-32	: Emergency measures in case of pollution of a stream or Well.
Section-33	: Injunction from court.
Section-33A	: Power to give directions for closure.
Section-41 to 50	: Penal Provisions.

The Water (Prevention and Control of Pollution) Cess Act, 1977 (Amendment 2003)

This Act is enacted for collection of cess on water consumed by persons carrying on certain (Schedule I) industries and by local authorities, with a view to augment resources of the Central and State Pollution Control Board(s). This Act aims to augment the resources of the Central and State boards for the prevention and control of water pollution. The industries specified in the schedule are to affix meters and submit reports of consumption in prescribed forms to the Central Board. There is a provision for 25 per cent rebate for industries, which install a plant for the treatment of trade effluents.

The Air (Prevention and Control of Pollution Act, 1981 (Amendment 1987)

The Air Act was enacted in 1981 under Article 253 of the Constitution of India, which gives power to the Central Government to make laws to implement decisions made at the United Nations Conference on the Human Environment held at "Stockholm in 1972. To counter the problems associated with air pollution, ambient air quality standards were established under the Air Act, 1981. The Air Act (1981) provides means for the control and abatement of air pollution. The Act seeks to combat air pollution by prohibiting the use of polluting fuels, explosives and appliances that causes air pollution. Under the Act establishing or operating of ay industrial plant/mining in the pollution control area requires consent from the State boards. The boards are also expected to examine the air in the air pollution control areas, inspect air pollution-control equipments and manufacturing processes. The Air Act provides for State boards even in states which do not have pollution control boards established under the Water Act. The Air Act provides power to State boards for the protection of environment".

Section-16 : Functions of the CPCB.
Sections-17 : Functions of the SPCB.
Sections-19 : Declaration of restricted areas.
Sections-23 : Information of SPCB.
Sections-24 : Power of Entry.
Sections-25 : Power of obtain information.
Section-31A : Power of order closure, prohibition or regulation of any industry.
Section-37 to 46 : Penal Provisions.

The ambient air quality must therefore, be measured before establishing the plant. The existing background ambient air quality levels for SO@, NOx, TSPM are to be provided in the Environmental Impact Assessment (EIA) report. The report comprises one full season other than the monsoon and information to be collected as per the CPCB guidelines. It the results of the mathematical modeling of air quality prediction indicate a significant change in the ambient air quality, it would be necessary to provide adequate air pollution control equipment as well as a system for measuring air quality and emissions. CPCB/SPCB prescribes standards for stack height of various plants for better dispersal of pollutants.

The Environmental (Protection) Act, 1986 (EPA)

The Act came into force on Nov. 19, 1986, the birth anniversary of our Late Prime Minister Indira Gandhi, who was a pioneer of environmental protection issue in our country. The Act extends to whole of India. The Act has given powers to the central Government to take measures to protect and improve environment while the state governments coordinate the actions. The most important functions of Central Government under this Act include setting up of:

A The procedure and safeguards for the prevention of accidents which may cause environmental pollution and providing for remedial measure for such accidents.

B The prohibition and restriction on the location of industries and to carry on process and operations in different areas.

C The prohibition and restrictions on the handling of hazardous substances in different areas.

D The procedure and safeguards for the handling of hazardous substances.

E The maximum permissible limits of concentration of various environmental pollutants (including noise) for different areas.

F The standards of quality of air, water or soil for various areas and purposes.

The power of entry and inspection, power to take sample etc., under this Act lies with the Central Government or any officer empowered by it.

For the purpose of protecting and improving the quality of the environment and preventing and abating pollution, standards have been specified under Schedule I-IV of Environment (Protection) Rules, 1986 for emission of gaseous pollutants and discharge of effluents/waste water form industries. These standards vary from industry to industry an also vary with the medium into which the effluent in discharge or the area of emission. For instance, the maximum permissible limits of B.O.D., of the waste water are 30 ppm if it discharged into inland waters, 350 ppm if discharged into a public sewer and 100 ppm, if discharged onto land or coastal regions. Likewise, emission standards vary in residential, sensitive and industrial area. Naturally the standards for sensitive areas like hospitals are more stringent. It is the duty of the Pollution Control Board to check whether the industries are following the prescribed norms or not. Laws existing prior to this Act generally focused on specific types of pollution, namely: water and air pollution, not on the general management principles for restoration and protection of the environment. Disposal of hazards waste and chemicals, biochemical and municipal solid wastes etc., were not covered. There were inadequate linkages in handling matters related to industrial and environmental safety. Thus, incorporating most of environmental issues, it was conceived as an Umbrella Act.

❖ *Section 3(1)*: Powers to and functions of the Central Government.

To set new national standards for the quality of the environment (ambient standards), as well as standards for controlling emissions and effluent discharges:

- to regulate industrial locations;
- to prescribe procedures for managing hazardous wastes;
- to established safeguards for preventing accidents; and to collect and disseminate information regarding environmental pollution;

❖ *Section 5:* Power to issue directions.

❖ *Sections 6*: Rules to regulate environmental pollution.

Ministry of Environment and Forest (MoEF) is responsible for making rules to implement the EPA and has adopted industry specific standards for effluent discharge and emissions for 24 designated industries.

❖ *Section 7*: This section states that those persons, who are carrying on industry, operations etc., are not allowed to emit or discharge environmental pollutants in excess of the standards.

❖ *Section 9*: Furnishing of information in certain cases.

- in cases where discharge of an environmental pollution occurs in excess of the prescribed standards, or there is an apprehension of this occurring due to an accident or some other unforeseen event, then the person who is in charge at that particular time is responsible for preventing environmental pollution due to the said discharge;
- it is the responsibility of the person to intimate the occurrence of the discharge to the CPCB/SPCB, and provide all possible assistance to the regulatory agencies to counter the effects of the discharge;
- all expenses incurred by the regulatory agency in undertaking remedial measures may be recovered from the polluter;
- central Government has the power under Section 3 and 5 of the EPA to levy and recover the cost of the remedial measures;
- the polluter pays principle was also held to be applicable and section 3 and 5 of the EPA were held to empower the Central Government to give directions and take measures;

❖ *Section 10*: Power of search and entry.

- the EPA empowers authorized officers to enter, at all reasonable times, any place, or premises for determining the infringement of standards and procedures set under the Act, and for testing any equipment, industrial plant, record, register or document or any other material object for determining offences under the EPA;

- a willful delay or an obstruction of such an inspection is an offence and the person in-charge is liable for prosecution.

❖ *Section 11:* Power to take samples of air, water, soil or any other substance from the factory premises. Collected samples are to be sent without delay to the environmental laboratories. CPCB/SPCB and the officers empowered by the respective Board under Section 21 and 23 of the Water Act, 1974 or under Section 24 of the Air Act, 1981 are empowered to enter and search the premises and take samples.

❖ *Section 12 and 13*: The samples collected are to be sent to notified environmental laboratories for analysis. Government analysis with specific qualifications is appointed under Section 13.

❖ *Section 14*: A document, which is a report signed by a Government analyst, can be used as evidence for any proceeding under the EPA.

❖ *Section 15*: Penal provision.

❖ *Section 18*: Protection of action done in good faith.

❖ *Section 19*: Cognizance of offences.

❖ *Section 22*: Bar of jurisdiction: No civil court has the jurisdiction to entertain any suit, or proceedings in respect of anything done, action taken, or order or direction issued by the Central Government or any other Authority or officer in pursuance of any power conferred by or in relation to its or his/her function under the Act.

❖ *Section 23*: Powers to delegate: The Central Government can delegate its functions.

Critique of the Environmental (Protection) Act, 1986

Section 3 of EP Act, 1986 provides for collection and dissemination of information regarding environmental pollution. However, the Government has not yet adopted regulatory provisions to implement this power. In the absence of such regulations a community may not be aware that a potentially hazardous operation is situated in their midst. Also, in such a situation the local authorities may not know what possible preparedness may be needed for emergencies. No minimum sentence is prescribed in the Section 15, which deals with penal provisions. Section 15 should provide some minimum punishment, so that the violators may have apprehension of such minimum punishment even in case of his smallest mistake.

Section 19 of the Act seemingly gives the public significant powers to enforce the Act. However, only Government officials are given the power under the Act to collect samples needed as evidence of violation of the Act. In addition, during the sixty days notice period required for the Government to decide whether to proceed against the alleged isolator, the offending industry has time to clean up and prepare itself for collection of samples. Section 24 of the Environment (Protection) Act 1986 is one of its controversial provisions.

Generally more recent legislation supersedes the previous legislation. Standards established under the EP Act are also dealt with under the Water Act and Air Act. In case of violation, both under the EP Act are therefore illusionary for those violations, where the Water Act and Air Act also apply. Suppose the Water Act allows discharge of a higher concentration of a particular pollutant than the concentration permissible under the EP Act and if a factory discharges wastewater containing the pollutant at a level higher than allowed under the EP Act but within the permissible limits of the Water Act, then whether the Water Act penalty provision applies become debatable. The Act is also criticized on the ground that it is absolutely silent with respect to civil liability and compensation to the victim. After all, The EP Act is far better than earlier Acts projecting wider perspective for preservation. Protection, conservation and restoration of environment and is good enough for curbing environmental pollution and disaster management.

The Environmental (Protection) Rules, 1986

Some relevant provisions of the rules are:

Rule-3 : Standard for emission or discharge of environmental pollutants.

Rule-4 : Issuance of specific directions to an industry.

Rule-5 : Prohibition and restriction on the location of industries in different areas.

Rule-6 : Procedure for taking samples.

Rule-8 : Procedure for submission of the sample for analysis.

Rule-9 : Functions of environmental laboratories.

Rule-11 : manner of giving notice.

Rule-13 : Prohibition and restriction on the handling of hazardous substances.

Rule-14 : Submission of Environmental Statement (Environmental audit report).

The Central Government has notified many rules and notifications under the Environmental Protection Act, 1986. Few of them are follows:

- Hazardous Wastes (Management and Handling) Rules, 1989: Provides safeguards in handling hazardous wastes.
- Manufacture, Storage and Import of Hazardous Chemical Rules, 1989: Provides safeguard in handling hazardous chemicals.
- Coastal Zone Regulation, 1991: Regulates activities in the coastal zone between the low tide line and 500 meters from the high tide line.
- Rules for the Manufacture, Use, Import, Export, Storage of Hazardous Microorganisms, Genetically Engineered Organisms or Cell, 1989.
- Rules on Emergency Planning, Preparedness and Response for Chemical Accidents, 1996: Provides safeguard against chemical accidents.

Ash Content Notification (1997)

- Notification of Compulsory Public Hearing, 1997: Makes compulsory, the public hearing for certain category of projects before EIA clearance.
- Notification for Environmental Impact assessment (EIA), 1994 and as amended in 1997, and 2006: makes it compulsory for certain category of projects to take prior EIA clearance from the central Government.
- Disposal of Fly ash Notification (1999): Provides safeguards for disposal of fly ash.
- The Noise Pollution (regulation and Control) rules, 2000: it is enacted to abate noise pollution.

The Environmental Impact Assessment (of Development Projects) Notification, 1994 (Amendment, 1997 and 2006)

Until January 1994, obtaining environmental clearance from MoEF was only an administrative requirement intended for mega projects undertaken by the Government or Public sector undertakings. The EIA notifications of September, 2006, make EIA statutory for 40 items (A and B category) under 8 projects/activities (Schedule of the notification). There will be a Central Expert Appraisal Committee for all projects includes under MoEF (A-category) and state level EIA Authority for B category projects.

The salient provisions of the notification are as follows:

A. All projects listed under Schedule are required to obtain environmental clearance (EC) from the MoEF/State Government.

B. Projects that all under "A" category need clearance from the MoEF.

C. All development projects whether under Schedule or not, if they are to be located in certain notified ecologically sensitive or fragile areas will have to obtain clearance from MoEF.

D. Industrial projects are further required to obtain a LOI (Letter of Intent) from the Ministry of Industry, and a NOC (no objection certificate) from the SPCB and the State Forest Department, if the location involves forestland.

E. Once the NOC is obtained, the LOI is converted to an industrial license by the State authorities. However, if the project falls under Schedule of the EIA notification (A-category), it must obtain an environmental clearance from the MoEF.

Environmental Clearance

Environmental Clearance (EC) will have four stages:

1. Screening for A, B1 and B2 categories of projects.
2. Scoping for A and B1 category of projects.

3. Public Consultation (for A and B1 categories-except building, township etc., defense infrastructure, expansion of roads and highways, modernization of irrigation projects and all B2 category projects).
4. Appraisal (detailed scrutiny by Central Expert Appraisal Committee (CEAC) or State level Expert Appraisal Committee.

The EIA report that is submitted after the site clearance contains the following:

A Description of site and site map.

B Land requirements, No objection certificate from State Forest Department if forest lands is involved.

C Rehabilitation plan for displaced people.

D Consent from SPCB (regarding effluents and emissions).

E Report on impacts on the environment during construction.

F Collection of ambient air quality and meteorological data.

G Report on hydrology and water quality.

H Report on occupational safety and health.

I Details of transport and handling of raw materials.

The National Environmental Appellate Authority Act, 1997 (NEAAA)

This Act was established to hear appeals with respect to an environment clearance given under the Environmental (Protection) Act, 1986. The NEAA is located in Delhi and Judge of the Supreme Court or a Chief Justice of any High Court as its Chairperson. A person aggrieved by an order granting environmental clearance in a given area for establishing an industry may, within 30 days from the date of such an order, appeal to the NEAA. The timeframe can be extended to 90 days if there are good grounds for delay. The appellant can be a person, who owns or controls the projects, an association of persons, Central or State Government or any local authority. No civil court or other authority has jurisdiction to entertain any appeal in respect of any matter with which the NEAA is empowered. All proceedings before the NEAA are deemed to be judicial proceedings. Failure to comply with any order made by the NEAA is punishable with imprisonment for a term of up to seven years or with a fine which may extends to one lakh or both. The corporate liability is pinned on the person in-charge of and responsible to the company. Ignorance and due diligence are considered adequate defense against corporate liability.

The National Environmental Appellate Authority Act, 1997

Section 3 : Establishment of Authority.

Section 4 : Composition of Authority.

Section 11 : Appeals to Authority.

Section 12 : Procedures and powers of Authority.

Section 15 : Bar of jurisdiction.

Section 16 : Proceeding before the Authority to be judicial proceedings.

Section 19 : Penal for failure to comply with orders of Authority.

Section 20 : Offences by companies.

Section 22 : Power to make rules.

Environmental Auditing

Environmental auditing is a management tool, which simply inspects the environmental management activities performed by industries or organizations and aware them with new cleaner technologies. It is the examination of accounts of revenues and costs of environmental and natural resources, their estimation, depreciations and values recorded in the books of accounts. In India, recognizing the importance of Environmental Audit (EA), procedure for EA was first notified under the Environmental Protection Act 1986 by the Ministry of Environment and Forestry by issuing of a gazette notification (No. GSR 329 (E)) on 13th March 1992. This makes the submission of the environmental audit reports mandatory. The industries are now required to submit their audit report to the concerned State Pollution Control Boards on or before 15th day of May every year beginning 1993. A large number of polluting industries were identified to submit their EA reports. The EA report has been renamed as Environmental Statement (ES) in 1993. The detail format prepared by the State Pollution Control Board is known as Form V. ISO-14000 is a methodology for environmental management. It provides necessary requirements and recommendations for any organization to develop and implement a cost effective system of management by introducing environmental auditing. ISO-14000 series covers environmental audit, audit procedure, audit criteria, audit management, site assessment, labeling, performance evaluations and life cycle assessment.

National Environmental Tribunal Act, 1995 (NETA)

The NETA prescribes the procedure and substantive law relating to compensation for the death of, or injury to, a person and damage to property and environment, by any industry wherein a hazardous substance is used or is a by-product. Where death and or injury have resulted from an accident due to the hazardous substance, the owner of the source is liable to pay compensation, irrespective of the wrongful act, neglect or default. Where the source of damage is multiple, the liability is split and apportioned on an equitable basis. A National Environmental Tribunal is established by the Central Government under NETA. The tribunal has jurisdiction over matters specified in the Public Liability Insurances Act. The Tribunal receives claims of compensation by the person who has sustained the injury or by his or her legal representative. The applications for claim are to be submitted within five years of the occurrence of the accident, otherwise it is liable to be dismissed.

The tribunal is not bound by the Code of Civil Procedure, but is guided by the principles of natural justice. For the purpose of NETA, the tribunal is vested with the powers of a Civil Court and can make its own rules of procedure, summon or enforce attendance of any person, examine witnesses on oath, require discovery or production of documents, and receive evidence on affidavits. The tribunal can sit in appeal over its own decisions, and its awards are executable as civil court decrees. Appeals against the award or other orders lie only to the Supreme Court.

The Indian Forest Act, 1927 (Amendment, 1930, 1933, 1937, 1947 and 2004)

Forest policy and management was introduced in India by British Government by setting up a Forest Department and enacting relevant legislation in the 19th Century. In 1878, British Government in India enacted the Indian Forest Act (IFA), 1878 relating to forests in British India. Subsequently it was felt that the provisions of this Act were not adequate. In order to consolidate the law relating to forests, the transit of forest produce and the duty livable on timber and other forest-produce, the Indian Forest Bill was introduced in the Legislature and received its assent on 21st September, 1927. It came on the Statute Book as The Indian Forest Act, 1927.

The Forest (Conservation) Act, 1980 (Amendment, 1988)

The forest (Conservation) Act (FCA) was adopted in 1980 to protect and conserve forest. The FCA restricts the powers of the State in respect of de-reservation of forests and the use of forestlands for non-forest purposes. An advisory committee has been created to oversee the implementation of the statute as per provision of FCA. According to Section 2 of the FCA "notwithstanding anything contained in any other law for the time being in force in a State, no State Government, or other authority shall, except with the prior approval of the Central Government, make any order directing-de-reservation of a reserved forest; use of any forest land for any non-forest purpose; assignment of any forest land to any private person or entity not controlled by the Government; and reforestation of any forest land of naturally grown trees.

This Act empowers type Central Government to constitute a seven-member committee to advise the Central Government on proposal made by a State Government for conservation of a forestland for a new project. The rules contain a detailed format for the State Government to follow, while asking for approval from the Central Government. The proposal requires reports on project details; location and land involved (legal status, details of flora and fauna, density, vulnerability to erosion, existence of a national park, wildlife sanctuary etc.); details of displacement of people due to the project; details of possible impact on the forest land; cost-benefit analysis; and opinion of the head of the State forest Department.

The Forest (Conservation) Act, 1980

Section 2 : Restriction on the de-reservation of forests or use of forest land for non-forest purpose.

Section 3 : Constitution of Advisory Committee.

Section 4 : Power to make rules.

Section 5 : Repeal and saving.

The Biological Diversity Act, 2002

The United Nationals Convention on Biological Diversity was signed at Rio de Janerio on the 5th day of June, 1992 and came into force on the 29th December, 1993. This Convention reaffirms the sovereign rights of the States over their biological resources. Being a signatory to the Convention, India has passed the Biological Diversity Act, 2002 to promote conservation of biological diversity. It is evident that India is rich in biological diversity and associated traditional and contemporary knowledge system. The Biodiversity Act, 2002 of India is meant for conservation of biological diversity, sustainable use of its components and fair and equitable sharing of the benefits arising out of the use of biological resources, knowledge and for matters connected therewith or incidental thereto. Scientific investigation of biodiversity is an essential prerequisite for its conservations, management and sustainable utilizations (Review literature).

The Coastal Regulation Zone (CRZ), 1991 (Recent Amendment 2011)

According to CRZ regulations, the coastal stretches of seas, bays, estuaries, creeks, rivers and backwaters, which are influenced by tidal action upto 500 meters from the High Tide Line (HTL) and the land between the Low Tidal Line (LTL) and HTL is termed as Coastal Regulation Zone. There are some restrictions on the setting up and expansion of industries on the setting up and expansion of industries, operations or processes, etc., in the said Coastal Regulation Zone (CRZ) such as:

(a) Setting up of new industries and expansion of existing industries, except those directly related to water front or directly needing foreshore facilities.

(b) Any construction activity between the Low Tide Line and High Tide except facilities for carrying treated effluents and waste water discharges into the sea, facilities for carrying sea water for cooling purpose, oil, gas and similar pipeline and facilities essential for activities permitted under these Notifications.

(c) Dressing or altering of sand dunes, hills, natural features including landscape changes for beautifications, recreational and other such purpose, except as permissible under this Notification.

Enforcement of the Environmental Norms

The Ministry of environment and Forest (MoEF), constituted in 1985, is the nodal agency at the central level for planning, promoting and coordinating environmental programmes. The MoEF formulates legislation to mitigate and control environmental pollution. A number of enforcement agencies assist MoEF in executing its assigned responsibilities.

Regional Office, MoEF

The major functions of the regional offices include:

(a) Follow up the implementation of conditions and safeguard laid down for projects, when environmental clearance is given.

(b) Follow up pollution control measures taken by various industries.

(c) Collect and furnish information relating to EIA of projects, pollution control measures, methodology and status, legal and enforcement measures, environmental protection of special conservation areas like: wetlands, mangroves and biosphere reserves.

CPCB and SPCB

The CPCB was established in September 1974 for the purpose of implementation of the Water Act. Later, in 1981 when the Air Act came into force the powers of the CPCB and SPCBs were expanded to include enforcement of the Air Act. Executive responsibilities for the prevention and control of industrial pollution are undertaken at the Central level by CPCB, which is a statutory body attached to the MoEF. The functions of the CPCB include promotion of cleanliness of the streams and wells, advising the Central Government on matters concerning abatement of water pollution, and laying down standards for water and air quality, and ensuring compliance with EP Act. The SPCBs were constituted to implement the Water Act in the states. The function of the SPCBs include planning and execution programmes for prevention and control of water and air pollution, advising the State Government on matters concerning abatement of water pollution, laying down standards for water and air quality, ensuring compliance with various laws, ensuring legal action against the polluters and evolving techno-economic methods for treatment, disposal and utilization of effluents.

Municipalities and Panchayats

Municipalities and Panchayats play an increasing role in the environmental management at the District level. Under the XIth schedule of the 73rd amendment, Panchayats would also be responsible for soil conservation, water management and non-conventional energy sources. Under the XIIth Schedule, Municipalities would also be responsible for water supply for industrial use, solid waste management and protection of the environment. No rule has, however, been made to put this amendment into practice.

India has an extensive framework of environmental laws. The conviction rate is extremely poor because of enforcement problems and some lacunae in the laws. Some reasons for poor implementation of environmental laws are:

A Relevance of standard lay down.

B Inadequate processes for environmental decision-making making and dispute resolution.

C Insufficient infrastructure in MoEF, CPCB and SPCBs for implementation.

D Government insensitivity.

E Poor legal infrastructure.

F Cost of compliance.

Despite the enactment of several environmental regulations, the desired results have not been achieved due to poor implementation. For effective implementation, coordination among all such agencies of government and private sector is imperative. Enforcement agencies and environmental authorities should work together at all levels to mitigate the gaps. For successful co-ordination, linkage at the field level among various government bodies is of the essence. Courts enforcing the law by calling upon the implementers to do their duties, by disciplining industries, through imposition of penalties, by awarding compensation and by-and-large allowing judicial activism to flourish through Public Interest Litigation (PIL) have all been welcomed (Rangarajan 2009).

Gape in Implementation, Enforcement and Co-ordination among the Environmental Agencies

MoEF is more involved in providing clearances instead of performing macro-tasks of environmental protection. The state and central MoEF authorities have been scuffling constantly for giving environmental clearances to projects. While the Centre want to retain control over such an authority, the State often feels trifling in the case of large development projects coming up in its territory-its role is limited to granting just a No Objection Certificate. This centre-state antipathy, have failed to enforce the environment regulations in many recent instances (Environmental Clearance for POSCO and Vedanta projects in Orissa). In a quasifederal democracy set-up in India, where the states are consulted after the centre decides a course of action, these issues will continue to be a hurdle for effective environmental enforcement unless states are democratically involved.

It is also pertinent to mention here that unfortunately, environmental legislations have been systematically diluted to pine away by removing legal impediments for development projects. For instance, the CRZ Notification, issued in 1991 and publicized as a progressive law, it is now a 'toothless tiger' due to innumerable amendments mostly on the nature of exemptions for developmental activities (Rangarajan 2009).

Thus, a comprehensive review of environmental legislation is necessary. Coupled with such a review, efforts to harmonise policy directives of states and state-level laws with existing environmental legislation should be undertaken. Such a review would be meaningless if agencies, implementers and regulators are not strengthened with provision of adequate technical support, financial autonomy, clear decision-making powers built into accountability mechanisms (Rangarajan 2009).

The absence of technical capacity is compounded by the lack of technical man power within the Pollution Control Boards. Due to lack of funding support and lack of revenue generation, the CPCB and the state boards are heavily reliant on the funds directly provided by the MoEF. The SPCBs especially receive only marginal funding from the Central Government and mostly through specific projects to be executed at a state level. According to the CPCB, the SPCBs are dependent on the reimbursement of cess/tax collected under the Water (Prevention and Control of Pollution) Act and other consent and authorization fees imposed on industries. The Department of Environment at the State level also faces a similar problem, being unable to enforce laws due to adequate financial support (Rangarajan 2009). For instance, a country with about 7500 kms of coastline, the Coastal Regulation Zone (CRZ) Notification 1991 set out a range of activities for its own implementation such as: preparation of maps, coastal zone management plans and zone demarcations. Such a significant stature was not supported with funding, thereby all the above activities necessary for its effective implementation did not quite stimulate the state government (Rangarajan 2009). Field-level monitoring of various pollutants by Board(s) needs to reinforced, if newer pollutants and forms of pollution need to be monitored and mitigated. Some of the modern and more hazardous pollutants are still not under the radar, nor are there any standard prescribed for them. These technological and financial gaps should be worked out by the monitoring and implementing agencies. Otherwise, aforesaid discussion on improvements in enforcement would go in vain. Thus to mitigate these gaps, multi-disciplinary training to control the various forms of pollution should be made available to the environment scientist of the CPCB and SPCBs. Moreover, the growing number of industries, the increasing types of industries and the growing number of functions of the Pollution Control Board(s) dictate an urgent need for capacity building within the SPCBs and the CPCB (Rangarajan 2009).

Methods to Propagate Environmental Awareness

Environmental awareness needs to be created through formal and informal education to all section of the society. Everyone needs understand it because 'environmental belongs to all' and 'every individuals matters' when it comes to conservation and protection of environment.

Various stages and methods that can be useful for rising environmental awareness in different sections of society are as follow:

1. *Among Students through Education*: Environmental education must be imparted to the students' right from the childhood stage. It is a welcome step that now all over the country we are introducing environmental studies as s subject at all stages including school and college level, following the directives of the Supreme Court.
2. *Among the Masses through Mass-media*: Media can play an important role to educate the masses on environmental issues through articles, environmental rallies, plantation campaigns, street plays, real eco-disaster stories and success stories of conservation efforts.
3. *Among the Planners, Decision-makers and Leaders*: Since this elite section of the society plays the most important role in shaping the future of the society, it is very important to give them the necessary orientation and training through specially organized workshops and training programmes.

Publication of environmental-related resources material in the form of pamphlets or booklets published by Ministry of Environment and Forests can also help in keeping this section abreast of the latest developments in the field. The social and environmental issues associated with any developmental and industrial project are both highly significant and complex to manage. There are environmental, social and health impacts of such project. The challenges with environmental assessment of projects are twofold-firstly, to ensure that the environmental, social and health costs are afforded by considering the economic viability and acceptability of the project; and secondly to ensure that adequate mitigation or protection measures are incorporated into project design. This requires effective enforcement of environmental legislations by regulatory institutions, proper co-ordination among the various law implementing agencies and sound environmental management practices by private and public sectors. Hence, a sagacious strategy should be implemented in industries of India to promote job-led economic growth through the adoption of employment generating, economically viable and eco-friendly technologies. No act however flawlwssly and thoroughly drafted can remain free from ambiguities, drawbacks, shortcomings and lacunae. These laws do not always clearly state the social obligations. The interpretations of some provisions of these laws are often not in conformity with intent and purpose of the law. In spite of everything, these acts provide for speedy, effective and planned strategy for preventing and mitigating environmental pollution. These laws also promote development and resource utilization for specific economic benefit along with careful analysis of the potential short and long deleterious effect on the environment. The current environmental laws put numerous obligations on Industry, which are required to be complied with, while establishing and operating an industrial unit. Environmental laws play crucial preventive as well as remedial roles and are prime catalysts for promoting environmentally responsible behaviour. Ignorance of laws is not excusable. Thus, policy makers' officers of CPCB, SPCBs, Ministry of Environment and Forest, NGOs, other Government officials should be aware of different provisions of existing environmental legislations and they also should implement relevant laws for sustainable management of the project.

Conclusion

India has an extensive framework of environmental laws. The conviction rate is extremely poor because of enforcement problems and some lacunae in the laws. As a rule of nature, man has been living with these members of his environment from times immemorial leading a peaceful life. Each member supported the existence of the other on the planet-one complemented the other, with no contradictions. But of late, as civilization progressed and science advanced, man started creating his own "artificial' environment. This made way for several serious problems for which solution are not that simple. These consequences are serious. Subsequently and traditionally we became a pollution loving nation and gradually forgot minimum civic sense. We need wholesome oxygen. However, we pollute air by bursting crackers on the occasions of festivals especially on the processions of idol immersions, wining of an election and many other things. India is the first country in the world to have made provisions for the protection and conservation of environment in it constitution. On 5th June 1972, environment was first discussed as an item of international agenda in the U.N. Conference on Human Environment in Stock-Holm and thereafter 5th June is celebrated all over the world as World Environmental Day. Therefore, different relevant environmental legislations should be implemented properly and strict action should be taken at all levels to change our polluting mindset and attitude to prevent and abate pollution. If the law does not eradicate human suffering, inequalities and operate without social goals and environmental goals, it becomes a meaningless.

REFERENCES

1. R. Rangarajan, A Review of Implementation Gaps in the Enforcement of Environmental Regulation in India, In: Environmental Policy: Citizens, Institutions Implementation, Working Paper, Institute for Financial Management and Research, 1-10, 2009. (www.indiapollutionmap.org/DownloadEnv).
2. Website of Central Pollution Control Board.
3. Website of MoEFE.
4. Website of SPCBs.
5. Website of FCO.
6. Website of Biological Diversity Board.
7. Website of Environmental Protection Agency.
8. Website of Water Board.

9. Website of Ministry of Environment and Forest.
10. Website Indian Pollution Map, India.
11. Website of Environmental Protection Agency.
12. Website of Environmental Policy.
13. Review Literature related to environmental rules and regulation.
14. Website of Food and Agricultural Organization.
15. Website of National Environmental Tribunal.
16. Website of WHO.
17. Website of Central Expert Appraisal Committee (CEAC).
18. Website of UNEP-GRID.
19. Website of Environmental Legislations.

Page 44-62

AGRICULTURAL PRACTICES AND CROP DISEASE CONTROL
Edited by : Dr. Alka Chauhan and Dr. Anubhuti Sharma
Edition : 2017
ISBN : 978-93-5056-859-0
Published by : Discovery Publishing House Pvt. Ltd., New Delhi (India)

3

Nutrient Analysis of some Common Indian Weeds as Biomarkers for Soil Conservation

Mital J. Kaneria[1]
Kalpna D. Rakholiya[2]
Rohit M. Patel[3]

ABSTRACT

The term 'weed' generally has a negative connotation, many plants known as weeds can have beneficial properties. A number of weeds, are edible, and their leaves or roots may be used for food or herbal medicine. Weeds may also act as a 'living mulch', providing ground cover that reduces moisture loss and prevents erosion. Weeds may also improve soil fertility, bring up nutrients like: calcium and nitrogen from deep in the soil with their tap root, and clover hosts nitrogen-fixing bacteria in its roots, fertilizing the soil directly. Some people have appreciated weeds for their tenacity, their wildness and even the work and connection to nature they provide. The objective of the present investigation was to study the chemical composition of eight weeds growing naturally in semi-arid agro-climatic region of Rajkot district, Gujarat, India, namely: Satodi (Boerhavia diffusa L. - Nyctaginaceae), Bhangro (Tridax procumbensi L. - Asteraceae), Kanajaro (Digera muricata (L.) Mart.- Amaranthaceae), Dhrokad (Cynodon dactylon (L.) Pers. - Poaceae), Congrass grass (Parthenium hysterophorus L. - Asteraceae), Pili talavani (Cleome viscosa L. - Capparaceae), Shayo (Cyperus rotundus L. - Cyperaceae) and Sudisopari (Euphorbia hirta L. - Euphorbiaceae).

1. Department of Biosciences, Saurashtra University, Rajkot - 360 005, India.
2. Main Dry Farming Research Station, Junagadh Agricultural University, Targhadia, Rajkot - 360 003, India.
3. Gujarat Institute of Desert Ecology (GUIDE), Bhuj, Kachchh - 370 001, India.

The sampleswere subjected to analyze in energy dispersive X-ray fluorescence (EDXRF) for different mineral composition. As the X-ray Fluorescence is one of the most reliable and accurate, as well as it is also a consistent and non-destructive method for analysis of major and trace elements. During the study it was found that Calcium, Magnesium, Potassium were noted in higher amounts, compared to that of other elements studied. The vanadium, arsenic, molybdenum, barium, hafnium and lead were not found in studied plant.

Keywords: Nutrient analysis, Weeds, XRF, Recycle, Soil fertility, Soil conservation.

INTRODUCTION

Weeds are plants that are unwanted in a given situation and may be harmful, dangerous or economically detrimental. Weeds are a serious threat to primary production and biodiversity. They reduce farm and forest productivity, displace native species and contribute significantly to land and water degradation. The costs of weeds to the natural environment are also high, with weed invasion being ranked second only to habitat loss in causing biodiversity decline. Weed management is an important component of plant protection improving the production potential of crops. It includes management of the weeds in a way that the crop sustains its production potential without being harmed by the weeds. Weed management is done through the mechanical, cultural and chemical means. Use of biological control methods in field crops is being considered, but still not much in use. Use of herbicides is an important method in the modern concept of much in use. Use of herbicides is an important method in the modern concept of weed-management technology. New hand-tools and implements have also been designed to assist in wed-management programme.

Organic farming is the backbone of sustainable agriculture. Organic farming mainly depend son Organic recycling: Industrial agriculture chemicals like: fertilizer, pesticide, herbicide etc., are not used or used to minimum extent necessary in this kind of farming. Organic farming may result in compatible performance as conventional agriculture and crops growth with high organic manure application could tolerate the pest and disease attack better. It is sound and sustainable way of growing more food.

Organic recyclable waste include: crop residues, waste, farm industrial waste, multiple and sewage wastes. They are valuable sources of plant nutrient and humans in tropical and subtropical soils found in India, there is general deficiency of organic carbon and plant nutrients due to rapid loss of this component by bio-degradation. To make u for these losses, extensive utilization of organic residues in agriculture is essential. In addition they also protect the soil from erosion.

FAO (2005) define the weed as a plant that growing where it is not wanted by human. However, Marshall *et al.* (2003) describes weed as the important components of agro-biodiversity by supporting the life of various dependent living organisms. It is also observed that some of weeds are the major food components of various birds and mammals as their direct role and indirectly they are hosts for various invertebrates. In addition, Hillocks (1998) describe weed as the secondary food sources for poor rural communities in the various countries including Africa. The roles of weeds in curing various diseases are already established by Stepp and Moerman (2001).

Boerhaavia diffusa belongs to Nyctaginaceae family of higher plants is a tropical plants and Known as Punarnava in Ayurveda. It is a creeping weed grows across the country. In-spite of its medicinal properties, it is also used as vegetables. *Tridex procumbens* is known as coat buttons is belongs to Asteraceae family which has wider distribution range across the globe. This species is native of tropical Americas and introduced to various tropical, subtropical and mild temperate areas worldwide. *Digera muricata*, which is an ephemeral herb, belongs to Amaranthaceae family. It grows up to 70-80 cm height and distributed from Eastern Africa to tropical and subtropical Asia. It can be used as vegetable and in some areas it is under cultivation and sold in local markets. *Cynodon dactylon* is a monocotyledonous plant belongs to Poaceae family. It is known as Durva or Dhokad in local language. It covers a large under its cover by vegetative reproduction by stolons and rhizomes. Ancient literature describes *C. dactylon* as a holy grass and used in various ritual ceremonies. This has native to India but now it become pan-tropical plant. *Parthenium hysterophorus* is an invasive alien annual species, which has antagonistically colonizes at the site of occurrence. This species is a native to southern United States, Mexico and Central and South America. This species has been accidently introduced in various counties of Australia, Asia and Africa continents including India. It has adverse impact on crop, animal, human health including ecosystem. *Cyperus rotundus* belongs to Cyperaceae family of monocotyledonous plants which is commonly known as nut sedge. It is a perennial weed having subterranean tuber. This species is native to Africa, Southern and Central Europe and Southern Asia. The tuber of this species is important food for various birds and mammals. *Euphorbia hirta* is a prostate herb Euphorbiaceae family. This is a pan-tropical species which is known as Asthma-plant. It has some medicinal importance. It can be grow in crop fields, gardens, grasslands, road sides etc. *Cleome viscosa* is an annual herb belongs to family Capparaceae of higher plants which is locally known as Pili Talvani. Maikhuri *et al.* (2000) stated this species as promising crop in few localities in the lower and middle altitude agro-climatic zones of Garhwal-Uttarakhand. The seed of this species is identified as Condiment.

Materials and Methods

Collection

The weed samples were collected from field dry under shade condition. Then crushed it in mixture to make in fine powder. The powder was stored in air tight bottles for further used.

Pellet Preparation

Sample Pellet were prepared by Hydraulic pressure and used for further elemental analysis in X-ray Fluorescence instrument.

Instrument Parameters

Benchtop energy dispersive X-ray fluorescence (EDXRF) spectrometers used for elemental analysis, X-ray Tube with high performance SDD detector with the use of Epsilon 3 software.

Results and Discussions

The elemental analysis of plants is an important tool for biologists in disciplines as diverse as ecology, physiology and agronomy (Reidinger*et al.* 2012). However, despite the routine application of digestion-based analytical techniques in many laboratories, the slow and often hazardous sample digestion process can create a bottleneck in the analysis of some elements, particularly where hundreds or even thousands of samples are to be analysed, as is the case for landscape-scale experiments in ecology or the rapid screening of new crop or biofuel varieties. Thus, the development of accurate and convenient high-throughput methods for assessing elemental concentrations in plants is of high importance. Here we describe a method for the rapid, safe and accurate elemental analysis of plant material using an X-ray fluorescence spectrometer (XRF).

The chemical composition of eight studied weed samples were analyzed by XRF spectrometer. The results are shown in Tables 3.1 to 3.8 and Figures 3.1 to 3.8. All the studied weed had higher amount of Si, K, Ca, Mg, P, S, Cl, Al and Fe, Mn, Zn, Cu, Ni, Sr, Hf, Cr were found in lower amount whereas Hf, Pd, Re, Au, Ba were not found in weed samples.

Table 3.1: Composition of *Cynodon dactylon* (L.) Pers. by X-ray Fluorescence

Oxide	% Mass	Element	% Mass
1	2	3	4
Na_2O	0.617	Na	0.145
$MgCO_3$	7.899	Mg	0.704
Al_2O_3	1.453	Al	0.221
SiO_2	32.839	Si	4.085
P_2O_5	3.807	P	0.363
SO_3	5.335	S	0.443
K_2O	25.229	K	3.461
$CaCO_3$	16.973	Ca	0.825
TiO_2	0.137	Ti	0.009
Cr_2O_3	0.013	Cr	0.001
MnO	0.088	Mn	0.007

Contd...

1	2	3	4
Fe_2O_3	1.248	Fe	0.093
NiO	0.01	Ni	0.001
CuO	0.051	Cu	0.004
ZnO	0.07	Zn	0.006
SrO	0.043	Sr	0.004
PdO	0	Pd	0
Ag_2O	0.112	Ag	0.018
CdO	0.035	Cd	0.005
In_2O_3	0.688	In	0.084
BaO	0.015	Ba	0.001
HfO_2	0.002	Hf	0
Cl	3.304	Cl	0.65
Br	0.032	Br	0.003
Re	0.001	Re	0

Table 3.2: Composition of *Digera muricata* (L.) Martby X-ray Fluorescence

Oxide	% Mass	Element	% Mass
Na_2O	1.226	Na	0.393
$MgCO_3$	22.158	Mg	2.707
Al_2O_3	0.674	Al	0.14
SiO_2	1.518	Si	0.273
P_2O_5	3.545	P	0.577
SO_3	3.971	S	0.565
K_2O	26.481	K	6.093
$CaCO_3$	35.96	Ca	3.012
TiO_2	0.04	Ti	0.004
Cr_2O_3	0.002	Cr	0
MnO	0.073	Mn	0.01
Fe_2O_3	0.332	Fe	0.042
NiO	0.001	Ni	0
CuO	0.01	Cu	0.001
ZnO	0.021	Zn	0.003
SrO	0.072	Sr	0.011
Ag_2O	0.059	Ag	0.016
CdO	0.051	Cd	0.013
In_2O_3	0.813	In	0.172
BaO	0.015	Ba	0.003
HfO_2	0	Hf	0
Cl	2.951	Cl	0.976
Br	0.028	Br	0.005

Table 3.3: Composition of *Boerhavia diffusa* L. by X-ray Fluorescence

Oxide	% Mass	Element	% Mass
Na_2O	0	Na	0
$MgCO_3$	2.632	Mg	0.124
Al_2O_3	0.503	Al	0.042
SiO_2	2.153	Si	0.152
P_2O_5	3.449	P	0.212
SO_3	2.89	S	0.149
K_2O	36.928	K	2.2
$CaCO_3$	39.563	Ca	0.655
TiO_2	0.128	Ti	0.003
Cr_2O_3	0.006	Cr	0
MnO	0.086	Mn	0.002
Fe_2O_3	0.949	Fe	0.021
NiO	0.004	Ni	0
CuO	0.031	Cu	0.001
ZnO	0.047	Zn	0.001
SrO	0.048	Sr	0.001
PdO	0.049	Pd	0
Ag_2O	0.347	Ag	0.027
CdO	0	Cd	0
In_2O_3	1.09	In	0.053
BaO	0	Ba	0
HfO_2	0	Hf	0
Cl	9.068	Cl	1.027
Br	0.027	Br	0.001

Table 3.4: Composition of *Tridax procumbensi* L. by X-ray Fluorescence

Oxide	% Mass	Element	% Mass
1	2	3	4
Na_2O	0	Na	0
$MgCO_3$	21.759	Mg	2.635
Al_2O_3	1.729	Al	0.356
SiO_2	7.271	Si	1.28
P_2O_5	3.292	P	0.509
SO_3	1.854	S	0.254
K_2O	17.285	K	3.865
$CaCO_3$	39.354	Ca	3.393
TiO_2	0.116	Ti	0.013

Contd...

1	2	3	4
V_2O_5	0.004	V	0
Cr_2O_3	0.013	Cr	0.002
MnO	0.05	Mn	0.007
Fe_2O_3	1.089	Fe	0.137
Co_3O_4	0.005	Co	0.001
NiO	0.005	Ni	0.001
CuO	0.016	Cu	0.002
ZnO	0.032	Zn	0.004
As_2O_3	0	As	0
Rb_2O	0.008	Rb	0.001
SrO	0.056	Sr	0.008
MoO_3	0	Mo	0
PdO	0	Pd	0
Ag_2O	0.065	Ag	0.017
CdO	0.03	Cd	0.007
In_2O_3	0.508	In	0.105
BaO	0.002	Ba	0
PbO	0.001	Pb	0
Cl	5.412	Cl	1.738
Br	0.045	Br	0.008

Table 3.5: Composition of *Euphorbia hirta* L. by X-ray Fluorescence

Oxide	% Mass	Element	% Mass
1	2	3	4
Na_2O	0	Na	0
$MgCO_3$	15.952	Mg	0.983
Al_2O_3	2.207	Al	0.227
SiO_2	5.798	Si	0.502
P_2O_5	3.429	P	0.256
SO_3	3.081	S	0.198
K_2O	16.178	K	1.556
$CaCO_3$	47.313	Ca	1.523
TiO_2	0.135	Ti	0.005
Cr_2O_3	0.014	Cr	0.001
MnO	0.104	Mn	0.005
Fe_2O_3	1.255	Fe	0.05
NiO	0.008	Ni	0
CuO	0.02	Cu	0.001

Contd...

1	2	3	4
ZnO	0.069	Zn	0.003
SrO	0.083	Sr	0.004
PdO	0	Pd	0
Ag_2O	0.169	Ag	0.019
CdO	0	Cd	0
In_2O_3	0.426	In	0.035
BaO	0.011	Ba	0.001
HfO_2	0.002	Hf	0
Cl	3.681	Cl	0.542
Br	0.064	Br	0.003
Re	0	Re	0
Au	0.001	Au	0

Table 3.6: Composition of *Parthenium hysterophorus* L. by X-ray Fluorescence

Oxide	% Mass	Element	% Mass
Na_2O	0	Na	0
$MgCO_3$	9.967	Mg	1.189
Al_2O_3	0.905	Al	0.189
SiO_2	2.826	Si	0.506
P_2O_5	2.827	P	0.452
SO_3	2.663	S	0.371
K_2O	42.803	K	8.788
$CaCO_3$	29.928	Ca	2.115
TiO_2	0.055	Ti	0.005
Cr_2O_3	0.005	Cr	0.001
MnO	0.028	Mn	0.003
Fe_2O_3	0.426	Fe	0.047
NiO	0.003	Ni	0
CuO	0.012	Cu	0.002
ZnO	0.019	Zn	0.002
SrO	0.076	Sr	0.01
PdO	0.026	Pd	0
Ag_2O	0.039	Ag	0.013
CdO	0.089	Cd	0.02
In_2O_3	1.344	In	0.248
BaO	0	Ba	0
HfO_2	0.001	Hf	0
Cl	5.854	Cl	1.874
Br	0.102	Br	0.016
Re	0	Re	0
Au	0.002	Au	0

Table 3.7: Composition of *Cleome viscosa* L. by X-ray Fluorescence

Oxide	% Mass	Element	% Mass
Na_2O	0	Na	0
$MgCO_3$	11.568	Mg	0.923
Al_2O_3	1.194	Al	0.164
SiO_2	2.576	Si	0.301
P_2O_5	2.19	P	0.227
SO_3	6.893	S	0.617
K_2O	12.952	K	1.75
$CaCO_3$	56.991	Ca	2.741
TiO_2	0.116	Ti	0.006
Cr_2O_3	0.011	Cr	0.001
MnO	0.066	Mn	0.004
Fe_2O_3	1.174	Fe	0.07
NiO	0.005	Ni	0
CuO	0.012	Cu	0.001
ZnO	0.03	Zn	0.002
SrO	0.062	Sr	0.004
PdO	0	Pd	0
Ag_2O	0.13	Ag	0.021
CdO	0	Cd	0
In_2O_3	0.34	In	0.04
BaO	0.003	Ba	0
HfO_2	0.001	Hf	0
Cl	3.63	Cl	0.726
Br	0.055	Br	0.005
Re	0	Re	0
Au	0.001	Au	0

Table 3.8: Composition of *Cyperus rotundus* L.by X-ray Fluorescence

Oxide	% Mass	Element	% Mass
Na_2O	6.457	Na	1.348
$MgCO_3$	9.719	Mg	0.722
Al_2O_3	2.858	Al	0.363
SiO_2	19.227	Si	2.017
P_2O_5	3.49	P	0.297
SO_3	3.392	S	0.251
K_2O	26.225	K	3.054
$CaCO_3$	19.944	Ca	0.785
TiO_2	0.269	Ti	0.014
Cr_2O_3	0.037	Cr	0.002
MnO	0.065	Mn	0.004
Fe_2O_3	3.092	Fe	0.18
NiO	0.014	Ni	0.001
CuO	0.042	Cu	0.003
ZnO	0.047	Zn	0.003
SrO	0.029	Sr	0.002
PdO	0	Pd	0
Ag_2O	0.165	Ag	0.023
CdO	0.022	Cd	0.003
In_2O_3	0.769	In	0.078
BaO	0	Ba	0
HfO_2	0	Hf	0
Cl	4.071	Cl	0.712
Br	0.065	Br	0.005
Re	0	Re	0
Au	0	Au	0

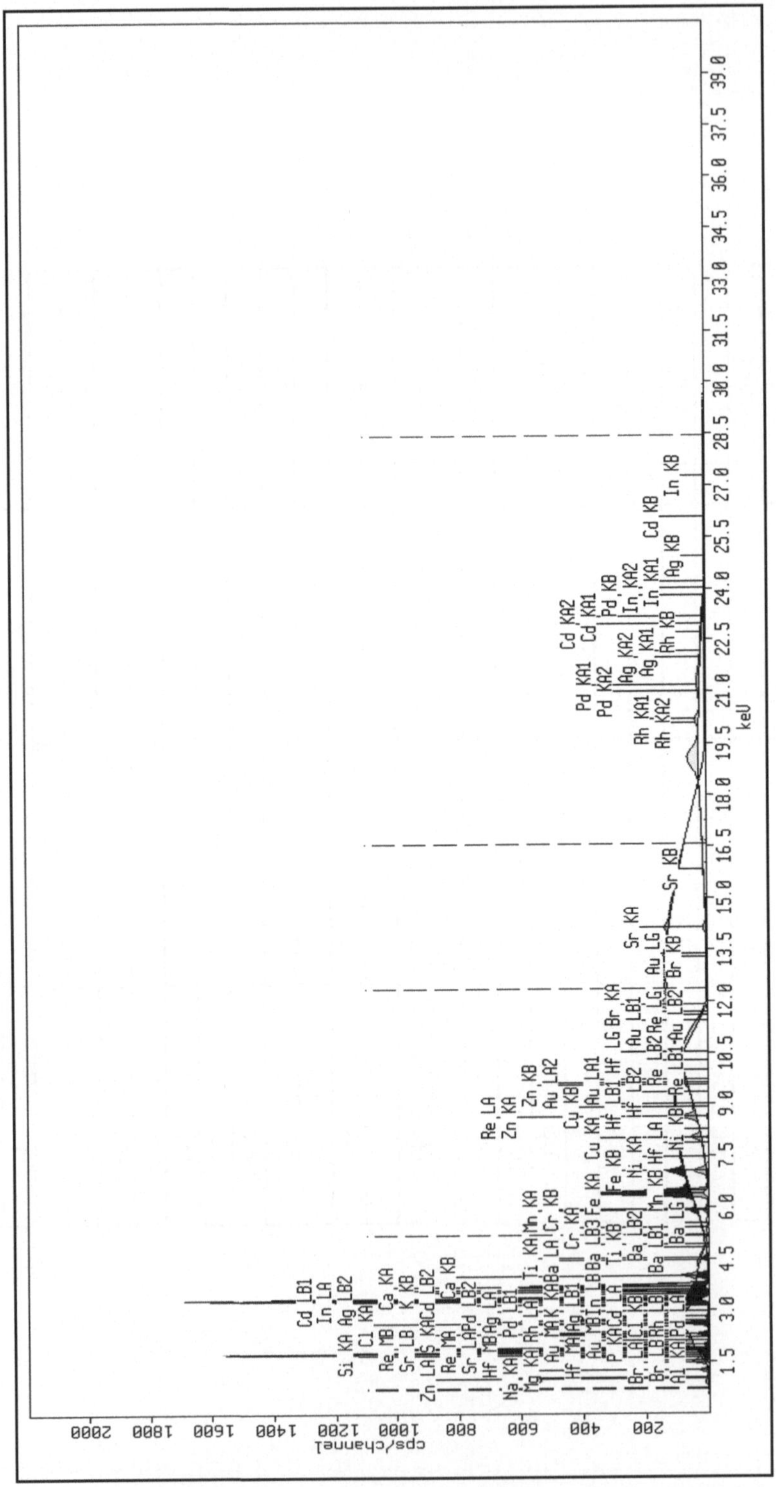

Fig. 3.1: **Spectra of XRF for mineral ion of *Cynodon dactylon* (L.) Pers.**

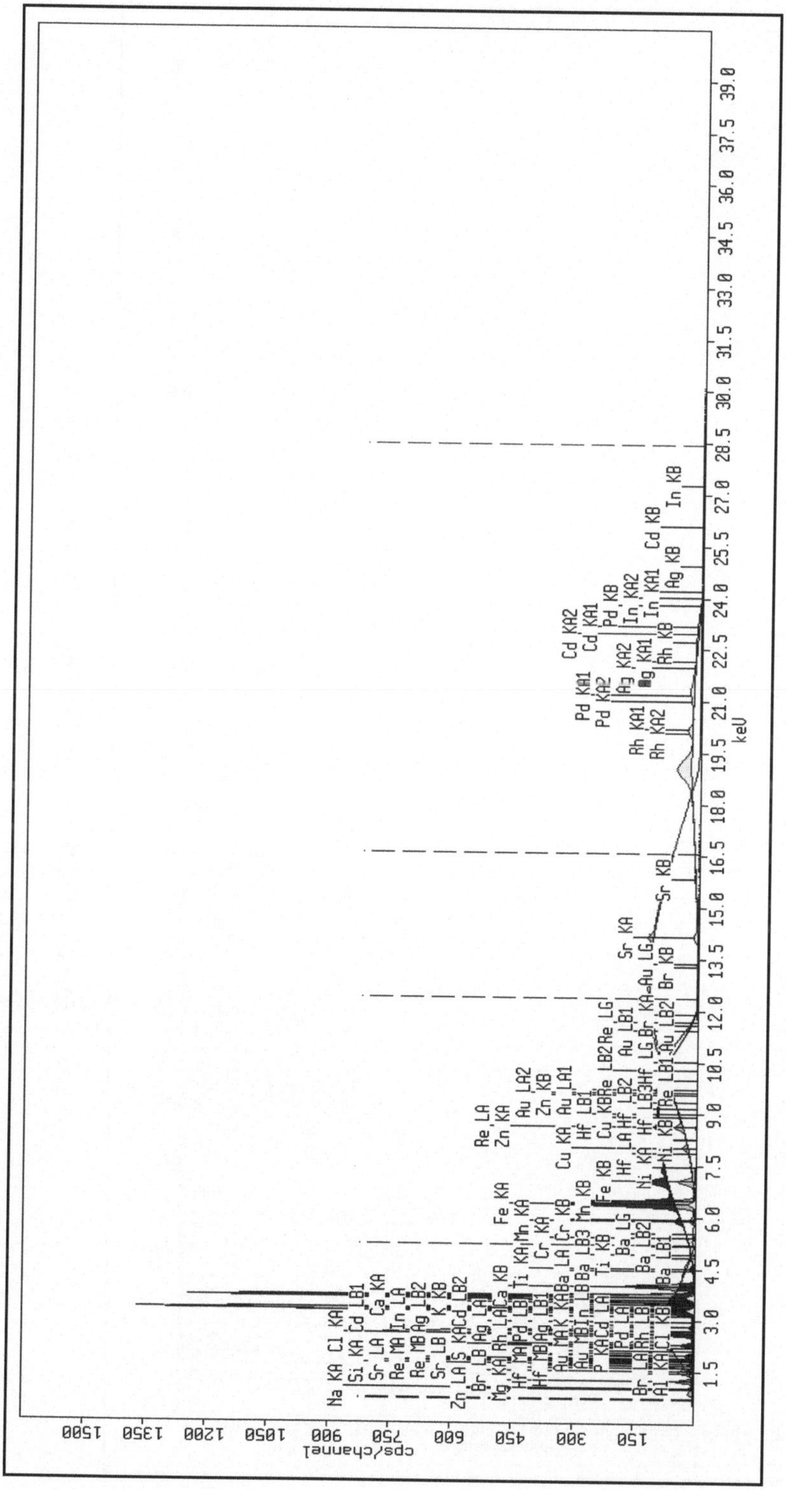

Fig. 3.2: **Spectra of XRF for mineral ion of *Digera muricata* (L.) Mart**

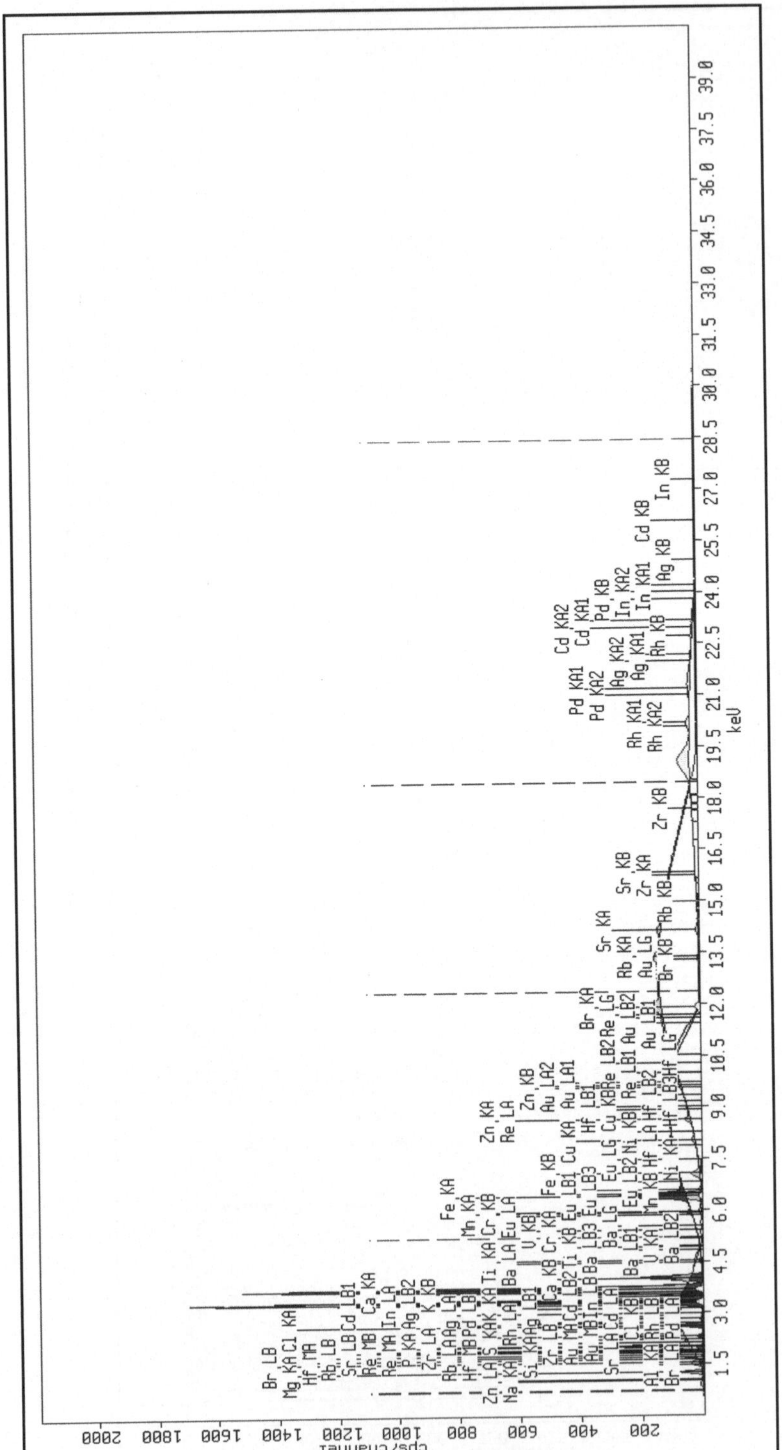

Fig. 3.3: **Spectra of XRF for mineral ion of *Boerhavia diffusa* L.**

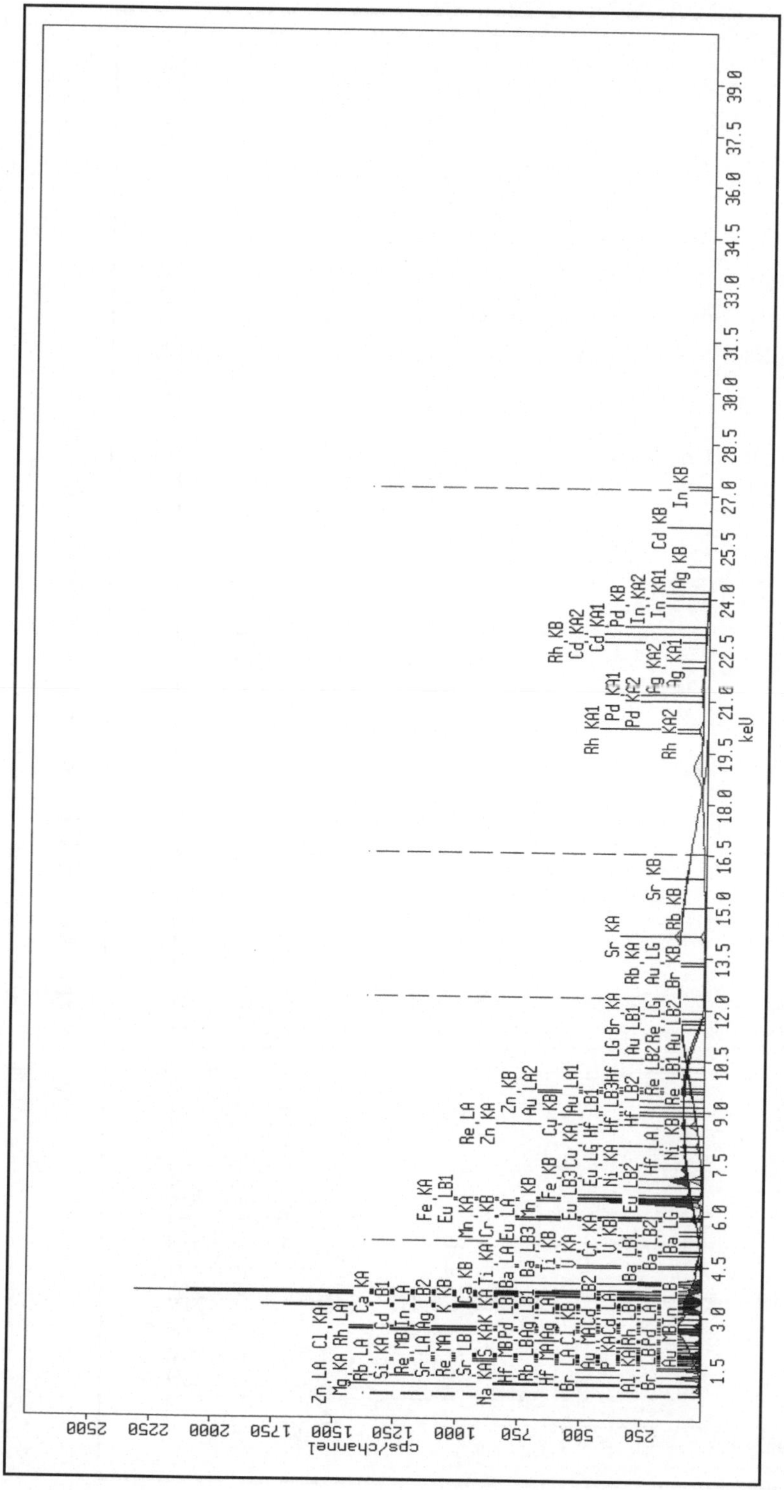

Fig. 3.4: Spectra of XRF for mineral ion of *Tridax procumbensi* L.

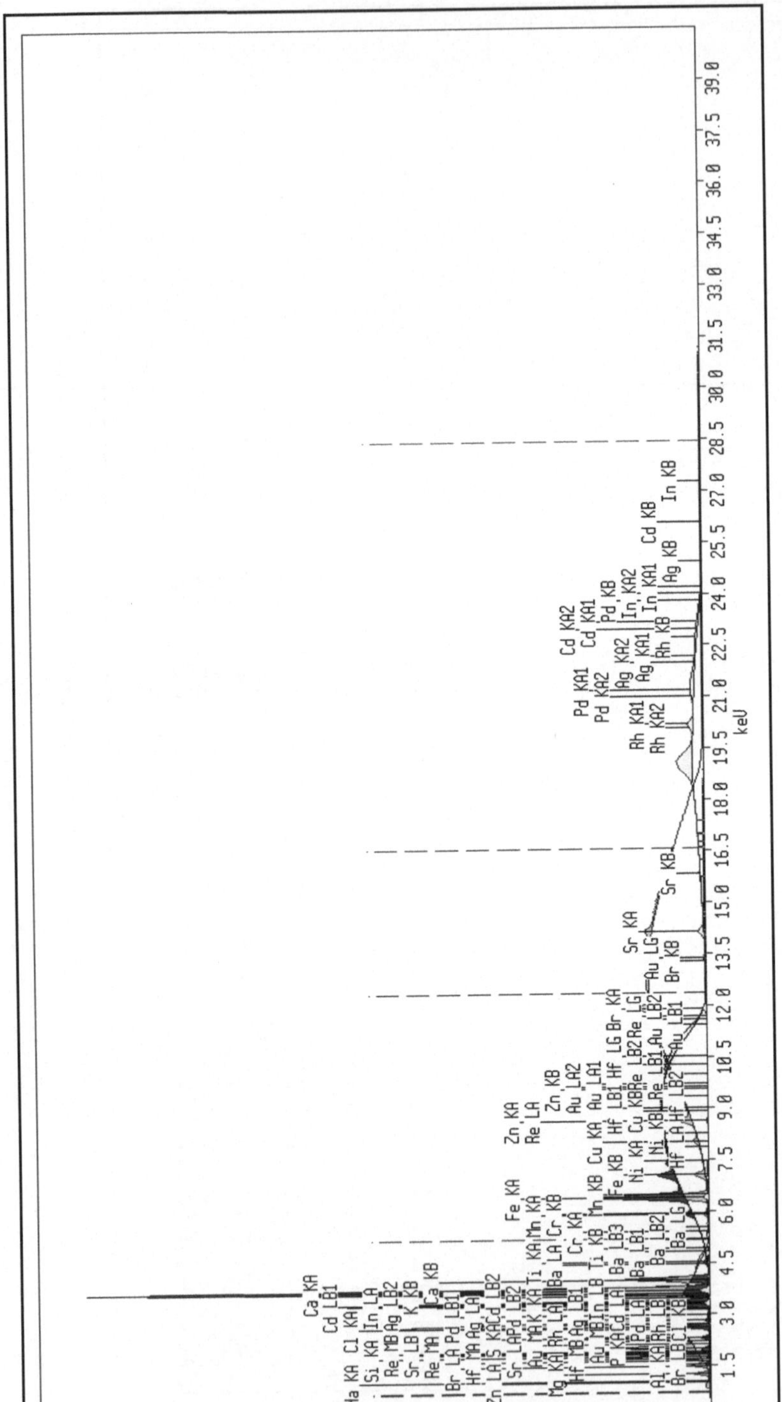

Fig. 3.5: **Spectra of XRF for mineral ion of *Euphorbia hirta* L.**

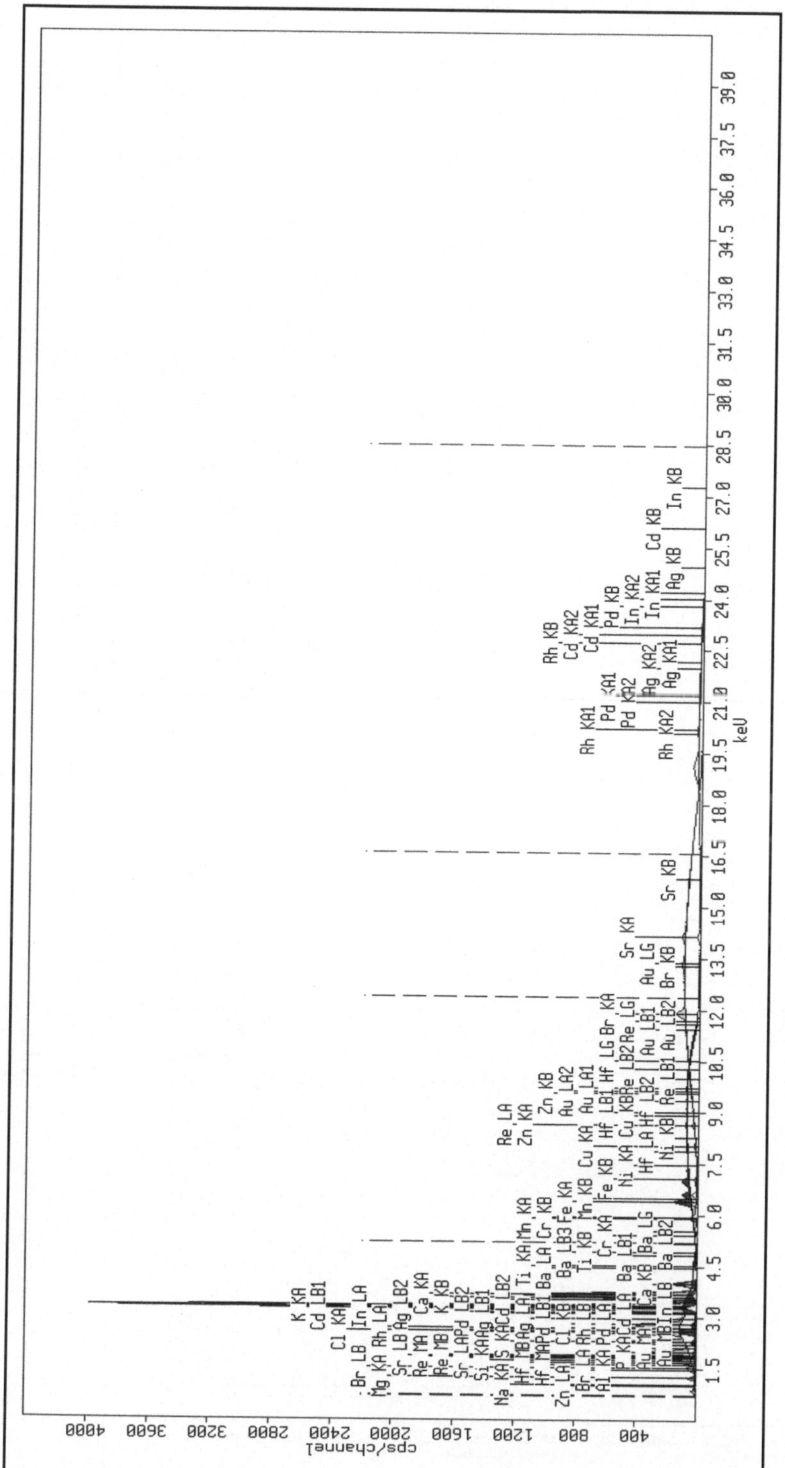

Fig. 3.6: **Spectra of XRF for mineral ion of *Parthenium hysterophorus* L.**

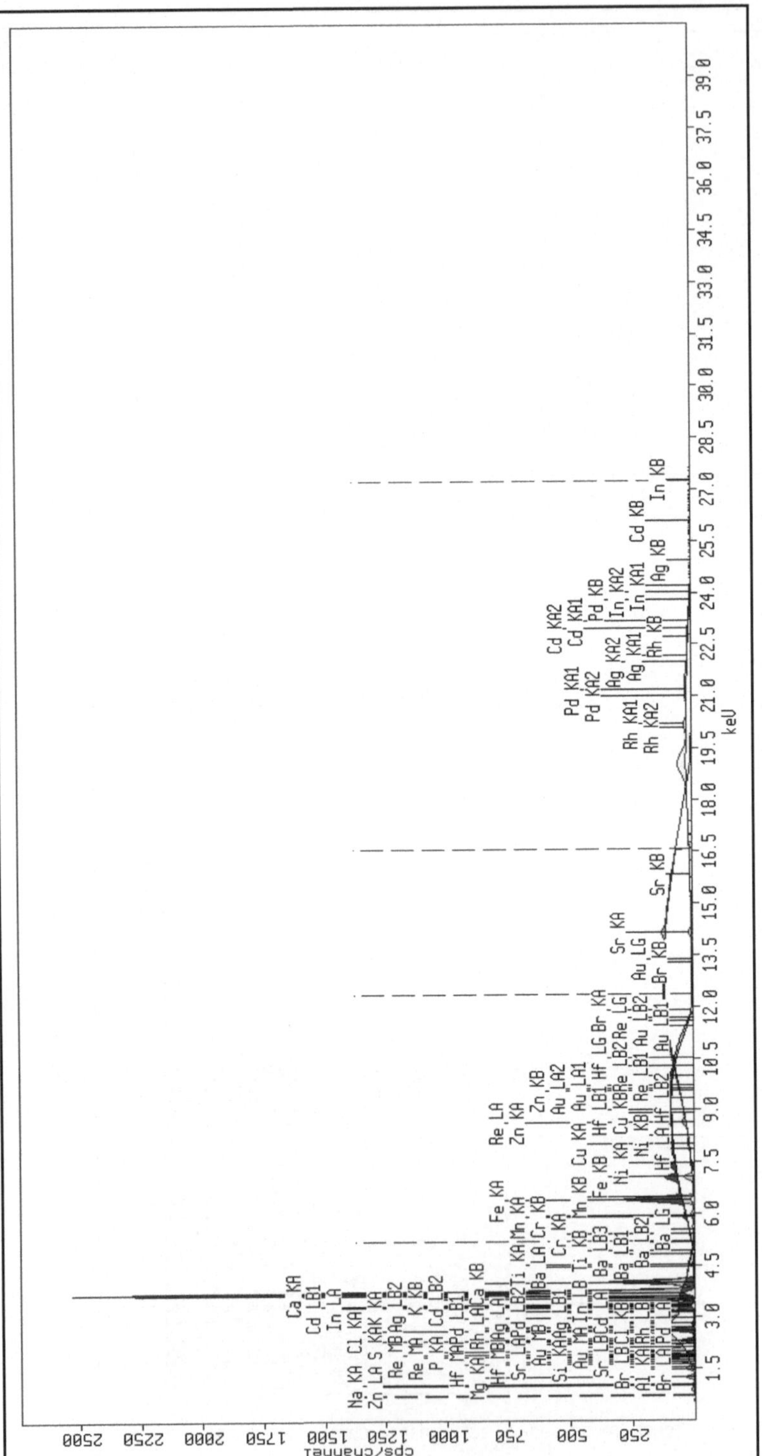

Fig. 3.7: Spectra of XRF for mineral ion of *Cleome viscosa* L.

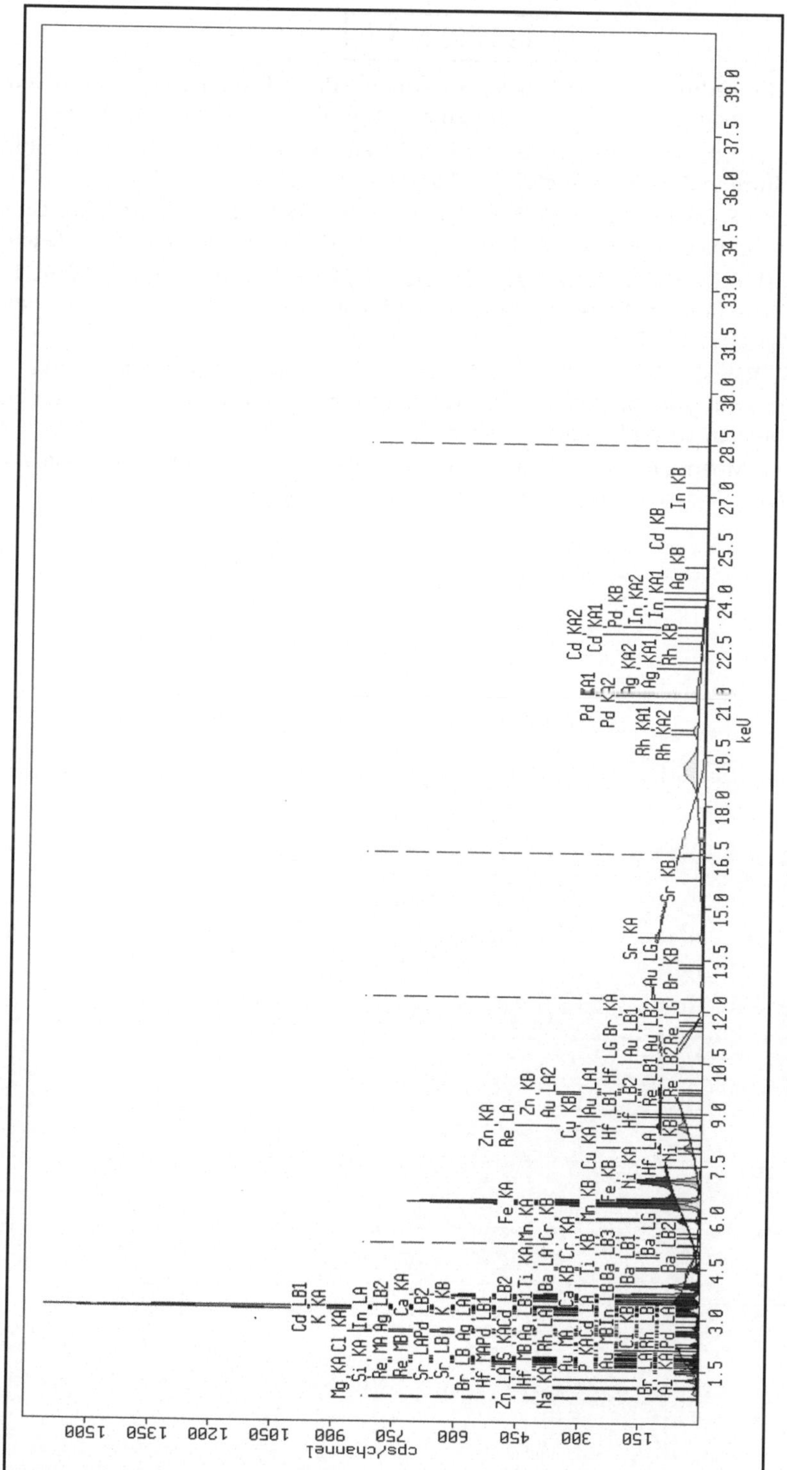

Fig. 3.8: **Spectra of XRF for mineral ion of *Cyperus rotundus* L.**

REFERENCES

FAO (2005). Procedure for Weed Risk Assessment. Plant Production and Protection Division, Food and Agriculture Organization of the United Nations, Rome.

Hillocks, R.J. (1998). The Potential Benefits of Weeds with Reference to Small Holder Agriculture in Africa. *Integrated Pest Management Reviews,* 3: 155-167p.

Maikhuri, R.K., Semwal, R.L., Rao, K.S., Nautiyal, S. and Saxena, K.G. (2000). *Cleome viscosa,* Capparidaceae: A Weed or a Cash Crop? *Economic Botany,* 54: 150-154.

Marshall, E.J.P., Brown, V.K., Boatman, N.D., Lutman, P.J.W., Squire, G.R. and Ward, L.K. (2003). The Role of Weeds in Supporting Biological Diversity within Crop Fields. *Weed Research,* 43:77-89.

Reidinger, S., Ramsey, M.H. and Hartley, S.E. (2012). Rapid and Accurate Analyses of Silicon and phosphorus in Plants using a Portable X-ray fluorescence Spectrometer. *New Phytologist,* 195: 699-706.

Stepp, J.R. and Moerman, D.E. (2001). The Importance of Weeds in Ethnopharmacology. *Journal of Ethnopharmacology,* 75: 19-2.

Page 63-88

AGRICULTURAL PRACTICES AND CROP DISEASE CONTROL
***Edited by*: Dr. Alka Chauhan and Dr. Anubhuti Sharma**
***Edition* : 2017**
ISBN : 978-93-5056-859-0
***Published by*: Discovery Publishing House Pvt. Ltd., New Delhi (India)**

4

Heat Shock Proteins

R.R. Dhutmal

In semi-arid and arid environments where water stress is associated with temperature stress, leaf temperature increases above air temperature as a result of stomatal closure and reduced respiration. The elevated leaf temperature under these conditions may limit dry matter accumulation because of increased respiration, reduced photosynthesis and cellular damage. High temperature stress is also known to severely reduce seed germination, pollen viability and pollen germination in several crop species. Plant can resist high temperature stress either by avoidance or by tolerance mechanism. Transitory or constantly high temperature causes an array of morpho-anatomical, physiological and biochemical changes in plants, which affect plant growth and development and may lead to drastic reduction in plant yield. The adverse effect of heat stress can be mitigated by developing crop plants with however, a thorough understanding of physiological responses of plant to high temperature, mechanisms of heat tolerance and possible strategies for improving crop thermotolerance is imperative. (Banu Efeoglu, 2009).

Heat induces a wide variety of changes in cellular structure and metabolic processes. When the magnitude and duration of heat stress exceeds a threshold, cells are irreversibly damaged and die. In higher eukaryotes heat stress perturbs many aspects of cellular physiology.

Asstt. Breeder, Vasantrao Naik Marathwada Krishi Vidyapeeth, Parbhani (M.S.), India.

Cellular Changes Induced by Heat Tolerance

Table 4.1: Cell stressors that induce heat shock proteins

Stressor or Stressor Type	Name or Description
Physical	Heat (including: fever), cold, several types of irradiation, including ultraviolet light and magnetic fields.
Nutritional	Starvation involving multiple nutritional components (carbon, glucose, nitrogen, phosphate, and nitrate) or anyone of these.
Oxygen	Oxygen-derived free radicals (reactive oxygen species), hydrogen peroxide, a shift from anaerobiosis toaerobiosis (*e.g.*, reperfusion), hypoxia-anoxia (ischemia).
Osmotic	Changes in the concentrations of salt, sugars, and other osmolytes (hyperosmotic or hypo-osmotic shock).
Antibiotics	Puromycin, tetracycline, nalidixic acid, doxorubicion.
Metals	Cadmium, copper, chromium, zinc, tin, aluminum, mercury, lead, nickel.
pH	Alkalosis, acidosis, pH shift.
Mechanical	Compression, shearing, stretching.
Other	Desiccation, benzene and derivatives, phenol and derivatives, teratogens, carcinogens, mutagens, arsenite, arsenate, amino acid analogues, nicotine, anesthetics, insecticides, pesticides.

These are the disruption of cytoskeleton and microtubules, fragmentation of golgi apparatus, an increase in the number of lysosomes, swelling of mitochondria, decrease in respiration and oxidative phosphorylation, disruption of normal protein synthesis, disappearance of polysomes, disruption of in the splicing of mRNA precursors, cessation of pre rRNA processing and a decline in the transcription of RNA polymerase I, perturbation in DNA synthesis, inhibition in chromatin assembly and a number of change in cellular membranes. Among these damages, synthesis of a set of proteins known as HSPs which is ubiquitous phenomenon in all prokaryotes and eukaryotes appears to be particularly important in the protection of cells from thermal damage.

Active plant growth in mesiphile organisms is in between 10-40°C. Any temperature which is under and below that range creates heat stress on metabolic activities of plants. Plant growth is a function of biochemical reactions and those reactions are controlled by enzymes. Most of the chemical reactions increase as two fold by every 10°C increase in between 20-30°C. Temperature above that range, reaction speed decreases since enzymes are denatured or inactivated. In addition, reactions catalyzed by enzymes depend on completeness of tertiary structure of enzymes. Increasing molecular collision as temperature increase harms tertiary structure and reduces enzymes activities and reaction rates. Faster increase in temperature brings faster denaturation. When an enzyme is inactivated, growth process related to that enzyme is depressed. Photosynthesis is an important reaction affected by heat Photosynthesis is performed in between 10-30°C range in temperate climate plants. Above 10°C, photosynthesis increases as temperature increases; it decreases above 30°C. Respiration generally adapt a normal course at 5-25°C, it is accelerated up to 30-35°C and reaccelerated above 3°C. It was reported that heat stress disrupts water, ion and organic solute movement across plant membranes, reduces chemical reactions, gas solubility, mineral absorption and water uptake, impairs photosynthetic electron transport systems, and increases oxidative degeneration of membrane lipids. Toxic material formation has been detected as a result of high temperature. Heat stress is a major factor limiting the productivity and adaptation of crops, especially when temperature extremes coincide with critical stages of plant development. The rate of temperature changes and the duration and degree of high temperature all contributes to the intensity of heat stress. Where heat stress occurs, it is important that plants possesses a certain degree of heat tolerance to survive the stress period. In addition, plant response to heat stress depends upon the thermal adaptation, the duration of the exposure and the stage of growth of the exposed time.

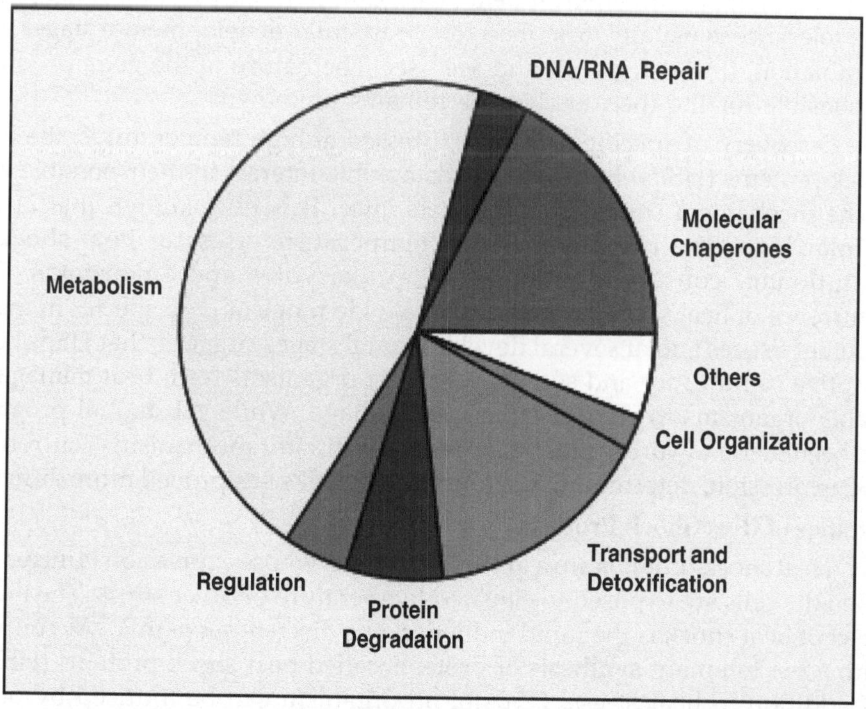

Fig. 4.1: **Summary of the functional classes of proteins upregulated during the heat shock response in *S.cerevisiae* after a shift from 25°C to 35°C for 10 min.**

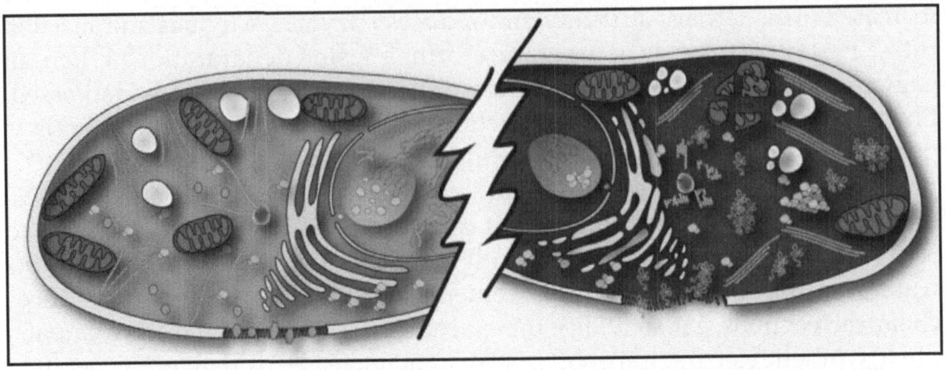

Fig. 4.2: **Effect of heat shock on the organization of the Eukaryotic cell. An unstressed eukaryotic cell (left) is compared to a cell under heat stress (right).**

Heat Shock Protein - Its Significance

Despite the crop losses suffered due to heat stress, breeding or selection of heat tolerant plant has not received much specific efforts. This is in part due to limited understanding of genetic basis of heat tolerance in plants, and in part due lack of accurate in laboratory tests to select for the components of heat tolerance. Variation in heat tolerance has been described to the native vegetation adapted to environments with different temperature ranges. The heat tolerance is usually described for a particular developmental stages *e.g.*, germination, flowering, fruit and seed set. The nature of the gene products responsible for the thermotolerance remains unknown.

Discovery of specific proteins expressed at high temperatures, the heat shock proteins (HSPs) has caused considerable interest in their possible role of the mechanism controlling heat tolerance. It is now known that at the cellular level, the response to high temperature stress or heat shock is evolutionary conserved among both prokaryotes and eukaryotes. The occurrence of heat shock response over a wide range of crop species in many different tissues and at several developmental stages suggests that HSps have adaptive significance and somehow protect organisms form heat damage or enable organisms to recover from heat damage. While substantial progress has been made towards understanding the regulator mechanisms controlling HSP expression, determining the functions of HSPs has proved more difficult.

Families of Heat Shock Proteins

Heat shock proteins are a group of proteins whose expression is increased when the cells are exposed to elevated temperature or other stress. The major effect of heat shock is the rapid induction of a discrete set of mRNAs coupled with a predominant synthesis of proteins called heat shock proteins (HSPs). IN addition to heat stress, HSps of an organism can be induced by other stresses. Imbalances in cellular metabolism are also able to activate the transcription of heat shock genes. Physiological studies of several organisms, including: plants, drosophila, yeast and human cells have correlated HSP synthesis with the development of thermotolerance. Heat shock response phenomenon was the first discovered by Ritossa in 1962 in drosophila larvae who observed the specific heat induced puffs in the polytene chromosomes of salivary glands following heat shock while other areas of gene activity regressed. The heat shock response has been documented in bacteria as well as in lower and higher eukaryotes where it occurs in almost in every cell and tissue type. HSps are referred by their molecular weights. Major HSPs synthesized by eukaryotes belong to six structurally conserved distinct classes: HSP 100, Hsp 90. Hsp 70, Hsp60, (Chaperonins), approximately 17-30 kDa molecular weight small Hsp (sHsps) and ubiquitin (8,5kDa).

Table 4.2: Families of Hsps in human beings, their site and suggested functions (Kregel, 2002)

Hsp Families	Cellular Location	Proposed Functions
Hsp27 (sHsp)	Cytosol, nucleus	Microfilament stabilization, antiapoptotic.
Hsp60	Mitochondria	Refolds proteins and prevent aggregation of denatured proteins, proapoptotic.
Hsp70		Antiapoptotic.
Hsp72 (Hsp70)	Cytosol, nucleus	Protein folding, cytoprotection.
Hsp73 (Hsp70)	Cytosol, nucleus	Molecular chaerones.
Hsp75 (mHsp70)	mitochondria	Molecular chaperones.
Hsp78 (GRP78)	Endoplasmic reticulam	Cytoprotection, molecular chaperones.
Hsp90	Cytosol, endoplasmic reticulum, nucleus	Regulation of steroid hormone receptor, protein translocation.
Hsp110/104	Cytosol	Protein folding.

High molecular weight Hsps are characterize by high sequence term of their specific function in different cell departments. Hsps horologes which belong to same family also function in different cell departments. Hsps show great difference in plants among eukaryotes.

(i) Hsp100

Members of these family are constitutively expressed, but they also up regulated by environmental stresses. Proteins of these families generally function to protect protein denaturation and/or aggregation of proteins. It was shown that Hsp104 in Arabidopsis and Hsp104 inn yeast play an important role in heat stress tolerance. It was stated that over expression of Hsp101 in Arabidopsis has positive effect on growth during recovery period. It was recently found that Hsp 101 homologue in Arabidopsis has positive effect on growth during recovery period. It was recently found that Hsp 101 homologue in Arabidopsis is involved in plastid differentiation mediating internal thylakoid membrane formation and conferring thermotolerance to chloroplasts during heat tolerance.

(ii) Hsp90

This family consists of proteins which conserved amino sequence. Proteins of these family especially are rich in cytoplasmic phopsho proteins. The major role of Hsp90 is to manage protein folding. But it also plays a key role in signal transduction networks, cell cycle control, protein degradation and protein trafficking. In addition, it might also plays a role in morphological evolution and stress adaptation in Drosssophilla and Arabidopsis. ATP is required its functions. It is among the most abundant proteins in cells: 1-2 per cent of total cellular proteins. Although Hsp90 chaperones are constitutively expressed in most organisms, their expressions increase in response to stress in both prokaryotes and eukaryotes. Decreasing the level of functional Hsp90 in Drosophila by genetic mutation or treatment with an Hsp inhibitor causes developmental abnormalities and morphological changes.

(iii) Hsp70

Members of the Hsp70 family have been highly conserved through evolution. In addition of Hsp70s strongly inducible by heat shock and other form of cellular stress, constitutively expressed Hsp70s have essential functions under no stressful conditions. These proteins include the E. coli dnak, the Yeast cytosolic proteins Ssa 1p and Ssa2p and the Hsp70 of mammalian cells, the so called clathrinuncoating ATpase. Horologes of these proteins are found within mitochondria, cytoplasma, nucleus ER and chloroplasts in eukaryotic cells. Hsp70s of mammalian and Drosophila cells are major translation products of heat shocked cells. Hsp70 accumulates in nucleus aftershock exposure. Organellarhsps have specific amino terminal target sequences. They provide Hsp 70 to translocate appropriate membrane sites. It has been shown that all Hsps have structural and functional properties following bellow:

1. They bind to AATP and highly conserved amino terminal ATP binding (450 amino acid) and following more variable carboxyl terminal substrate binding domain. This is most likely responsible for peptide binding.
2. They bind to unfolded of partially denatured polypeptides.
3. They use the energy coming from ATP hydrolysis to release the substrates.
4. Members of Hsp 70 family are at least 50 per cent homlog at amino acid sequence level. ATPase domain is placed in amino terminal region. Some members of Hsp70 family are phosphoryleted and/or methylated in vertebrates, yeast, bacteria and plants. Arabodopsis genome has at least 18 genes coding proteins of Hsp 70 family. There has been at least 12 Hsp70 in spinach members are also expressed in environmental stresses like: heat, cold, chemicals. Over expression of Hsp70 genes induces thermal tolerance and increase resistance to environmental stresses.

(iv) Hsp60

This family of highly conserved proteins of approximately 60 kDa is chaperons helping proteins folding and submits assembly. Their prokaryotic and eukaryotic members are dimeric and have phosphorylated isoforms. Members of this family are 14 subunit oligomers. They found in bacteria cytoplasm. While members of their stress inducible and non-inducible members found in bacteria cytosol and in the inner space of mitochondria and chloroplast, they have not been detected in ER and cytoplasm. The hsp60s functionally co-operate with a smaller cochaperonin protein of 10 kDa subunit. Their eukaryotic horologes constitute majority of total cellular proteins. They are developmentally controlled and found in mitochondria and chloroplast. 61 and 60 kDa of Rubisco subunit binding proteins, which are nuclear encoded, synthesized on cytoplasmic ribosomes and imported into chloroplasts and bind to large subunit encoded in chloroplast of Rubisco. Chloroplastchaperion is required for the assembly of Rubisco, hence the name Rubisco binding protein. This assembly is not covalent and requires ATP hydrolysis. In plants the molecular weights of these heat shock proteins range in size from 110 to 15 kD. In general these proteins are classified as high molecular weight, 110, 80, 70, or 60 kD, or lower molecular weight of 30-15 kD. The lower molecular weight class of Hsps is particularly abundant and complex in plants (Mansfield and Key, 1986).

Small Heat Shock Proteins (sHsps)

In somatic tissues of plants sHsps are the most abundant group of Hsps and 17-30 kDa are unique to higher plants. The abundance and heterogeneity of sHspa suggest that they may have physiological functions. Mammalian and Yeast cells hace only one sHsp located in cytosole. However, plants usually produce more than 20 Hsps and they are often the most abundant and stress responsive group of hsps in plants. Heterogenetety of sHsps is unique to plants and plants are only eukaryotes in which organelle localized sHsphaver been described, sHsps show very low sequence similarity. This applies not only to comparisons of sHsps between divergent species, from different organisms are related with each other and even their sequences structure show difference; their structural properties are conserved (Waters *et al.* 1996).

Plant sHps are all encoded by nuclear and are divided into six classless: three classes of (classess CI, CII, and CIII) of sHsps are localized in the cytosols or in the nucleus and the other three in the plastids, the endoplasmic reticulum and mitochondria (CIV, CV, and CVI). The organellar forms of sHsps appeared to be unique to plants with the exception of the mitochondrial hsp22 in Drosophila. Classes CI and CII of cytosolic/nuclear sHsps are generally encoded by multigene families within the same classes, different members of ShSPS Share high sequence homology at the amino acidic level. sHsps of the same class are also homologues among different plant species; however sHsps from different classless share low sequences similarities. All Hsps share a conserved 90 amino acid carboxyl-terminal domain called the alfa-crystalline domain or heat shock domain.

This domain distinguish Hsps from other small protein induced by heat and might have an important role in chaperon activity. This domain can be subdivided into consensus I and consensus II domains separated by hydrophilic domain of variable length. It was determined that consensus I and II have similar hydrophobicity and secondary structure (Sun and Montague, 2002).

Amino terminal domain of the plant sHsps are quite divergent between classless. For the chloroplast, ER and mitochondria localized proteins, amino terminal sequences typical of organelle targeting peptides are present. Within the amino terminal regions of the mature proteins there are consensus domains that are unique to each class of sHsps. There is methionine rich 28 amino acid long consensus III domain in sHsps targeted to chloroplast and represents the most highly conserved domain in sHsps. The presence of these highly conserved domains unique to different classes of sHsps suggests that they serve important roles in the function of these proteins. It has been shown that shsps located in mitochondria and chloroplasts protect respiratory electron transport in mitochondria and PSII electron transport in chloroplast.

Some sHsps have been demonstrated to act as molecular chaperon in vitro and in vivo. 18.1 kD as Hsp has been shown to prevent protein aggregation and maintain them refolding by other chaperon. There is no evidence that sHsps are required for normal cellular functions. They are typically found in heat stressed plants. sHps are also produced in other environmental stresses and some developmental stages (embryogenesis, germination, pollen growth and fruit maturation). Including sHsp gene expression and accumulation of sHsps in environmental stresses indicate important role of these proteins in stress. The extent of sHsp accumulation depends on temperature and the duration of the stress period. sHsps accumulate significantly in couple of hours. They show a heterogenic structure according to their molecular weight, isoelectric point and satiability. After the heat stress has been released, the sHsps are quite stable with half-lives of 30-50 h. suggesting thats Hsp may be important for recovery as well, sHp gene are expressed under control of the heat shock transcription factor (HSF). It has been believed that sHsps play role in transcriptional control on heat stress. It is also unique for plant sHsps to form heat shock granules which are approximately 40nm diameter, 200-400kDa molecular weight during long-term heat stresses. Ongoing heat stress induces accumulation of unfolded proteins bound to sHsp oligomers in the cytoplasm. The complexes of denatured proteins-sHsp oligomers can be stored transiently in HSGs that disintegrate during the recovery period. HSGs contain mainly cytosolic sHsps,

Hsp 70 and heat stress transcription factor HSF 2 are also present in HSG complexes. Oligomers formed by Shps go under structural modifications and change their surface hydrophobicity; thus increasing affinity of substrate binding.

Table 4.3: Stress proteins

Name	Molecular Size	Location	Remarks
Ubiquitin	8	Cytosol/ nucleus	Facilitates targeting and removal of proteins denatured by stress.
Hsp10	10	Mitochondria	Cofactor for Hsp60
Low-molecular weight hsps	20 to 30	Cytosol/nucleus	Some may be responsible for regulating the cellular cytoskeleton and migration, and others regulate vascular tonne and vessel wall remodeling.
Hsp56	56	Cytosol	Binds and stabilizes the steroid hormone receptor complex.
Hsp60	60	Mitochondria	Molecular chaperones.
Hsp72	70	Cytosol/nucleus	Highly stress inducible (tolerance).
Hsp73	70	Cytosol/nucleus	Constitutively expressed molecular chaperone.
Hsp90	90	Cytosol/nucleus	Part of the steroid receptor complex.

Ubiquitin (Hsp 8.5 group)

Ubiquitin is a highly conserved, low molecular weight protein with 75-76 amino acid residues and found in every eukaryotic cell. It is either found as free or bound to various proteins by their terminal Glycin amino acid (Nover *et al.* 1989). Heat stress induced synthesis of ubiquitin may have a vital function for stress tolerance and recovery. Plants use are pertoire of method to control the level and activity of their constituent proteins. One method is selective protein breakdown by the ubiquitin/26S proteasome pathway.

Remarkably, recent analyses of the near complete Arabidopsis thaliana genome identified > 1300 genes, or 5 per cent of the proteome, involved in the ubiquitin/26S prteasome pathway, making it one of the most elaborate regulatory mechanisms in plants (Vierstra, 2003).

Molecular Regulation of Heat Shock Response

Threshold temperature for inducing Hsp synthesis is generally related to temperature at which each species ordinarily grows (Feder and Hofman, 1999). Major prokaryotic hsps are constituently expressed by special genes at all temperatures. After switching temperature or treatment with any agent harming to proteins expression of these genes speed up and reaches in the level that is characteristics for that species in a few minutes. Heat shock responses are controlled by alfa 32 polypeptide (rpoH gene product) at transcriptional level.

Table 4.4: Location of sHsps types in plant cell

Species	Protein
1	2
Chloroplast-localized proteins	
Arabidopsis thaliana	HSP21
Glycine max	HSP22
Petunia hybrida	HSP21
Pisumsativium	HSP21
Triticumaestivum	HSP26A
Triticumaestivum	HSP26B
Zea mays	HSP26
Mitochondrial-localized protein	
Chenopodium rubrum	HSP23
Endoplasmic reticulum-localized proteins	
Arabidopsis thaliana	HSP22
Glycine max	HSP22
Class I Cytocolically localized proteins	
Pisumsativum	HSP22
Arabidopsis thaliana	HSP17.6
Arabidopsis thaliana	HSP17.4
Arabidopsis thaliana	HSP18.2
Chenopodium rubrum	HSP18.3
Daucuscarota	HSP18.0
Daucuscarota	HSP17.8
Glycine max	HSP17.5
Glycine max	HSP17.6
Glycine max	HSP18.5
Helianthus annuus	HSP17.6
Lycopersiconesculentum	HSP17.8
Medicago sativa	HSP18.1
Medicago sativa	HSP18.2
Oryza sativa	HSP16.9
Oryza sativa	HSP17.4

Contd...

1	2
Pisumsativum *Triticumaestivum*	HSP18.1 HSP16.9A
Triticumaestivum	HSP16.9B
Triticumaestivum	HSP16.9C
Zea mays	HSP17.2
Class II Cytocolically localized proteins	
Arabidopsis thaliana	HSP17.6
Glycine max	HSP17.9
Ipomea nil (Pharbatis nil)	HSP18.8
Ipomea nil (Pharbatis nil)	HSP17.2
Lilium longiflorum	HSP17.6
Lilium longiflorum	HSP16.5
Pisumsativum	HSP17.7
Triticumaestivum	HSP17.3
Zea mays	HSP17.5
Zea mays	HSP17.8

There is an analog situation an eukaryotes. Expression of Hsp genes are primarily regulated at transcriptional level (Weng and Nguejen, 1992). Heat shock response is controlled by heat shock transcriptional factors (HSF) binding to specific DNA sites (HS elements) at transcriptional level. HSF specifically binds to heat shock elements (HSEs) in promoters and activates the transcriptional of HS genes. HSFs, once plant has sensed an increase in temperature, go from amonomeric state in the cytoplasm to a trimeric state in the cell nucleus where they can bind the HSEs. HSF binding recruits other transcription components, resulting in gene expression within minutes. Unlike animals and yeasts, which may have 4 of fewer HSFs, plants have been shown to have multiple copies of these genes: tomato has at least 17 and Arabidopsis has 21 different HSF genes (Krishna, 2004). HSFA2 of Arabidopsis has been shown as a key regulator in response to several types of environmental stress.

An important component of thermotolerance is heat tolerance of gene expression. Heat stress is known to swiftly alter the pattern of gene expression, including the Hsp complement and inhibiting expression of many genes expressed under temperature. The mRNAs encoding non-heat stress-induced proteins are destabilized during heat stress. Heat stress inhibits splicing and it was hypothesized that Hsp encoding mRNAs can be processed properly due to the absence of introns in the corresponding genes (Maestri *et al.* 2002). The heat shock response is connected with profound changes of intracellular protein distribution in general. This is observed in 'microscale' *e.g.*, the migration of

RNAPII control from gene to heat shock activated gene or binding of activated cytoplasmic heat shock transcription factor to nuclear heat shock promoter sites, but also in microscale. Examples are the reorganization of the cytoskeleton, the massive accumulation of nonhistone proteins in the chromatic or formation of HSG. Restoration of normal protein pattern of protein distribution is an essential part of the recovery period. It is improved in thermo-tolerentcells and precedes the recovery of normal cellular functions.

Plant sHsps are controlled at transcriptional level in heat stress. sHsps might protect and keep stable untranslated normal cellular mRNA during heat stress. Describing some isoforms of sHsps indicates those proteins are coded by different post-translation modifications. The high selectivity of Hsp synthesis depends on the massive synthesis of new mRNAs encoded bu the Hsp genes and the number of alterations of translation apparatus leading to an efficient discrimination of non-Hsp mRNAs. The selectivity of Hsp synthesis in heat shocked cells does not correspond to the composition of the mRNA fraction. Most of the 'control' mRNAs, though not translated, are maintained intact and can be reactivated in the recovery period. Heat shock mRNAs rapidly accumulate during heat shock and preferentially occupy the polysomal apparatus (Nover *et al.* 1989).

A hypothetical multistep model of essential translation events during heat shock can be put forward:

In 0-5 min, an immediate initiation deficiency and the collapse of the cytoskeleton lead to destruction of polysomes, 15 min. After stress, formation of Hsgs (non-translated control mRNAs are protected from) degradation by increasing of Hsps); in the late phase of the stored mRNAs are reactivated. Slow adaptation to heat or pre-stimulation increase translation at strong heat shock situations. Many modifications of translation process were described in microorganisms, plants and animals. Storing of transiently untranslated mRNAs is needed to efficiently recover synthesis of control proteins.

Thermal Tolerance and Molecular Chaperones

Biologically function of proteins is critically dependent on the formation/ dissolution of weak chemical bonds. This requirement irrevocably synthesizes organism to environmental factors that affect weak bonds. If these factors are present in excess or in insufficient quantity, the result is departure from the native structure of proteins, with ultimate divesting consequences for protein functions. Non-native proteins expose regions that are satisfied in the native structure; these exposed unsatisfied regions can bind other such regions in other proteins and so lead to aggregations of proteins that at worst are cytotoxic and at best reduce the pool of functional protein in the cell. This problem is ancient and widespread as life and so is one major biological solution: molecular chaperones. Molecular chaperones can recognize and bind to non-native proteins and release them in highly related fashion, allowing the bound proteins to attain/retain their native conformation and/or be targeted for degradation and removal from the cell (feder, 1999). Chaperons are responsible for protein folding, assembly, translocation and degradation in many cellular processes.

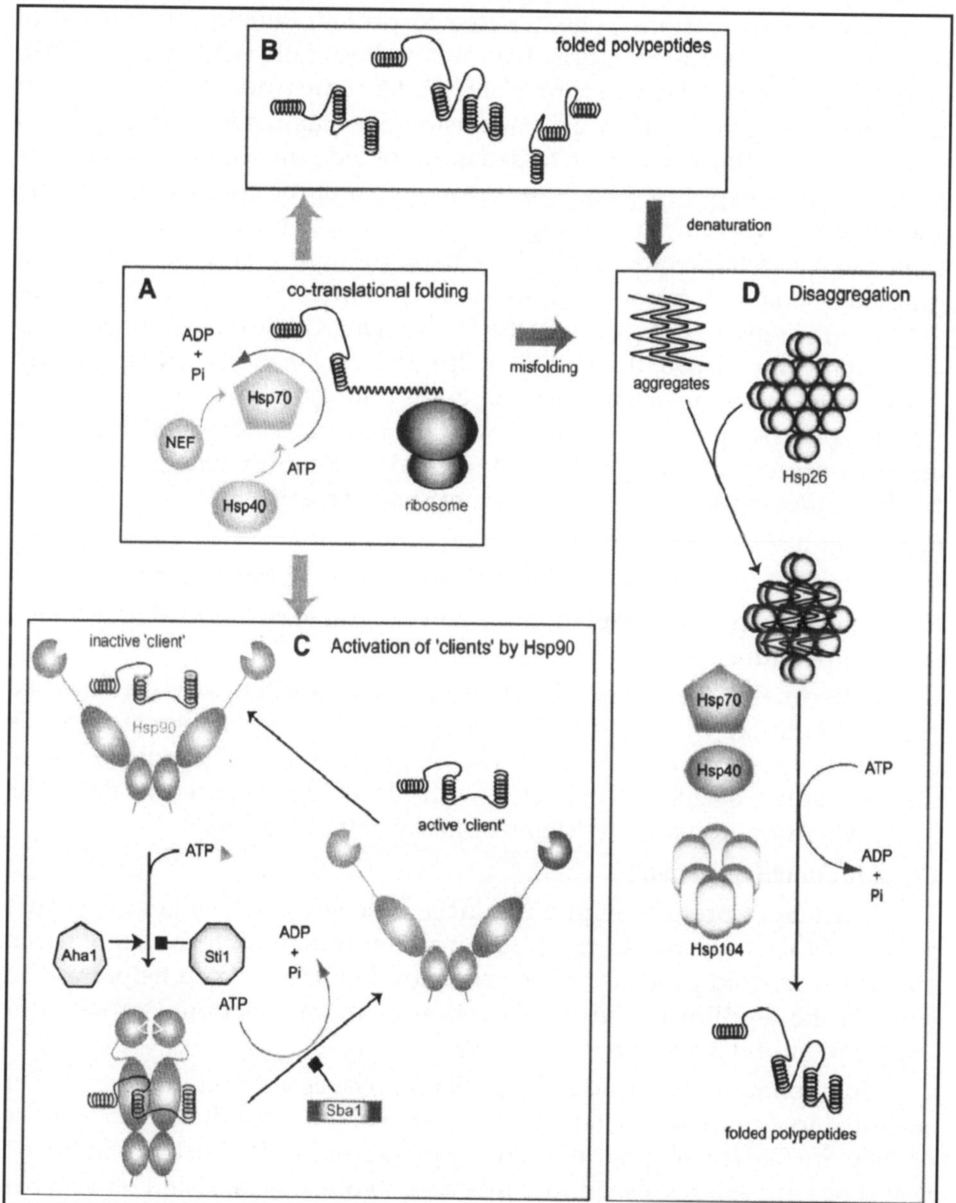

Fig. 4.3: **Simple illustration of part of the chaperone machines that operate in the cytosol**

They stabilize proteins and membranes and can assist in protein refolding under stress conditions. Hsps function as molecular chaperones *i.e.,* they interact with other proteins and in so doing, minimize the probability that these other proteins will interact inappropriately with one another. Hsps recognize and bind to each other proteins when these other proteins are in nonnative conformations, whether due to protein denaturation stress or because the peptide they comprise have not yet been fully synthesized, folded, assembled or localized to an appropriate cellular compartment. Typically Hsps functions as oligomers. They are responsible for maintaining 'Hsps' partner proteins in a folding competent, folded or unfolded state; Organellar location, import, and/or export; minimizing the aggregation of non-native proteins; and targeting non-native or aggregated proteins for degradation and removal from the cell. Chaperones generally should recognize structural elements exposed by non-native proteins (Hendrick and Hartl, 1993). Five major families of Hsps are known as chaperones: the Hsp70 (DnaK), the chaperones (GroEL and Hsp60), the Hsp90, the Hsp100 (Clp) and the small Hsp (sHsp) family. Aside from these major families, there are other proteins with chaperone functions, such as protein disulfide isomerase and calnexin/calreticulin, which assist in protein folding in the endoplasmic reticulum (Wang *et al.* 204). Evident differences of the thermotolerent states observed:

(a) After a short and mild heat shock.

(b) After a moderate to severe heat shock applied to few hours.

(c) After a long-term adaptation to growth or at least survival at elevated temperatures.

Experimental heat shock research mostly concentrates on conditions a and b. If both are compared two different states of thermotolerance can be defined.. Long-term heat shock (c) has two important effects: destruction of the chloroplast structure connected with bleaching observed in the virus infections from growing meristems of many cultural plants.

Cellular Functions of hsp's

The fate of proteins with non-functional conformations after exposure may be either to re-obtain the functional conformation, form aggregation with other misfold proteins or become degraded. Hsps play a helper role in shifting the equilibrium in the direction of more functional proteins or degradation of damaged proteins (Soransen, 2003).

For thermotolerance induction in plants, tissues or cell cultures are either subjected to a continuous, moderate heat shock, to a preinduction procedure or they are slowly adapted to increasingly severe heat shock. Preinducion heat shock procedures also induce tolerance to other stresses and other types of stresses induce tolerance to heat stress. Two tightly related aspects have to be considered:

Table 4.5: Other chaperones and stress related proteins

Name	Synonyms	Function/Structure
Calnexin	CNX, P90	Calcium-binding ER protein that interacts transiently with newly synthesized N-linkedglycoproteins, facilitating protein folding and assembly; it may also play a central role in the quality control of protein folding by retaining incorrectly folded protein subunits within the ERfor degradation. Transmembrane.
CHIP	STUB1, UBOX1, HSPABP2	E3 ubiquitin ligase; co-chaperone that associates with HSP70 and HSP90.
ERdj5	JPDI, DnaJC10	Expression induced by ER stress; also a member of the DnaJ family.
ERp27	NA	Interacts with PDIA3; does not contain a CXXC active site motif indicating that it is a catalyticallyredox-inactive member of the protein disulfide isomerase family.
ERp44	TXNDC4	Induced by ER stress.
ERp57	Grp58, PDIA3	ER protein with protein disulfide isomerase activity that interacts with the lectin chaperonescalreticulin and calnexin to modulate the folding of newly synthesized glycoproteins.
HO-1	Heme oxygenase (decyclizing) 1,HMOX1, HSP32	Highly inducible by heavy metals, endotoxin, oxidizing agents, UVA; cleaves heme ring at the α methene bridge to form biliverdin.
HO-2	Heme oxygenase (decyclizing) 2,HMOX2	Non-inducible; cleaves heme ring at the α methene bridge to form biliverdin.
ERp18	TXNDC12, AGR1, ERp19	Member of the thioredoxin superfamily; expressed in ER lumen.
ERp29	ERp28, ERp31, PDI-DB	Similar in sequence to the PDI family, but lacks a thioredoxin motif, suggesting it does not function as a disulfide isomerase; the protein dimerizes and is thought to play a role in the processing of secretory proteins within the ER; two alternative splice forms.
HSF-1	HSTF1	Regulates the programme of heat shock gene expression. Expression repressed by HSP90; positively and negatively regulated by phosphorylation; modified by SUMO-1 and SUMO-2 in a stress-inducible manner.
HSP47	SerpinH1, Colligin, Gp46	ER-localized member of the serpin family of serine protease inhibitors; expression induced by heat shock; binds collagen and thought to be a chaperone involved in the maturation of collagen; auto-antibodies found in patients with rheumatoid arthritis.
KDELR3	ERD2L3	Two alternative splice forms.
UGG T	UDP-glucose: glycoprotein glucosyltransferase, HUGT1, UGCGL1, GT, UGT1, UGTR	Misfolded part of the protein, thus providing quality control for protein folding in the endoplasmicreticulum; reglucosylated proteins are recognized by calreticulin for recycling to theendoplasmic reticulum and refolding or degradation.

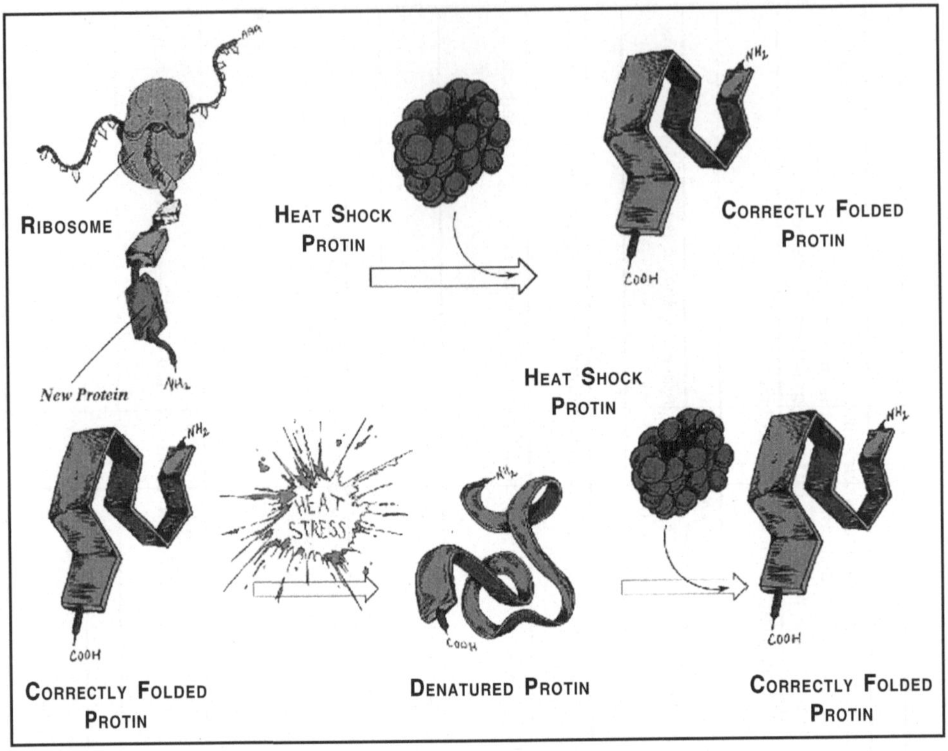

Fig. 4.4: **Functions of heat shock protein**

1. The protection of cellular fine structure during the stress period.
2. The effective repair of eventual damages with restoration of the normal metabolic and gene expression activities mainly in the recovery period. Similar to animal systems, the 3 phases of heat shock induction (few minutes), expression (1-3 hra) and decay (12-48 hrs) of Hsps and thermotolerance are very similar also in plants. Generally it is not justified to conclude from analyses of growth of survival curves that Hsps are required or not required for thermotolerance. For example, growing pollen tubes of Tradescantia paludosa, though unable to Hsp synthesis, exhibit certain aspects of induced thermotolerance simply demonstrate that other protective agents contributes as well. Variation in Hsp production among closely related species from thermally contrasting habitats has been observed even when these species are grown and heat stressed under identical conditions. This variation I Hsp production is often correlated with organismal thermotolerance (Downs *et al.* 1998). There are many studies showing quantitative variations for their tolerance degrees among genotypes. The acquisition of thermotolerance appears to depend on not only upon the synthesis of Hsps but also on their selective cellular localization. Lin *et al.* 1984, reported that in the soybean seedlings, several

Hsps become selectively localized in or associated with nuclei, mitochondria and ribosomes at 40ºC , they were absent in other parts. The selective localization odHsps is temperature dependent. Genotyping variations have been observed for thermo sensitivity in studies up to date. Heat shock sensitive genotypes synthesized Hsps earlier than tolerant genotypes (Krishnan, 1989). Especially very early detected (in a few minutes in heat shocks) specific hsp transcript might have effect on order of Hsp gene expression and cause different tolerance levels among species (Wang *et al.* 2002). Tolerance to heat shock cannot be controlled by only one gene. The heat shock tolerance is determined by different genes sets in different stages of life cycle and in different tissues. Hsp70 was shown to be casually involved in the capacity to acquire thermotolerance in Arabidopsis. Hsp27 in another thermo sensitive Arabidopsis mutant. Hsp27 was identified as a factor of acquired thermo tolerance in the study of transgenic cells (Maestri *et al.* 2002).

Table 4.6: Transgenic attempts to enhance plant temperature stress tolerance

Phenotypes	Function	Plant	Gene
Hs tolerant; Hs sensitive	TF	Tomato	HsfA1
HS tolerant	TF	Arabodopsis	Hsf3
HT sensitive	HSP	Arabodopsis	Hsp70
Abolished acquired thermotolerance	HSP	Maize	Hsp101
HT tolerant	HSP	Carrot	Hsp17.7
HT tolerant	Fatty acid denaturation	Tobacco	Fad7
HS tolerant	AOS metabolism	Barley	Hvapx1

Sung *et al.* (2003)

Abbreviations: AOS: active oxygen spacies; Hsf, heat shock factor; Hsp, heat shock protein; HT, high temperature; TF, transcription factor; APX, ascorbate peroxide; fad7, fatty acid desaturation.

Heat Shock Proteins of Pigeon pea (*Cajanuscajan*)

The proteins synthesized in response to higher temperature in a tropical legume-plant pigeon pea have been studied using polyacrylamide gel electrophoresis. Ten to twelve heat shock proteins (hsps) of molecular weights ranging from 15 to 81 kDa are synthesized by excised roots when temperature is raised by 10°C above their normal growth temperature (30°C). The heat shock response is rapid and the presence is rapid and the presence of hsps can be detected just 30 min after raising the temperature. Hsps cannot be seen in stained gels, and their presence can only be monitored by fluorography. The results indicate the transient nature of their synthesis. Most of the hsps are of nuclear origin, however, at least two of them, 18 and 60 kDa proteins appear to be synthesized in mitochondria.

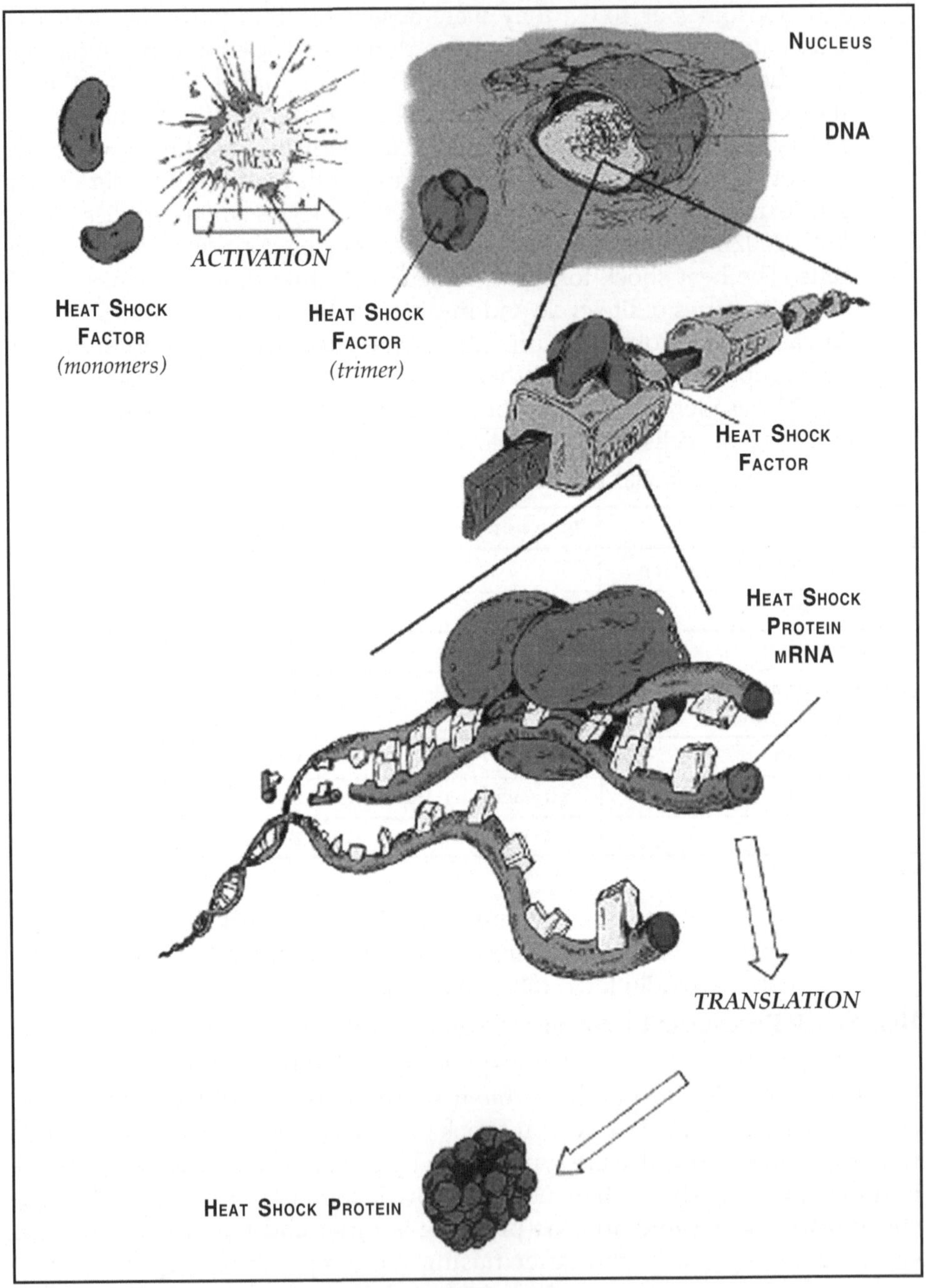

Fig. 4.5: **Upregulation of heat shock protein**

Heat Shock Triggers Rapid Protein phosphorylation in Soybean

Heat shock rapidly triggers phosphorylation of a set of proteins in soybean seedlings. Although the kinetics of phophorylation and the heat shock response are similar, the major identified phophorylation products do not co migrate with heat shock proteins on polyacylamide gels. Cadmium, which is known to induce the heat shock response, stimulates phosphorylation of the same set of proteins. The rapidity of phosphorylation suggests that it may play a pivotal role in sensing and transduction elevated temperature stress in plants.

Characterization of the Heat Shock Response in Cultured Sugarcane Cells

Effect of heat shock on the growth of cultured sugarcane cells was measured. Heat shock treatment at 36 to 38°C (2 hours) induced the development of maximum thermotolerance to otherwise no permissive heat stress at 54°C (7 min) optimum thermotolerance was observed 8 hours after heat shock. Development of thermotolerance was observed initiated by treatments as short as 30 minutes at 36°C. Temperature below 36°C or above 40°C failed to induce maximum thermotolerance. In vivo labeling revealed that HS at 32 to 34°C induced several high molecular mass heat shock proteins (HSPs). A complex of 18 kilodaldon HSps required at least 36°C treatment for induction. The majority of the HSps began to accumulate within 10 minutes, whereas the synthesis of low molecular mass peptides in the 18kDa range became evident 30 min after initiation of HS. HS above 38°C resulted in progressively decreased HSP synthesis with inhibition first observed for HSPs larger than 50 kDa.

Expression of a Unique Plastid-localized Heat-shock Protein in Wheat

Joshi *et al.* 1997 have used a combination of molecular and classical genetic approaches to delineate the relationship between a specific HSP member and cell viability under heat stress. Using recombinant inbred lines (RILs) of wheat, derived from a cross of the thermotolerent cultivar 'Mustang' and the thermo suceptible cultivar 'Sturdy', we have identified a unique HSP and a differtially expressed cDNA sequence, both related to the plastid-localized HSP26 gene family, that are closely associated with acquired thermotolerance in wheat. An isoform of HSP26 was synthesized under heat stress in all examined thermotolerent RILs and 'Mustang' and was absent in all examined thermo suceptible RILs and 'Sturdy'. Using a modified differential-display method, we have also identified a gene specific cDNA sequence that is similar to other known members of the wheat HSP26 gene family and is selectively expressed in 'Mustang' and the most of the examined thermotolerent RILs, but not expressed in 'Sturdy' and all the thermosuceptible RILs. These results suggest a genetic linkage between the acquired thermotolerance trait and the differential expression of a unique member of the HSP26 gene family.

Enhanced Expression of Heat Shock Proteins in Thermotolerant Lines of Sunflower

The major lacuna in developing stress-tolerance lines through breeding is the lack of suitable technique for screening the segregating population. Kumar *et al.* 1999, developed an efficient technique for identifying high temperature tolerant lines in sunflower. The rationale behind this technique is that the stress responsive genes are expressed during sub-lethal (induction) stress, and its products impart tolerance at subsequent lethal stresses. The genetic variability in gene expression upon induction stress is responsible for the differential survival and recovery following exposure to severe lethal stress ina heterogeneous population. Optimization of induction and subsequent lethal temperature levels is a pre-requisite for developing a standardized screening protocol. The optimum induction temperature in sunflower was identified by subjecting the germinated seedlings to various sub-lethal temperatures followed by exposure to a specific lethal temperature for a fixed duration. Gradual temperature induction was found to be optimum in bridging about a maximum response in terms of the recovery growth of seedlings after exposure to lethal temperature. The seedlings were subjected to a specific high temperature for different periods to arrive at a high-stringency lethal temperature treatment. By adopting this approach an open-pollinated population of sunflower. Was screened for high temperature tolerance.. The seedlings which survived at the high-stringency lethal temperature following the optimum induction treatment were identified as thermotolerent lines. At the plant level too these identified lines showed higher tolerance as reflected by a higher membrane integrity and recovery leaf-area. The progeny population of these identified lines also exhibited higher tolerance to temperature compared to the original population, indicating the persistence of the selected trait. This tolerance was associated with a higher accumulation of heat shock proteins (HSPs).

Biochemical and Biophysical Characterization of Small Heat Shock Proteins from Sugarcane

The diversity of small Hsps in plants is intriguing and characterization of their chaperones activity is important to understand plant tolerance to heat stress. A previous study showed that small Hsps mainly represented by class I (cytosolic), correspond to about 5 per cent of all sugarcane ESTs belonging to the molecular chaperones category. Ana O Tiroli and Carlos, 2007 characterized sugarcane small Hsps from class I, which were named HsHsp 17.2 and SsHsp 17.9 accordingly to their monomer molecular mass of 17.2 and 17.9 kDa, respectively. The recombinant proteins have identify of about 75 per cent to each other and similar structural characteristics.. However, their stability and their chaperone activity were not equivalent: SsHsp 17.9 was more efficient in protecting citrate synthase and malate dehydrogenase from aggregation. Whereas SsHsp17.2 was more efficient in protecting luciferase from aggregation. There is only one region, which is located at he N-terminus, of low homology between these two proteins. Based on that and on previous works pointing to multiple sites, mainly at the N-n terminus, involved with substrate specificity in small Hsps, we suggest that this specific region is one of these sites. In addition, this is the first report on the chaperone activity of sugarcane small Hsps.

Expression of the Chloroplast-localized Small Heat Shock Protein by Oxidative Stress in Rice

A rice cDNA clone, Oshsp26, encoding the chloroplast-localized small heat shock protein (sm HSP) was isolated. Southern blot analysis of genomic DNA and the result of screening of a cDNA library indicated that Oshsp26 gene is encoded by single gene in rice genome. The Oshsp26 gene was expressed following heat stress: the transcript level was highest when rice leaves were treated at high temperatures for 2 h at 42ºC, and the transcript became detectable after 20 min and reached a maximum level after 2 h. It was also found that the Oshp gene was expressed following oxidative stress even in the absence of heat stress. Treatment of rice plant with methyl vilogen (MV) in the light and treatment with hydrogen peroxide either in the light or in the dark, both caused a significant accumulation of the transcript and the protein. Since MV treatment in the light leads to the generation of H_2O_2 inside the chloroplast, it is likely that H_2O_2 by itself acts to induce the expression of the Oshsp26 gene. These results suggest that the chloroplast ssmHSP plays an important role in protecting the chloroplast against damage caused by oxidative stress as well as by heat stress.

Molecular Cloning and Sequence Analysis of cDNAs cytoplasmic hsps in Wheat

In an effort to study the low molecular weight HSPs in cultivated wheat, Jiang Weng *et al*. 1993 have cloned and characterizes three cDNAs from wheat, Tahsp 16.9B and tahsp 17.4, respectively that encode peptides having homology to the cytoplasmic LMW HSP family. Nucleotide sequence comparisons indicated that: 1. Tahsp 16.9 A and Tahsp16.9B belong to the LMW HSP class I; there is 82 per cent identity of whole cDNA sequence between them, but only 58 per cent identity at the 3′ non-coding region 2. Tahsp 17.4 belongs to LMW HSP class II. Amino acid sequence comparisons indicates that there is a 97 per cent similarity between Tahsp 16.9A and tahsp 16.9b and 57 per cent between class I and class II (Tahsp 17.4) members in wheat. There is a 93 per cent similarity between Tahsp 17.4 and Zmhsp 17.9 from maize which belong to class II of LMW HSps. Northern blot hybridization analysis was performed using poly (A)+ RNA from green leaf tissue treated at different temperatures (250, 280, 310, 340, 370 and 400C) for 60 min or at 37°C for different time periods (0,7.5,15, 30, 60, 120 and 240 min).

These experiments revealed that the expression of Tahsp 16.9 B and Tahsp 17.4 was induced beginning at 31°C and reached maximum levels at 37°C. The onset of mRNA induction occurred within about 7 min, reached a peak at 60 min and declined after 240 min when treated under the optimal heat stress condition (370C). In vitro hybrid selection and Southern blot analysis data indicate that Tahsp 16.9A and Tahsp 16.9B belong to a 12-member class I multigene family. Tahsp 17.4 on the other hand belongs to a 14-member class II multigene family. These cDNAs, which encodes cytoplasmic LMW HSPs in hexaploid wheat, will provide us with tools to investigate the role of HSps in an agriculturally important cereal crop species.

Sporophytic and gametophytic Heat Shock Protein synthesis in sorghum

The general characteristics of the heat shock response in the sporophytic and gametophytic phases of Sorghum bicolor, species well adapted to tropical environments, were studied. At the sporophytic level, heat shock protein (HSP) synthesis in sorghum is still induced after an extreme (over 50°C) or prolonged heat stress: the so called late HSps are first induced after 14 h continuous exposure at 45°C, and persist up to at least 28 h shock. A normal protein pattern is not resumed, as is the case in most organisms. In contrast to plant species typical of temperature climates, sorghum pollen also retains the capability to synthesize HSps in post-germinative stages. In addition to several classic Hsps, those synthesized in all sporophytic tissues, some gametophyte specific heat inducible polypeptide are expressed in both immature and germinating pollen. Taking in to account the likely role of Hsps in cellular thermo-protection, these data support the hypothesis that acquition of thermotolerance shows between species variability, in relation to climatic adaptation. In addition, the results concerning Hsp synthesis in the male gamrtophyte suggest the possible use of gametophytic selection in crop improvement for thermotolerance.

Genotype-specific Heat Shock Proteins in two Maize inbreds

Leaf blade tissue of maize inbred lines B73 and mo17 was anlysed for interspecific genetic variability in the heat shock response. The maize inbred were characterizes for acquired thermal tolerance and patterns of heat shock protein synthesis. The leakage conductivity assay of membrane stability during stress indicated that Mo17 possess greater potential than B73 to acquire thermal tolerance. Poly (A)+ RNA, extracted from leaf blades, was translated in vitro in the presence of 35S-methionine and the translation product separated by two diamentional gel electrophoresis. Major genotypic difference were observed in the translation product. Mo17 synthesized twelve unique heat shock proteins in the 15-18 kDa range, but B73 polymorphisms were observed between the maize lines using 32P labeled heat shock protein gene probes (Julie *et al.* 2004).

Heat Shock Proteins during Grain Filling in Wheat

Skylas *et al.* 2002 used two complementary approaches to determine the effect of heat shock on wheat grain quality. Heat susceptible (cv. Wyuns) and the heat tolerant (cv. Fang) cultivars of wheat were compared after heat shock, utilizing both dough quality testing and protein analysis. Plants were grown at day/night temperatures of 24/18°C during development, with stressed plants being subjected to heat shock at day/night temperature of 40/25°C on 15, 16 and 17 days post anthesis. Grainsamples were taken during development (17 days post-anthesis) and at maturity (45 days post anthesis). Dough quality testing of flour indicated that the Wyuna cultivar exhibited a decrease in dough strength after heat shock, whilst the fang cultivar exhibited an increase. Proteome studies conducted on endosperm (at 17 days post anthesis) showed that the heat tolerant fang cultivar exhibited a stronger and more diverse heat shock response than Wyuna. In total, 48 protein spots exhibiting differtial expression between control and heat shock treatments were excised from gels and analyzed by mass spectrometry. The resultant triptic-peptide mass fingerprint data was submitted to SWISS-PROT and TrTREMBL databases for protein identification. The majority of heat shock associated proteins had low molecular mass and showed database similarity to previously characterized small heat shock proteins. Several discrete isoforms of the low molecular weight heat shock protein were observed as differtially expressed between the two cultivars. Furthermore, seven protein spots were expressed in heat shocked fang but not in heat shocked Wyuna, thus were further characterized utilizing tandem mass spectrometry. These possible marker proteins for heat tolerance may assist breeders in the selection of heat tolerant cultivars that would not be expected to lose dough strength in such an environment.

Class I small Heat Shock Proteins in Tobacco

A class I cytisolic small HSP gene, TLHS1, whose protein showed a stronger molecular chaperone activity among the class I cytosolic small HSPs in tobacco, and constitutively expressed it in tobacco. Bioassay of transgenic tobacco seedlings at T_2 generation for thermotolerance was performed as the rates of cotyledon opening after heat stress. Transgenic tobacco seedlings with the constitutively expressed TLHSI showed up to two times higher cotyledon opening rates compared to the transgenic tobacco seedlings caring TLSHI gene in antisense orientation and the expression vector only after the high temperature stresses of 40°C and 45°C for 1 to 4 h. When the correlation between the level of thermotolerance was examined, a strong correlation between them could be observed. Together these results support the thermo protective function of a class I small HSP plants.

Identification of pea genotypes with Enhanced thermotolerance

Thermotolerance is one of the various acquired stress tolerance phenomenon observed in all living organisms, when the stress is imposed gradually. Based on this fact a very efficient technique termed As Temperature Induction Response (TIR) technique has been developed to identify and select the thermo tolerentgenotypes. It involves exposing seedlings and or plants to induction stress and subsequently challenging with sever temperature and selecting the surviving seedlings at the end of a challenge temperature, exhibited higher recovery growth compared to seedlings which were directly exposed to challenge temperature. Moreover, the induced seedlings accumulated higher levels of hsp18.1 and hsp70 transcript as well as HSP 104 and HSp90 proteins. A similar response was also seen when the experiment was done in mature plants as well. Using TIR technique 32 pea genotypes were screened. Genetic variability for thermotolerance was seen only upon induction treatment. Further, by employing Z analysis they have grouped genotypes into thermotolerent (Acc. 623, Acc 765) and susceptible (Acc. 476, Bonnevile) genotypes. Amongst the tolerant lines one of the cultivars, Acc, 623, showed a higher threshold temperature for thermotolerance compared to the other. The tolerant genotypes Acc. 623 showed higher expression of a few HSP genes compared to the susceptible genotype Acc. 476 upon temperature induction. Thus, it confirms that through TIR, thermotolerent genotypes can be identified from a large germplasm. The advantage of this technique in identifying tolerant lines from segregating populations and subsequently developing tolerant progenies has been discussed.

Summary

Abiotic stresses especially temperature, salinity and drought, are the primary causes of plant loss worldwide. The adverse effect of heat stress can be mitigated by developing crop plant with improved thermotolerance using various genetic approaches. Plant can experience wide fluctuations of temperature on a daily or seasonal basis and they are constantly exposed to changing environments and genetic threats. The Hsps buffer this environmental fluctuations and are therefore important factors for the maintenance of homeostatic across environmental regimes.. Heat shock proteins are important in relation to stress resistance and adaption to the environment. For this purpose, however, a thorough understanding of physiological responses of plants to high temperature, mechanisms of heat tolerance and possible strategies of improving crop thermotolerance of imperative. Based on a complete understanding of such mechanisms, potential genetic strategies to improve plant heat stress tolerance include traditional and contemporary molecular breeding protocols and transgenic approaches. Although biochemical and molecular aspects of aspects of thermotolerance in plants are relatively well understood, further studies focused on phenotypic flexibility and assimilate partitioning under heat stress and factors modulating crop heat tolerance are imperative. Such studies combined with genetic approaches to identify and map genes (or QTLs) conferring thermotolerance will not only facilitate marker assisted breeding for heat tolerance but also pave the way for cloning and characterization of underlying genetic factors which could be useful for engineering plant with improved heat tolerance.

REFERENCES

Banu Efeoglu. (2009). Heat Shock Proteins and Heat Shock Response in Plants. G.U. *Journal of Science*, 22 (2):67-75.

Dash, S., Mohanty, N. (2002). Response os Seedlings tom Heat Stress in Cultivars of Wheat: Growth Temperature-Dependent differtial Modulation of photosystem I and 2 Activity, and foliar Antioxidant Defense Capacity. *J. Plant Physiol.* 159:49-59.

Downs, C.A., Hechathorn, S.A., Bryan, J.K. and Cleman, J.S. (1998). The Methionine-Rich Low Molecular Weight chloroplast Heat Shock Protein: Evolutionary Conservation and Accumulation in Relation to thermotolerance,. *American Journal of Botany*, 85(2):175-183.

Feder, E.M., Hofman, G.E. (1999). Heat-shock Proteins, Molecular Chaperons, and the Stress Response. *Annial Review of Physiology*. 61: 243-282.

Feder, E.M. (1999). Organismal, Ecological and Evolutionary aspects of Heat Shock Proteins and the Stress Response: Established Conclusions and unresolved Issues, *American Journal of Zoologist*. 39(6): 857-861.

Hendrick, J/ P. and hart, F.U. (1993). Molecular Chaperone Functions of Heat-Shock Proteins, *Annual Review of Biochem.*, 62:349-384.

Julie Jian Weng, Tuan Huo Daivid Huop and Henry T. Nguyen. (2004). Genotype-specific Heat Shock Proteins in Two Maize Hybrids – *Plant Cell Reports*. 11, 9110:576-580.

Kregel, K.C., (2002). Heat Shock Proteins: Modifying Factors in physiological Stress Responses and Acquired Thermos Tolerance. *J.Appl. Physiol.* 92, 2177-2186.

Krishnan, M., Nguyen, H.T., Burke, J.J. (1989). Heat Shock Protein Synthesis and Thermal Tolerance in Wheat, Plant Physiol. 90: 140-145. Krishna, P. (2004). Plant Responses to abiotic Stress, Springer, Berline, 73-93.

Kumar, G., Krishnaprasad, B.T., Savitha, M.R., Gopal krishna, G., Rammohan, M., Udaykumar, K. Mukhopadyay. (1999). Enhanced Expression of Heat Shock Proteins in Thermotolerant Lines of Sunflower and their Progenies Selected on the Basis of Temperature-induction Response (Kumar, *et al.* 1999), Theret. *Appl. Genet.* 99:1-2.

Lin, C.Y., Roberts, J.K., Key, L.L. (1984). Acquisition of Thermotolerance in Soybean Seedlings, *Plant Physiol.* 74:152-160.

Maestri, E., Klueva, N., Perrotta, C., Gilli, M., Nguyen, H.J., Marmiroli, N. (2002). Molecular Genetics of Heat Tolerance and Heat Shock Proteins in ceareals, *Plant Molecular Biology*. 48: 667-681.

Nover, L., Neumann, D., Scharf, K.D., (1989). Heat Shock and other Stress Response Systems of Plants. Springer, New York. 155p.

SKylas, D.J. Cordwell, S.J. hains, P.G., Larsen, M.R., Basseal, D.J., Walsh, B.J., Blumenthal, C., Rathmell, W., Copeland, L., and Wrigley, C.W. (2002). Heat Shock of wheat during Grain Filling: Proteins Associated with Heat-tolerance. *J. of Cereal Science*, 35(1): 175-188.

Sorransen, J.G., Kristensen, T.N., Loeschcke, V., The Evolutionary and Ecological Role of Heat Shock Proteins, *Ecology Letters*, 6:1025-1037.

Sun, W., Montagu, M.V., (2002). Small Heat Shock Proteins and Stress Tolerance in Plants, Biophysica Acta., 1577:1-9.

Sung, D.Y., Kaplan, F., Lee, K.J., Guy, C.L., (2003). Acquired Tolerance to Temperature Extremes. *Trends Plant Sci.* 8,179-187.

Vierstra, R.D., (2003). The ubiquitin/26S Proteosome Pathway, the Complex last Chapter in the Life of Many Plant Proteins, Trends in Plant Science, 8(3):135-142.

Waters, E.R., Lee, G.J., Vierling, E., (1996). Evolution, Structure and Function of the Small Heat Shock Proteins in Plant. *Journal of Experimental Botany*. 47(296):325-338.

Wang, W., VInocur, B., Shoseyov, O., Atman, A. (2004). Role of Plant Heat Shock Proteins and Molecular Chaperons in the abiotic Stress Response, *Trends in Plant Science*. 9(5):1360-1380.

Weng, J., Nguyen, H.T. (1992). Differences in the Heatshock Response between Thermotolerant and Thermo Susceptible Cultivars of Hexaploid Wheat, *Theor. Appl. Genet*. 84:941-946.

Page 89-103

AGRICULTURAL PRACTICES AND CROP DISEASE CONTROL
Edited by : Dr. Alka Chauhan and Dr. Anubhuti Sharma
Edition : 2017
ISBN : 978-93-5056-859-0
Published by : Discovery Publishing House Pvt. Ltd., New Delhi (India)

5

'E-Farmer' - The 3E Concept for Sustainable Agricultural Development for Farmer's Revolution in India

Prasann Kumar

ABSTRACT

Our trip to India in January of 2012 with the International Agriculture Rural Development Programme 6020 class allowed us to observe firsthand many facets and issues of agricultural systems in India. Despite the fact that our travels were limited to the southern part of the country, we still discerned the immense diversity of Indian agriculture and the clear necessity of an integrated and thorough method of combating a wide range of issues. This overarching theme pointed us in the direction of technology transfer, which presents solutions as well as its own problems. A major challenge that tramples down most of the extension measures is the illiteracy of the farmers which is a serious concern and impediment to the extension workers. This motivated me to put forth the concept of an 'E-farmer' an enlightened, educated and enthusiastic farmer who could lay the foundation for the dawn of a farmer's revolution in India.

Keywords: *Agriculture, Crop, Development, E-farmer, Farmer.*

INTRODUCTION

This was true in my trip with Cornel University Geneva, NY, student to India - the nation of a fascinating agrarian culture which etched a deep and permanent change on my ideas about agricultural extension systems. In south, it awakened my senses to the reality of agricultural jeopardy in the

Department of Plant Physiology, Institute of Agricultural Sciences, Banaras Hindu University, Varanasi, 221 005, India.

developing nations. It also vividly animated the fact that Indian agriculture is in peril today. It was startling to see how a nation that flourished with food grains and spices for many centuries is now crippled with a serious agrarian crisis that has wrecked have on the lives of the rural poor and made their future gloomy. Weaving my experiences in India to the extant hunger reports, left me perplexed with the question: *Why, is a nation blessed with such a mind-boggling diversity of climate, soils and natural wealth, entangled in hunger and malnutrition?* The only possible answer that flashes in my mind is that farmers who are supposed to be the pillars of Indian agriculture are like bent reeds today. They are still walking on the roads of Stone Age men and updates are almost turned off for their agricultural version. The stagnancy and dormancy in Indian agriculture can be attributed to the poor adoption of advanced technologies by the farmers. Neither agriculture nor the conventional farmers have progressed even a bit from the starting line to be on track with India's increasing population in the race of progress. The trip gave us a panoramic view of the impoverished and the illiterate condition of the farmers in South India besides highlighting the real need for our overarching theme. At this golden era of communication, where scientists have been even able to communicate with satellites in other planets, the irony is that the communication strength between the scientist and the farmer inside the same city is too weak. Though there are several extension measures taken by the public, private sectors as mentioned in the previous chapters, very little improvement has been made and this sector still remains at its infancy. A major challenge that tramples down most of the extension measures is the illiteracy of the farmers which is a serious concern and impediment to the extension workers. This motivated me to put forth the concept of an 'E-farmer' - an enlightened, educated and enthusiastic farmer who could lay the foundation for the dawn of a farmer's revolution in India. Based on my experiences in the Tamil Nadu Agricultural University (TNAU), I believe that the Agricultural Universities can play a mammoth role in catalyzing this paradigm shift in the lives of the Indian farmers. This chapter analyzes the role played by TNAU in the transfer of technologies and how agricultural students can augment its role effectively.

The Vision for an 'E-farmer - An Enlightened, Education and Enthusistic Farmer

The farmers are the backbone of India and they play a pivotal role in its growth and economy. The success of a farmer is a herald of dawn whereas his failure is a harbinger of doom for the whole nation. In the past two decades India has witnessed an alarming increase in the number of farmer's suicides. A closer look at the data on farmers suicides from the National Crime Report Bureau (Accidents and suicides - ADSI reports [updated 2010]) shows a dismal picture of 2,56,913 farmers suicide cases from 1995-2010. This is the most awful recorded wave of suicides of its kind in the history. The farmer hooks himself in a knot when all his hopes of living have been enervated. But, the unpalatable truth is that science and technology are least bothered about the suicide spate and the farmers fate. I would say that more attention is given to a potato plant's life in the greenhouse than a farmer's life in the open field! Is Indian going to tread over these farmers graves or triumph in ceasing this disaster? My answer to this question also brought in me the passion to reciprocate the 'I-farmer' who is ignorant, illiterate and incompetent to the 'E-farmer' who is enlightened, educated and enthusiastic. Just as it is true that a 1st grade kid cannot solve complicated engineering mathematics problems it is also true that an uneducated farmer cannot solve the complicated crisis of the Indian agriculture. Our visit to the groundnut lab in ICRISAT, presented a huge contrast before me. Though ICRISAT uses all the cutting edge technologies in groundnut breeding, what is the whole point in successfully developing a 'super groundnut hybrid variety' when an Indian groundnut farmer is still cultivating a variety that is sixty years old and achieving very poor yields? Though it is not possible to transform every farmer into a scientist, it is feasible to teach him more about his crop, the management practices and the technologies available to ensure better productivity. It is time to rehabilitate the farmer's life and salvage the drowning extension sector.

The Role Played by State Agricultural University and the Need for Students' Participation

Realizing the vision of 'E-farmer' is in the hands of the agricultural extension workers as Eugene F. Ware says *'The farmer works the soil, the agriculturist works the farmer.'* The major reason why technology transfer to the farmers still stands as a flimsy hanging bridge is that less than 1 per cent of the population comprising the agricultural extension workers cannot revolutionize a sector that involves 58.4 per cent of the country's population. The role of the public, private sectors in extension is complemented by the State Agricultural Universities who play a commendable role in technology transfer. The visit to TNAU helped me to comprehend its key role and envisage how it has been transforming the lives of the farmers in the state. In this chapter besides discussing the strategies adopted by TNAU in transferring technologies, I was also curious to look into the role that I, as an agricultural student can play in strengthening the nerves of this extension. There were two episodes in the Indian trip that motivated me to think about a student's role in agricultural extension: *(i)* the girl named Selvi at Keystone who had completed only 8th grade but now runs a newspaper for her tribal community; *(ii)* the little boy at the 5th grade in the Earth Trust School who told that he would become a farmer and also spread the awareness about organic farming to his family and friends. *If they can do why can't we as agricultural graduates? If not we, then who?* Students can effectively augment the role played by

Universities in bridging the gap between the agricultural scientists and the farmers. Their participation would drive a new era of farmer's revolution and also give the students a chance to interact with the farmers and realise the crucial role they can play in a farmer's life. Besides, it would also be a bilateral approach where both the farmer and the students are mutually benefitted and would be of great aid to the Universities in extension activities. But, this revolutionary change can be brought about only when a student realizes his/her role and steps into this mission that can make a difference, just as *Mahatma Gandhi said, 'Be the change you want to see in the world'. Now, let us now look into some of the extension strategies adopted by the Tamil Nadu Agricultural University (TNAU) and how they can be synchronized with the participation of the students in paving the way to an 'E-farmer'.* Strategies adopted by TNAU in transferring technology to the farmers and participation of students to enliven the vision of an 'E-farmer'. The printed media that are used successfully by TNAU in the transfer of technology include:

(i) *Pamphlets and Leaflets:* They are printed media distributed to the farmers which epitomize the technology in a nutshell. The best example is the dynamic participation of TNAU in the Tamil Nadu Irrigated Agriculture Modernization and Water-Bodies Restoration and Management Project (TN-IAMWARM) where pamphlets about the significance of crop diversification and soil testing were distributed to the farmers and it achieved a tremendous success during its initial implementation. (TN-IAMWARM, Annual report, 2007-08).

(ii) *Magazine:* 'Valarum Velanmai' is a monthly magazine published by TNAU Besides the only monthly magazine, there is absolutely no printed media in Tamil Nadu to update the farmers on a regular basis. The overwhelming number of entertainment and sports magazines published in India and the trivial importance given to agricultural magazines led me to conceptualize a 'Farmer's magazine' that can enlighten and educate the farmer.

(iii) This strategy can be effectively implemented by the agricultural students by the members of the Arts and photography club of TNAU who can organize competitions every week where students exhibit their creativity and artistic skills on themes related to 'New technologies in agriculture'. The best entries can be awarded with prizes and be published in the farmer's magazine. This would be a mutual benefit for both as:

- the farmer benefits from the simple and creative way that the technology is delivered which would address the major illiteracy challenge;
- the student's benefit from this as it boosts their creative skills and enables them to artistically illustrate what they study in order to understand better.

Radios in Enlightening the Farmers

Radios are a thrifty and efficacious medium of communication due to the simplicity of operation. The All India Radio has been the key driver of agricultural technology dissemination for decades. But of late, community radios are gaining popularity due to their role as effectors of social change. They have a good reception as the local dialect is used to share locally relevant information involving the participation of communities. They are found to be one of the best ways to reach excluded or marginalized communities in targeted, useful ways, and in rendering them a 'voice' that can effectuate social development and change (Dagron 2001). TNAU has inaugurated a community radio station with an average coverage of 15-20 kms., and organizes informative programmes for farmers. Some of the programmes broadcasted in the community radio are:

(i) Talks by village leaders and successful farmers.

(ii) The wonders of technology sung to the rhythm of cultural folk music.

(iii) Interviews of farmers by visiting them in their fields and villages.

Students can effectively involve in radio programmes and be the voice of modern technologies to the farmer. They can advocate great changes in the farmer's lives by investing the knowledge they gained from their courses. For example, the students learning a course on Agro forestry can have a group discussion after each chapter which can be broadcasted to the farmers. The students can eloquently express their views and opinions to the farmers besides acquainting them with its benefits. This would be a mutual benefit as group discussions would inculcate critical thinking and analysis in the students besides providing insight to the farmers on those topics. Students can interview successful and innovative farmers which would aid in passing on the torch of a successful technology to other farmers and also upgrade the student's knowledge. This programme would become an enormous success if maneuvered in the right direction and scaled up by involving all the departments' students in it *viz;* Horticulture, Sericulture, Apiculture, Entomology etc., thus catering to the farmer's needs. As TNAU handles 797 agricultural courses in total, one programme broadcasted for each course would be a giant stride in technology transfer.

Televisions in Enlightening the Farmers

Televisions have a paramount role to play in extension because of the fact that they blend the visual content with audio and portray technologies in real time. They act as a major source of agricultural news and technology dissemination to the farmers (Behrans and Evans, 1984). They transmit the wave of technologies to the farmer's via dramatizations, animations, explanations and skits. The credit of making televisions more common in

Tamil Nadu than any other essential commodity goes to the freebies policy of the DMK government which ensured that every house had a color television. So, now farmers can sit back at home and nourish their brains with new inputs of agricultural information. TNAU hosts 2 programmes namely: 'Pon Vilayum Bhoomi' in Podhigai Channel and 'Malarum Bhoomi' in Makkal channel. In these programmes, the extension officers and the scientists give clear explanations of new technologies and demonstrate them. Participation of the students in television programmes would set ablaze the dramatic skills of the students. The dramatics society of the students club that plays a major role in organizing students' cultural programmes can be a major contributor to farmer's programmes. The students can direct and enact at least one short film per semester portraying and depicting the new technologies that they study during the course which can then be telecasted. A few examples of short films are: Biotechnology students on Bt cotton, Agro informatics students on precision farming, Horticulture students on hybrid vegetable seeds. Though the Indian farmer is not as glamorous as the Bollywood movies of today, which draw the student's attention, I believe that he deserves more attention than these ruining movies and we students have a stupendous mission ahead!

Tele-communication in Enlightening the Farmers

The Kisan Call centre is a marvel of the telecommunication infrastructure which effectively bridges the digital divide between the farmer and the agricultural experts. The Directorate of Extension education in TNAU operates a Kisan Call Centre and farmers can get expert guidance by dialing the toll free number 1800-180-1551. The lecture presented in TNAU during the trip affirmed that this center was indeed a boon to the farmers encumbered with loads of queries and burdens. The operation of the KCC involves three levels.

(i) *Level - I:* Agricultural graduates function as call centre agents (CCA's) and try to resolve the farmer's questions. If they are unable to resolve then they are referred to the Level II experts.

(ii) *Level - II:* This involves the scientists from various agricultural institutes who answer technical questions from their field of expertise.

(iii) *Level - III:* The calls that cannot be answered by the scientists are escalated to the nodal agencies in the state which is the Department of Agriculture.

Mobile phones are turning the tide in agricultural communication systems and are the recent efflorescing tools in agricultural extension. Mobile based agro-advisory services can be a valuable aid of the farmers. TNAU has collaboration with Nokia and works on harnessing mobile technology in agriculture with the objective of developing a mobile village where the farmers can interact, exchange ideas and share information. The results of a recent study reveal that the quality, timeliness and trustworthiness of information are the three major aspects that drive the use of mobile phones in improving the farm productivity of the small farmers (Surabhi Mittal *et al.* 2009). TNAU also sends SMS about the daily market prices to about 25,000 farmers who have subscribed to this service. Inspired by the success of mobile technology in agriculture in several countries, I have a few suggestions that would help TNAU's harness the mobile technology to a greater extent. They are:

(i) To alert farmers about the vagaries of the monsoon and other climatic variations by an SMS which would help him to take timely action and save his crops.

(ii) To enable farmers get information about loans, credits and subsidies by sending an SMS.

(iii) To establish a user friendly system of market price enquiry via SMS and provide the farmers with comparative market prices so that they can sell their produce for a higher profit. For example if the farmer wants to know the price of brinjal in Coimbatore farmers market, he can send an SMS with 'brinjal' followed by 'Coimbatore'.

(iv) To create networks for linking the farmers, middlemen and the buyers for effective bartering and bargaining of the produce.

(v) To act as a source of information for the farmers about the planting time, the amount of fertilizers required the timings for pesticide sprays etc.

The major challenges that all the above suggestions face is the illiteracy of the farmers. Hence students can play an important role in teaching the farmers the basic operations in mobile phones. Based on my personal experiences, a student in TNAU sends a minimum of 10 SMS's per day with the maximum peaking upto 200 and hence, their participation in updating the farmer would be a great way to channelize their interest towards the interest of the farmers.

Internet in Enlightening the Farmers

The internet is an ocean of knowledge and its resources are a treasure to the farmers. There are several internet based technology transfer services in India like: e-Choupal, Agriwatch, e-Sagu, IKisan etc. TNAU has also designed an 'Agritech portal' which transforms the lives of the farmers by providing a complete package of knowledge about the crops, management practices, weather, market prices etc. Besides it also hosts the DEMIC (Domestic and Export Market Intelligence Cell) website which provides price information, price behaviour, forecasts the future prices of commodities to enable the farmers in planning, production and holding their stocks. To overcome the illiteracy barrier, TNAU conducts training sessions for farmers about computers and students can effectively volunteer their leisure time in training farmers on the basics.

Trainings, Campaigns and Courses in Educating the Farmers

Trainings, demonstrations, interaction sessions, exposure visits, exhibitions and field diagnostic visits are conducted by the Universities to train the farmers and mobilize a change in them. The successful transfer of the System of Rice Intensification (SRI) technology by TNAU was evident by observing the farmers at the wetlands who were well trained. The precision farming technology also witnessed a huge success in Tamil Nadu mainly because of the efforts of TNAU which conducted several training sessions, campaigns and demonstrations to promote the technology. An article published in 'The Hindu' on September 29th, 2011 highlights the irrigation park that TNAU has set up in Tiruchi to train the farmers about the latest irrigation technologies like: drip irrigation, sprinklers etc. The University also conducts awareness programmes about the pests and diseases outbreak and the management technologies that farmers can adopt. Besides these the farmers are also taken to the University periodically and trained about various technologies using media aids; the new implements developed are taken to the farmers fields and demonstrated and several exhibitions are conducted to update the farmers. TNAU also coordinates the functions of several Krishi Vigyan Kendra's (KVK's) who are exclusively devoted to training the farmers. TNAU has also introduced several certificate courses for farmers like: Cotton cultivation, bee keeping, vegetable seed production, repair and maintenance of farm equipments and machineries, mushroom production, coconut cultivation etc. A remarkable mile stone in TNAU's accomplishments is the introduction of a Bachelor of Farm Technology degree (B. Ft) exclusively for the farmer which is the first of its kind. This programme extends for 3 years with a major objective of imparting practical skills and latest agricultural technology knowledge to the farmers which is a remarkable way of enlivening an 'E-farmer. Besides these, the Farmer's Field Schools (FFS) also play a major role in educating and empowering the farmers to solve their own problems. It is a process of learning from experimenting and observation in the fields. They inculcate decision-making skills in the farmers and make them self-reliable. Realizing the tremendous amount of input needed in training the farmers, I believe that students can involve themselves by:

(i) Organizing rallies and carrying placards to create technology awareness among the farmers. This can be effectively done by the students as part of the National Social Service (NSS) scheme that is mandatory for students until they complete their sophomore year.

(ii) Student presentations for the courses can be hooked up to a seminar day for the farmers where they get to hear information from young budding minds which can motivate them.

The vision of an 'E-farmer', the current extension strategies that are adopted by the Tamil Nadu Agricultural University and the ways to synchronize the participation of the students to realize the vision were discussed in this chapter. The printed media, radios, televisions, telecommunication networks, internet and different forms of oral communication play a pivotal role in transferring technology. In addition to these existing strategies, I strongly recommend the University to follow a bottom-up strategic participatory approach which is to first adopt a target farmer audience, then identify their needs/problems and come up with solutions for their problems. It is also important for the University to join hands with other public and private sectors in building a strong extension network. The Agri-Business Incubator (ABI) which is a joint initiative by ICRISAT and TNAU to develop and commercialize technologies is a good example. Thus, I definitely see a promising future for the University's mode of extension and it can be further augmented by the participation of enthusiastic and innovative students. All the suggestions made in this chapter are based on my personal experiences in the trip and also in TNAU and the conviction that I have about my role as an agricultural student. The trip and the paper were instrumental in building a keen desire in me to serve the farming community of my nation. It also made me realize that the journey is not over yet and there are miles to go before I sleep. I also understood that if I am a computer student, I can rest a while or remain idle because I have an option to shut down the computer and put it in a sleep mode till I choose to resume it. But, it is not the case being an agricultural graduate. I cannot sleep during my degree programme and dream of publishing my research paper when a farmer outside is hanging himself, shutting down his life and seeking an eternal sleep! I finally conclude that the future of agricultural extension and the vision of an 'E-farmer' lies in the hands of the agricultural students as rightly said by Joel Arthur Barker, *"Vision without action is merely a dream. Action without vision just passes the time. Vision with action can change the world!"*

Private Sector Extension with Special Reference to Self-Help Group and NGOs

The problem that India is currently encountering with the transfer of agricultural technology is an adult problem. Private companies and NGOs provide personalized amenities unfound within the public sector, but in order for them to really help the agricultural sector, they must be able to work with both the public sector and the farmers together through a participatory approach. It may sound like a Nicholas Sparks cliché (because it is: see *Suzanne's Diary for Nicholas*), but like most adult solutions, the resolution to improving India's national food problem is like a juggling act of 6 glass balls: the stockholder, the environment, the market, the culture, the public-private sector relationship, and the goal. Each private company and NGO is different, but each must learn to juggle. On my trip to India, I was exposed to different kind of private companies and NGOs. I am not an expert, but through my experiences I have seen not only where the juggling is working but also where balls may be getting a bit loose.

Private Businesses

There are three types of private sector companies that are not categorized as NGOs that provide important systems for the transfer of agricultural technology: the 'sellers', the 'buyers' and the donors. 'Sellers' are private businesses that sell the agricultural technology such as: the new seeds and varieties. Though we didn't get to see a farm that partnered with a 'seller' in India, it is well known that a 'seller' company is monetarily driven by the stockholders, the farmer themselves. Private 'sellers' can allot direct transfer of agricultural technology by not only selling their innovative products, but by also by imparting extension to help farmers understand the latest technologies the companies are selling. Seller businesses are useful in that they provide unique access for farmers to be directly exposed to agricultural technologies for mutual gain. A famous example of a type of 'seller' company is Monsanto that produces herbicides, pesticides, and seeds. Big enough to provide major impact on the transfer of technology to the farmers who partner with them, on their website, it says they strive to make products that help produce more, conserve more, and improve lives (Monsanto). Reading off their website, the consumer may believe they are a well-rounded and deserving company. However, in reality, 'sellers,' like Monsanto, are profit driven. Therefore, when the company itself provides its own benchmark of what they believe to be a sustainable company, they will only make positive advertisements. For this reason, it shouldn't be the 'sellers' responsibility to make that call. A third party, such as: that in the public sector, is needed to put pressure on companies, such as: Monsanto, to have to reach a standard. 'Seller' businesses should and could never be the only solution for technology transfer. The public-private sector relationship and the technologies' effects on the environment seem to be harder to regulate in 'seller' companies since most of their focus is on the advancement of their products for quick profit. Therefore, if farmers are looking for a product that will create higher yield, the seller company may ignore the environmental costs for instant cash flow. In reverse, if farmers understand the importance of environmentally friendly technology then 'seller' companies are more likely to respond. Public sector extension and regulation is necessary to remind 'seller' companies about environmental impacts of technology. In addition, farmer-to-farmer extension is also favorable to increase the efficiency of the direct extension provided by private businesses. Therefore, though private businesses that sell technology are useful for transfer of technology, it should never be the end all form of transfer. 'Buyers', are a lot like 'sellers', in that they provide direct transfer of agricultural technology for monetary gain. The difference is in the private companies' stockholders. 'Buyers' sell products produced by farmers by processing them to add additional value. These type of companies are unique because they have great potential as intermediaries by providing unique access to local and global markets that farmers may never reach on their own.

However, these companies also depend on uniformity in their products. Therefore, though they provide farmers with varieties and technologies, these systems are purely to induce profit (Klasfeld 2012). According to our travel guide, India accounts for 31 per cent of the global production of tea (2012 6020 IARD Travel Guide 47). Mr. Sri RAM, CEO of Contemporary Tea Auctioneers, explained to us, in terms of quality of tea, leaf appearance is most important. A lot of work, he explained, goes into making sure the tea he auctions off is of only the highest of quality. Contract farming is often used for tea companies. In Ooty, we saw how this could be beneficial. Tea contract farming opened up markets for farmers in Ooty, but not everything seemed black and white. Tea plants covered the land in almost every direction where it naturally wasn't before, potentially disrupting natural habitats. This monocropping could have negative effects on the quality of the soil and economically, having an entire community dependent on the fluctuations of the tea market may not be financially sustainable. In addition, when your stockholder is a farmer, they can tell more easily whether the technology is more environmentally sustainable. However, investors such as: those that buy Birds Eye, Pepsi, companies that use contract farmers or other 'buyer' related products, may realize the need to conserve our planet, but he or she cannot measure the sustainability of each technology used to make a product from the supermarket unless it is certified by a trustworthy third party. Time and time again we see either false or lack of labeling within 'buyer' companies. These companies are ideal for bringing farmers to the global market, but regulation from the public sector is obviously needed. Private companies run by donors are completely different from the buyers and the sellers. Donor companies are usually large corporations that are useful in setting aside money to implement specific goals. Looking specifically at donors who put money aside for farmers, however, I have come to understand that private companies that are run by donors are also harder to regulate in terms of meeting social demand. The best example of a private organization run by donors in India is the Tata Trust. The Tata Trust is a professional organization that identifies strategic plans in order to provide grants to organizations, institutions, or even individuals to help social development. Examples of truly successful projects they have funded are the development of KVKs (there will be more about these in the next chapter) and the activation of mKRISHI, a cell phone service that provides farmers with agricultural-based information and services. Unfortunately, though, not all service projects have gone to plan even in such a disciplined organization as the Tata Trust. In 2009, the Tata Trust helped fund a five-year programme for Indian students to participate in a two dual degree programme offered by Cornell with India's Tamil Nadu Agricultural University 'to fill a critical need for agriculture and rural development managers who are well versed in global issues and perspectives (Cornell Chronicle 2011).' However, when representatives of the Tata Trust visited Cornell this year, one of the women explained that the Tata's project failed. Indian students exposed to the US find that they like it here better. They want to do research for the global community and focus less on the not-so glamorous life of an extension officer. Having had the entire trip to get to know these students, I know they are grateful for the programme. However, perhaps, a more organized programme would have made extension work a necessary part of the programme after they earned their degree in return for the opportunity. This example proves that donors can be a great form of agricultural extension but a true multifaceted approach must always work in unison, and it is not easy. NGOs (Non-Governmental Organizations) are usually made up of a small group of people with no technical background who have a social goal. Like most of the private sector, they usually specialize on one specific goal and hope the rest falls into place. Like donors, and unlike 'buyers' and 'donors,' however, sometimes the goals and outcomes of some NGOs may not be clearly defined and the outcomes are then random. On our trip to India we specifically learned about 3 different NGOs. The first one we were exposed to was a Non-conventional Energy and Rural Development (NERD) self help group (SHG). Self-help groups are formal groups of a small amount of usually all men or all women. They provide support for each other, which in India usually means on a financial basis. Many of the women we met on farms on our trip were a part of a self-help group. It is used as a form of microfinance, and under NERD the members have been trained in interloaning and account keeping according to the pamphlet they gave us (Sodhi and Santhaijothi 2011). The women were very friendly. They showed us some of their products, which included dresses and spices, and the interpreter told us that the women also make feminine products. Perhaps biased by American culture, but some of the women from our trip wondered whether we would buy feminine products made by self-help groups. For this NERD provides a great example of a shortfalls that some NGOs fall weak to. Unlike 'buyers' and 'sellers,' NGOs may forget to think about the market when trying to provide a social goal. However, if women are less willing to buy self-help group feminine products, then this could be a limitation that the NGO should consider. The original goal of the NERD society, however, was not to support self-help groups. They wanted to bring electricity to these small villages that were dependent on kerosene. By collaborating with the Small Grants Programme (SGP), NERD established this idea of this community based approach to the problem by helping to set up these SGRs to then charge them for the fixing and maintenance of biogas plants. Whether biogas is a better alternative fuel than kerosene can be debated, but I believe the NERD society handles a great show. In the Nilgiri Hills of South India, we spent even more time understanding the Earth Trust NGO. Focused on educating farmers about sustainable agricultural practices, Earth Trusts sets up programmes to teach organic agriculture and biodynamic farming. While organically grown food has become a hot topic in the US, biodynamic farming is a bit less understood. In Otty, the speakers we talked with promote it as a religious practice that has to do with using different products made by the holy cow to release positive energy that should cover the farm. Depending on the cycles of the moon and other spirtual climates, one must follow certain procedures on certain days. There are so many practices so we only got to see a few. While the efficacy is undocumented, we did get to see some practices that scientifically made logical sense. Not only did the stockholders of Earth Trust seem to truly buy into the ideas of biodynamic farming, they also felt the need to focus their organization on promoting these practices. One of programmes we got the chance to see was an Earth Trust school. I understand this structure and believe it is brilliant. A child that uses sustainable practices in school is going to want to show off to their parents. In addition, parents want to encourage their children's education and good health. Presenting this subject of organic farming through the children, parents are directly hit with this idea that can do both. Not only did the older generation not grow up with Internet but also the ideas behind sustainable practices in everyday life are fairly modern. Why shouldn't they be taught the same way?" (Klasfeld 2012). During my visit in India, I saw this programme as a well-balanced form of transfer of technology. The Earth Trust School provides a unique foundation for these children. However, over all the practices of organic agriculture are not sustainable for the India's growing population and having school farm costs money that many schools cannot afford without contribution. Therefore, while the Earth Trust School worked on a small scale, the technology it was transferring is not the end-all solution. The last small and probably most intriguing NGO we saw was at the Nilgiri Bioreserve. The Keystone foundation had a rocky start and their not afraid to admit it. In an area with so much culture, tradition, and environmental sensitivity, they needed to not only build a formal relationship with the various villages but also with the state government, the mandate of extension. The goal of their programme was also a bit murky. When the Tata Trust visited Cornell, I asked a representative why the Trust didn't help fund Key Stone. She denied that she was speaking on the behalf of the trust, but she did giggle at my recommendation. Key Stone made their mark on the Nilgiri Bioreserve studying bee hunters and harvesters. You would have thought they were studying how to improve honey collecting. They were, but at the same time they used honey as the in to the cultures of the villages, and looking for ways to bring better capitalism into the society. The woman of the Tata Trust saw this to be a bit shady. According to the workers at the NGO and the website, 17 years after they originated, Key Stone has become more organized. They have set up business ventures for many of the products these villages had already been producing for generations. While expanding the market for these mountain villagers, Keystone has also tried to balance strengthening the culture and traditions of these areas, producing current research on the communities natural resources, and improving the education system within the villages by mapping out the traditional cultural sites, setting up community newspapers in the local languages, and establishing educational programmes. Many of my fellow classmates were thoroughly impressed and believed this to be the ideal NGO. However, while I agree that science done on the reserve may be better for the developed world, I believe Keystone may exemplify the complication of whether western ideology such as: capitalism is necessarily better for tribal villages. Though, Key Stone could provide a unique resource for the tribal villages, it is understood why it took so long for Key Stone to "establish" itself. It is as if Key Stone had no right being there in the first place. Continuing my discussion with the representative from the Tata Trust I asked her what qualification helped an NGO qualify to obtain a grant. She explained that it is difficult because many NGOs in India are corrupt. Groundwork must be to be done. Key Stone seemed to be doing so much. They showed us a newspaper that was made, sold us locally made products, and gave us a tour through all their corporate buildings filled with research done in each of the areas including the maps of the culture sites and books on the diversity of birds. However, we didn't get to see an actual village working with Key Stone due to dilemmas with traveling. I would have loved to see their work in action so I could gain a deeper opinion. ICRISAT, International Crops Research Institute for the Semi Arid Tropics, could be in its own separate catefory because unlike the smaller NGOs its it not only large but global. Supported by the Consultative Group on International Agriculture (CGIAR), the goal of ICRISAT is not a social one like: the smaller NGOs. Instead, ICRISAT produces technical information as an agri-business incubator for all regions described as the semi arid tropics. More specifically ICRISAT is a non-profit organization that develops systems for rainfed agriculture through establishment of water management technology and research on drought-tolerant crops (specifically chickpea, pigeonpea, pearl millet, sorghum and groundnut). They seemed to have a great focusing on improving agricultural technology in the semi arid tropics. However, their relationship with the state government didn't seem to be as stable as ideally it would be. The Indian government is very strict and in order for ICRISAT to transfer technology to Indian farmers they must goes through a series of regulations and then jump through some hoops in order to get technology passed through the strict regulations of the state government. Fenced and gated away from the farmers of India, ICRISAT has proved that it could be a resource for Indian farmers. In this case, ICRISAT was given permission from the Andhra Pradesh state government to set up a Community-Participatory Integrated Watershed Management model. On our trip we got the opportunity to visit these lands and it was proved to be successful. However, this was a rare opportunity for ICRISAT to be given so much permission even though it is such a great resource.

Conclusion

Ending with ICRISAT is ideal because it is the perfect example of a resource the public sector of India does not use to its full potential. The private sector can only be as great as the government allows. With that being said, it is not typical for an NGO or private business to be able to perform a perfect juggling act that can both help their farmer reach a market and do it in a sustainable way. Therefore, a balance of regulation must also be put in place. While corruption and the dilemma of global capitalism may also be difficult to distinguish, the private sector is different from the public sector in that its goal can be more focused. Risks may have to be taken.

REFERENCES

Accidents and Suicides in India. Data compiled from ADSI reports from 1995-2010 [Internet].

The National Crime Records Bureau [Updated 2010]. Available from http://ncrb.nic.in/

Behrens JH, Evans JF. (1984). Using Mass Media for Extension Teaching. Agricultural Extension: A Reference Manual, 2nd Edition. FAO, Rome, Italy. p. 144-155.

Dagron AG. (2001). Making Waves. Stories of Participatory Communication for Social Change. A Report Published by the Rockefeller Foundation, New York. p. 15.

IARD. (2012). Available from: teamuseumooty.com, pp. 47.

Klasfeld S. (12:36:35 PM January 4, 2012) [A Self-Help Group at TNAU].

Klasfeld S. (12:55:39 PM January 9, 2012) [A Student from the Earth Trust School].

Klasfeld S. (3:52:13 PM January 9, 2012) [A glimpse of the Ooty tea plantations].

Klasfeld S. (2012). The Girl with the Bright Yellow Homer Simpson Bag Encompassed by the 7th Grade Agriculture Einsteins [Web log post]. Available from 2012 IARD 6020 Wordpress: http://2012iard6020.wordpress.com/2012/01/14/the-girl-with-the-bright-yellow-homer-simpson-bag-encompassed-by-the-7th-grade-agriculture-einsteins/

Ramanujan, K. [Internet]. (2011, January 24). First Students of Dual Degree Programmes in India Graduate. Cornell Chronicle Online. Available from: http://www.news.cornell.edu/stories/Jan11/TNAUGraduation.html

Sodhi P., Santhaijothi K. (2011). Alternate Energy Electrification of Thalingi Tribal Area [Pamphlet]. Tamil Nadu, India: GEF Small Grants Programme.

Surabhi M., Gaurav T. (2009). Role of Mobile Phone Technology in Improving Small farm Productivity. *Agricultural Economics Research Review*, Vol. 22. p. 451-459.

Tamil Nadu Irrigated Agriculture Modernization and Water-Bodies Restoration and Management Project (TN-IAMWARM). [Internet]. Annual report, 2007-08. Available from http://www.iamwarm.gov.in/pdf/annual_report.pdf.

Who we are. [Internet]. (Updated 2011). *Monsanto* (about Monsanto) Available from: http://www.monsanto.com/whoweare/Pages/default.aspx.

Page 104-132

AGRICULTURAL PRACTICES AND CROP DISEASE CONTROL
Edited by : **Dr. Alka Chauhan** and **Dr. Anubhuti Sharma**
Edition : **2017**
ISBN : 978-93-5056-859-0
Published by : **Discovery Publishing House Pvt. Ltd., New Delhi (India)**

6

Toxins in Food

Sources and Effect

Priyanka Shukla

Food contains natural chemicals, including: carbohydrates, sugars, proteins and vitamins. But some foods contain potentially harmful natural toxins. Sometimes a toxin is present as a naturally occurring pesticide to ward off insect attack or to protect the plant from spoilage when damaged by weather, handling, UV light or microbes.

Although many foods contain toxins as a naturally-occurring constituent or, are formed as the result of handling or processing, the incidence of adverse reactions to food is relatively low. The low incidence of adverse effects is the result of some pragmatic solutions by the US Food and Drug Administration (FDA) and other regulatory agencies through the creative use of specifications, action levels, tolerances, warning labels and prohibitions. Manufacturers have also played a role by setting limits on certain substances and developing mitigation procedures for process-induced toxins. Regardless of measures taken by regulators and food producers to protect consumers from natural food toxins, consumption of small levels of these materials is unavoidable. Although the risk for toxicity due to consumption of food toxins is fairly low, there is always the possibility of toxicity due to contamination, overconsumption, allergy or an unpredictable idiosyncratic response. The purpose of this review is to provide a toxicological and regulatory overview of some of the toxins present in some commonly consumed foods, and where

National Institute of Food Technology, Enterpreneurship and Management, Sonipat, Haryana, India.

possible, discuss the steps that have been taken to reduce consumer exposure, many of which are possible because of the unique process of food regulation in the United States.

Historically, we have learned that everything is toxic; it is only the dose that separates the toxic from the non-toxic. Even water is toxic if a large amount (4-5 liters) is consumed in a relatively short time (2-3 hours). The pathogenesis of water intoxication includes hyponatremia, followed by cerebral edema, seizures and death.

Like water, too much of a good thing such as: the antioxidant vitamin A, can have acute toxic effects leading to hepatotoxicity or chronic high levels can have a pro-oxidant effect. Something as innocent as licorice, when consumed in large amounts may be harmful. For example, Bannister and associates reported hypokalemia leading to cardiac arrest in a 58-year-old woman who had been eating about 1.8 kg., of licorice per week. This licorice intoxication (dubbed 'glycyrrhizism' after glycyrrhizic acid, the active component of licorice), has an effect resembling that of aldosterone, which suppresses the renin-angiotensin-aldosterone axis, resulting in the loss of potassium. Clinically, hypokalemia with alkalosis, cardiac arrhythmias, muscular symptoms together with sodium retention and edema, and severe hypertension are observed. The syndrome may develop at a level of 100 g licorice per day but gradually abates upon withdrawal of the licorice.

Recently, public health and social agendas have become more proactive in food toxicology, such as: regulating (or outright banning) trans fats or 'endocrine disruptors' in foods on the basis of public safety, including a suggestion of removing the generally recognized as safe (GRAS) status for salt. These agendas lose sight of the basic principle of toxicology that 'the dose makes the poison' and that demanding 'safety *per se*' or 'safe at any dose', for all foods and ingredients is a non-starter and as a concept, was abandoned with the adoption of the Federal Food and Drug Act (FFDCA) in 1958. For their part, the regulators can limit amounts of potentially toxic substances allowed in food and in those circumstances where setting limits is not effective and public health policy-makers provide the public with sufficient information (*e.g.*, label information), where possible, to protect the consumer from reasonably foreseeable problems. Labeling requirements by the FDA provide the consumer with helpful information about content of fats, carbohydrate, protein, potential allergens, caloric value, etc., but do not provide information about toxins that may be inherent in the foods or formed during processing. Because some food toxins cannot be removed from foods and others may be created during processing or cooking, consumption of small quantities of food toxins is unavoidable. The purpose of this review is to illustrate the potential risks of these toxins when consumed at concentrations normally present in foods and the steps taken by regulators to mitigate exposure where possible. Although regulatory information from countries other than the United States is included, FDA legislation is emphasized. Readers from other countries are advised to consult regulations for their specific region, because regulations and regulatory practices in other countries may differ from those in the United States.

The term 'food' means *(i)* articles used for food or drink for man or other animals; *(ii)* chewing gum, and *(iii)* articles used for components of any such article.

The framers are to be congratulated on their realistic approach, but a little interpretation is required. In the first clause '...articles used for food...' includes what humans and animals will eat as such (including: eggs, meat, kohlrabi, Velveeta cheese and angel food cake). The third clause 'articles used for components of any such article,' are simply those substances used to make food (defined in the first clause)-therefore, anything approved for addition to food, becomes a part of the food. The second clause was more of a political consideration than anything else, as there was some disagreement whether chewing gum was swallowed or expectorated; the swallowers prevailed and chewing gum is regulated as a food. Had the majority determined that chewing gum was expectorated (as is evident on a sidewalk outside of any theater or church), it would have been classified with breath mints (which are not swallowed) and are therefore regulated as a cosmetic, whose function is to '...promote attractiveness...' of the body. It has also been ruled by the FDA that proposed dietary supplements (which are regulated as a subset of foods) meant to be held in the mouth, followed by expectoration, are not dietary supplements, because they are not swallowed.

The definition of food has generally held since the 1958 definition, although it was changed slightly in the 7th Circuit in 1983, to now indicate that a food is something consumed '...primarily, for [it's] taste, aroma or nutritive value.' This court decision did not radically change the definition of food from the original context, but in this particular case, prohibited the use of a food extract for therapeutic intent (*i.e.*, amylase isolated from kidney beans as an inhibitor of carbohydrate breakdown and marketed for weight loss-so-called 'starch blockers').

In general, the law prohibits the sale of food 'if it consists in whole or in part of any filthy, putrid, or decomposed substance, or if it is otherwise unfit for food' (in practice, 'fitness' can be quite subjective).

A few potential foods are banned outright by regulation such as: the slaughter of companion animals (cats, dogs and horses) for food, offal and colostrum or those foods whose preparation is regulated by guidelines other than current good manufacturing practices (*e.g.*, puffer fish preparation). Some naturally sourced substances (while present in some foods) are banned for addition to food for reasons of safety and include safrole, calamus and coumarin (a full list of which may be seen in 21 Code of Federal Regulations (CFR) 189). Other foods which may contain toxic substances, such as: prussic acid in peach leaves, β-thujone in wormwood, saxitoxin in seafood, etc., are controlled by regulation through the use of tolerances, or more correctly, specifications for the product that limit the amount of toxin that may be present. For those foods or ingredients with potential for harm, but not addressed by a specific regulation, action level, etc., the reference in the FFDCA to substances 'unfit for food' and flowing from that provision, Sections 402 and 406 of the FFDCA, apply. That is, the lack of a specific action taken by the FDA (or any regulatory agency), for a potentially harmful substance is not a license to market that substance.

Toxin Incorporation during Growth, Storage or Processing

Environmental Contaminants

Selenium in grain

Selenium (Se) enters the food chain via plant and microorganism conversion of inorganic selenium to organically bound forms. Selenium toxicity (*i.e.*, selenosis), caused by excessive selenium intake, has occurred on a large scale in seleniferous regions in China as the result of increased consumption of selenium-containing foods (approximate daily intake of 3-6.5 mg Se/day). The most common symptoms of selenosis are loss of hair, deformity, and loss of nails. Other reported symptoms include: increased blood selenium levels, diarrhoea, fatigue, a garlic-like odor of the breath and bodily secretions, irritability, peripheral neuropathy, and skin lesions. Selenium intake levels that cause selenosis have not yet been well defined. Studies in China suggest that approximately 3-5 mg/day (0.05-0.08 mg/kg/day) will cause selenosis. Residents of seleniferous regions in South Dakota who consumed approximately 700 μg selenium/day (0.01 mg/kg/day) showed no symptoms of selenosis. The EPA has proposed an oral reference dose (RfD) of 0.005 mg/kg bw/day, or 350 μg/day.

Methyl mercury in seafood

Exposure to elemental mercury is relatively rare, although was once an occupational disease of hat manufacturers as elemental mercury was used for the curing of animal pelts. Inhalation of the mercury fumes led to mental deterioration and subsequently named 'mad hatter syndrome'.

Of interest to food toxicology, is the methyl derivative, methyl mercury, formed by bacterial action in an aquatic environment from anthropogenic and natural sources of elemental mercury. Anthropogenic sources include burning of coal (which contains mercury), chloralkali process and other sources of elemental mercury into aquatic environments. In the case of Minamata, Japan, there was a direct discharge of methyl mercury into the environment. Methyl mercury exposure may cause neurological paresthesias, ataxia, dysarthria, hearing defects and death. Developmental delays have been documented in children borne of mothers exposed to methyl mercury. Other than direct exposure to methyl mercury, exposure usually comes about as the result of methyl mercury becoming incorporated into the food chain, moving up as each predator consumes the smaller and less fortunate animal. Near the peak of the food chain, methyl mercury becomes concentrated in fish including: bonito (*Sarda* spp.), halibut (*Hippoglossus* spp.), mackerel (*Scomberomorus* spp.), marlin (*Makaira* spp.), shark (all species), swordfish (*Xiphias gladius*), and bluefin tuna (*Thunnus* spp.). The selection of these species was based on historical data on levels of methyl mercury found in fish consumed in the U.S. The selection was also based on an FDA action level of 1.0 ppm in the edible portion of fish. However, the allowable level of mercury depends on whether the mercury was 'added'; that is, did the presence of mercury arise from an anthropogenic source (*i.e.*, was the fish caught in an area known for mercury discharge), or was not added and the result of mercury naturally present in the environment.

Naturally Formed Substances

β-Thujone

Thujone, a monoterpene ketone, is the primary constituent of essential oils derived from a variety of plants, including: sage (*Salvia officinalis*), clary (*Salvia sclarea*), tansy (*Tanacetum vulgare*), wormwood (*Artemisia* spp., and white cedar (*Thuja occidentalis* L.). Essential oils from these plants are used in herbal medicines, as flavorings in alcoholic drinks and fragrances throughout the world. Thujone is potentially toxic and the presence of alpha or beta-thujone in food and beverages is regulated by law in several countries. In the US, thujone as an isolated substance is banned as an ingredient to be added to food and many of the natural thujone-containing plant oils (*e.g.*, wormwood, white cedar, oak moss (*Evernia prunastri*) and tansy) are used as flavorings in food under the condition that the finished food is thujone-free. Absinthe (made from wormwood) contains significant levels of thujone and is available in Spain, Denmark and Portugal. Wormwood itself is a popular flavoring for vodka in Sweden, while vermouth, chartreuse, and Benedictine all contain small levels of thujone. Sage oil is used to provide the characteristic flavor in sausages, meats, condiments and sauces, and contains approximately 20-30 per cent thujone (alpha and beta). Both alpha and beta-thujone act as non-competitive blockers of the gamma-aminobutyric acid (GABA)-gated chloride channel. The essential oils of sage, hyssop (*Hyssopus officinalis* L.), and cedar all contain thujone and have been cited to have caused central nervous system effects characterized by tonic-clonic or solely clonic convulsions. Thujone is believed to be the toxic agent in absinthism, a syndrome produced by the chronic use of absinthe, made from the essence of wormwood. The syndrome is characterized by addiction, hyperexcitability and hallucinations. The debilitating illnesses suffered by Vincent Van Gogh and Henri de Toulouse-Lautrec have been linked to absinthism, while the toxicity of thujone was a major factor in banning absinthe in the early 1900s. A published case report detailed a male subject that drank about 10 mL of essential oil of wormwood (believing it was absinthe) and became agitated, incoherent and disoriented, subsequently developing renal failure. The no observable effect limit (NOEL) for convulsions in subchronic toxicity studies in female rats was 5 mg/kg bw/day. Detoxification of thujone is thought to occur via CYP450-dependent oxidation and subsequent glucuronidation and excretion. The FDA limits exposure to β-thujone from *Artemisia* spp., when used as a natural flavoring substance or natural substance used in conjunction with flavors.

Prussic acid in cherry, apple and peach pits

Prussic acid (also known as hydrocyanic acid, hydrogen cyanide, or cyanide) is formed when cyanogenic glycosides found in leaves, cherry, apple and peach pits, oak moss and other plant tissues are damaged and come into contact with *beta*-glycosidase or emulsion enzymes. The enzymes release the cyanide from the glycoside, and the cyanide prevents the body's cells from utilizing oxygen, resulting in cellular necrosis and tissue damage. The mucous membranes and blood are bright red as they are oxygenated, but the cells in the tissues cannot utilize the oxygen. Clinical signs of prussic acid poisoning include: rapid breathing, trembling, in co-ordination and in extreme cases, respiratory and/or cardiac arrest. Many fruit trees contain prussic acid glycosides in the leaves and seeds, but only negligible levels are present in the fleshy parts of the fruit. In the west African tropics, cassava is consumed as a dietary staple and inappropriate handling of the cassava prior to processing and consumption can result in a chronic form of cyanide poisoning termed 'tropical ataxic neuropathy', the result of demyelinization of the optic, auditory, and peripheral nerve tracts.

Prussic acid as found in flavoring ingredients is limited to 25 ppm in cherry pits (*Prunus avium* L. or *P. cerasus* L.), cherry laurel leaves (*Prunus laurocerasus* L.), elder tree leaves (*Sambucus nigra* L.), and peach leaves (*Prunus persica* (L.) Batsch); although the extract of bitter almond (*Prunus amygdalus* Batsch, *Prunus armeniaca* L., or *Prunus persica* (L.) Batsch) must be prussic acid free (21 CFR 182.20). There are no FDA regulations or guidelines restricting the presence of prussic acid in apple seed (*Malus* spp.), probably because extracts of these seeds have no economic value as flavor ingredients.

Hypericin in St. John's wort

St. John's wort (*Hypericum perforatum*; Figure 6.1) is an herbal thought to alleviate symptoms of depression, and standardized extracts of St. John's wort are consumed typically in tablet or capsule form. The major active antidepressive constituents in St. John's wort are thought to be hyperforin and hypericin. The mechanism of action is not fully understood, but may involve inhibition of serotonin (5-HT) reuptake, similar to conventional antidepressive drugs. In this manner, hyperforin and hypericin taken in conjunction with other serotonin reuptake inhibitors may contribute to *serotonin syndrome,* a potentially life-threatening elevation of serotonin in the central nervous system. Hyperforin is also known to induce cytochrome P450 enzymes CYP3A4 and CYP2C9, which can lead to increased metabolism of certain drugs and decreased clinical response.

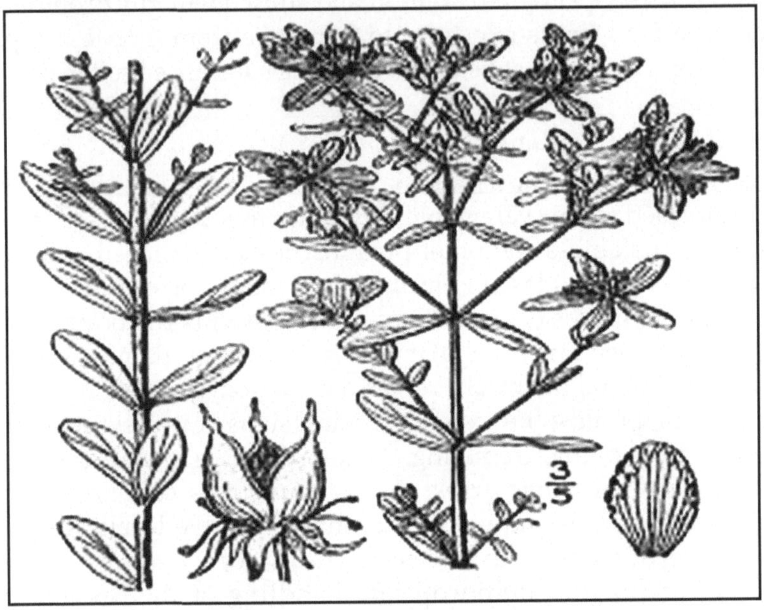

Fig. 6.1: **St. John's wort (*Hypericum perforatum*)**

In large doses, St. John's wort is poisonous to grazing animals, with published cases of livestock poisoning characterised by general restlessness and skin irritation, hindlimb weakness, panting, confusion, depression and in some instances, mania and hyperactivity resulting in the animal running in circles until exhausted. In humans, consumption of St. John's wort may result in photosensitization, and at high continuous doses, some liver damage may occur. The FDA limits exposure to St. Johns wort (*Hypericum perforatum*), including: the leaves, flowers, and caulis, by mandating that only hypericin-free alcohol distillate form may be used and then, only in alcoholic beverages.

Goitrogens (glucosinolates) in brassica spp.

Certain raw foods have been found to contain substances that suppress the function of the thyroid gland by interfering with the uptake of iodine, an essential nutrient in growth, cognitive function, and hormonal balance. A lack of functional iodine is known to result in cognitive deficiencies (*e.g.,*

Cretinism). The decrease in iodine uptake causes the thyroid gland to enlarge, forming a goiter. Foods that have been identified as goitrogenic include: spinach, cassava, peanuts, soybeans, strawberries, sweet potatoes, peaches, pears, and vegetables in the *Brassica* genus, which include: broccoli, brussels sprouts, cabbage, canola, cauliflower, mustard greens, radishes, and rapeseed. Goiter has also been attributed to the consumption of large quantities of uncooked kale or cabbage.

High temperatures (*i.e.*, cooking) inactivate the goitrogenic substances, collectively termed glucosinolates. Cassava (*Manihot esculenta*) is an essential dietary source of energy in the tropics, but contains high levels of linamarin, a glucosinolate. Cassava must be properly processed-dried, soaked in water or baked to effectively reduce the linamarin content. Glucosinolates are sulfur-containing substances that are metabolized in the body by thioglucosidase to form thiocyanate, isothiocyanate, nitriles and sulfur. Under certain conditions the isothiocyanates undergo cyclization to form goitrins, increasing their potent goitrogenic activity. The oils from rapeseed (*Brassica napus*) must be analyzed for potential goitrins to circumvent potential goitrogenic activity when consuming these oils. No FDA regulations were located for permissible concentrations of glucosinolates in human food. Glucosinolates (calculated as epi progoitrin) and goitrin are limited to not more than 4 per cent and 0.1 per cent (respectively) of the seed meal of *Crambe abyssinica* (Crambe meal) obtained after the removal of the oil and used as an animal feed ingredient.

Erucic acid in rape

Rape (*Brassica napus* L. or *Brassica campestris* L.) is an annual herb of the mustard family native to Europe and is grown in the United States because it produces oil-rich seeds for cooking oil. Rapeseed oil had been used for hundreds of years as oil for lamps and more recently as machine oil lubricant. Widespread use of rapeseed oil as a food ingredient was not considered until the late 1940s and 50s. However, early studies found that feeding high levels of rapeseed oil to rats significantly increased cholesterol levels in the adrenal glands and lipidosis in the cardiac tissue. This effect was also noted in chickens, ducks and turkeys fed high levels of rapeseed oil, resulting in growth retardation, mortality, and a thickening of the epicardium and increased fibrous tissue in different areas of the myocardium. Erucic acid was identified as the causative agent of these effects of rapeseed oil. Erucic acid is a long-chain fatty acid with one unsaturated carbon-carbon bond (C22:1). High levels of erucic acid have been liked to fatty deposit formation in heart muscle in animals. Erucic acid is poorly oxidized by the mitochondrial β-oxidation system, especially by the myocardial cells, which results in an accumulation of erucic acid, producing myocardial lipidosis which has been reported to reduce the contractile force of the heart. Although myocardial lipidosis due to erucic acid consumption has not been confirmed in humans, animal feeding studies confirmed the formation of myocardial lipidosis in a variety of animal species in a dose-dependent manner, which has been the standard assessment by government agencies of potential adverse effects in humans. Canola oil is obtained from Canola (Canadian oil, low acid), a rapeseed variety that was conventionally bred in the late 1970s in Canada to contain reduced levels of erucic acid and glucosinolates. The FDA limits the amount of erucic acid in Canola oil to no more than 2 per cent of the component fatty acids..

Amylase inhibitors

Naturally occurring inhibitors of α-amylase are found in aqueous extracts of wheat, rye and kidney beans. The physiological role of α-amylase inhibitors in plants is not well understood, but may protect them against insect infestation. In mammals, some amylase inhibitors have been shown to attenuate the normal increase in blood glucose that occurs after ingestion of starch. However, since α-amylase inhibitors have been shown to be inactivated by gastric acid, pepsin or pancreatic proteinases, their potential as 'starch blockers' is limited. α-Amylase inhibitors were once added to foods as 'starch blockers' to limit carbohydrate absorption for the purpose of weight loss; however, the FDA later determined that at least this use of α-amylase inhibitors was as drug, and they were consequently taken off the market.

α-Amylase inhibitor protein is a major allergen (referred to as Asp o 2) that has been implicated in the development of occupational toxicity known as 'baker's asthma disease'. Although α-amylase inhibitor protein is naturally found in wheat flour, it is also found in flour in which α-amylase from *Aspergillus oryzae*has been added to enhance carbohydrate fermentation by yeast. Consequently, α-amylase inhibitor protein can be potentially found in baked products that are derived from sources other than wheat. Cases of food allergy have been reported in people ingesting bread containing α-amylase inhibitor protein. Symptoms of allergy include: sneezing, rhinorrhea, oropharyngeal itching, hoarseness, cough and dyspnea.

High α-amylase inhibitor activity against human salivary α-amylase has been found in wheat flour (590 units/g), whole wheat flour (351 units/g) and whole rye flour (186 units/g). Bread baking reduces the activity by 80-100 per cent, depending on type. The activity in uncooked spaghetti (248 units/g) is reduced more than 98 per cent by 15 minutes of boiling. Boiling of red beans for 1.5 hours reduces activity to undetectable levels. However, α-amylase has been shown to retain some allergenic activity when heated to 200°C.

Lectins in legumes

Lectins are a group of glycoproteins that are present in high levels in legumes (*e.g.*, black beans, soybeans, lima beans, kidney beans and lentils) and grain products. Lectins can reversibly bind to carbohydrates without altering their covalent structure. The ability of lectins to bind to and agglutinate red blood cells is well known and used for blood typing-hence the lectins are commonly called hemagglutinins. Lectins also can bind avidly to mucosal cells and interfere with nutrient absorption from the intestine. Because the ability of the lectins to cause intestinal malabsorption is dependent on the presence of enteric bacteria, it has been hypothesized that lectins may also produce toxicity by facilitating bacterial growth in the GI tract.

Lectins isolated from black beans can produce growth retardation when fed to rats at 0.5 per cent of the diet, and lectin from kidney beans causes death within two weeks when fed to rats at 0.5 per cent of the diet. Soybean lectin produces growth retardation when fed to rats at 1 per cent of the diet. The castor bean lectin ricin (one of the most toxic natural substances known) is notorious for causing deaths of children, and has been used as an instrument of bioterrorism.

Phytohaemagglutinin (PHA) is a lectin found in significant quantities (as much as 2.4-5% of total protein) in legumes such as: red or white kidney beans, green beans and fava beans. PHA has a number of different properties, including the ability to induce mitosis, affect membrane transport and permeability to proteins, and agglutinate red blood cells. Rats fed a diet containing 6 per cent PHA exhibit weight loss, associated with malabsorption of lipid, nitrogen and vitamin B12. PHA from red kidney beans inhibits sodium and chloride absorption in the rabbit ileum, indicating that PHA can affect electrolyte transport in the gut. Symptoms of toxicity to PHA in humans such as: nausea, vomiting, or diarrhea occur within three hours of ingestion. Recovery generally occurs within four or five hours of onset.

There are no FDA regulations or guidelines restricting the presence of lectins in food, but the FDA does provide recommended cooking practices prior to consuming legumes. Concentrations of PHA (and other lectins) are higher in uncooked than cooked beans. A raw, red kidney bean can contain up to 70,000 hemagluttinating units (hau). Most lectins are reduced by moist, but not dry heat. Therefore, steaming or boiling causes a significant reduction in concentrations of lectins in beans. Boiling for at least ten minutes has been shown to reduce hau in beans by 200-fold. Because cooking temperatures under 176 °F do not destroy lectin, use of slow cooking and/or a crockpot is not advised for cooking beans.

Anti-thiamine compounds

Substances that act on the availability of vitamins are commonly referred to as antivitamins. These include materials that can cause a deficiency of vitamins by competing with vitamins in various metabolic reactions as the result of similar chemical structure or destroying or decreasing the effects of a vitamin by modifying the molecular conformation or by forming a complex.

Thiaminase cleaves thiamine (vitamin B1) at the methylene linkage, rendering it biologically inactive. Activity of thiaminase requires a cosubstrate-usually an amine or sulfhydryl-containing protein such as:

proline or cysteine. Thiaminase is found in fish, crab, clams and in some fruits and vegetables such as: blueberries, black currants, red beets, Brussels sprouts and red cabbage.

Thiamine is an essential vitamin involved in energy production. Thiamine deficiency is associated with impaired pyruvate utilization, resulting in a shortage of cellular ATP. In humans, thiamine deficiency may lead to weakness and weight loss. Severe thiamine deficiency produces 'beri-beri', a disease characterised by anorexia, cardiac enlargement, and muscular weakness leading to ataxia. Cooking destroys thiaminases in fish and other sources. There are no FDA regulations or guidelines specific to the presence of thiaminase in food.

Pyrrolizidine alkaloids

Pyrrolizidine alkaloids (PAs) are found in some plants of the Apocyanacae, Asteraceae, Boraginaceae, Compositae (*Senecionae* and *Eupatoriae*), Fabaceae, Leguminosae (*Crotalaria*), Rannuculaceae and Scrophulariaceae families. Herbs such as: comfrey root and leaf (*Symphytum* spp.) (Figure 6.2), coltsfoot leaf and flower (*Tussilago farfara*) and borage leaf (*Borago officinale*), and several species of *Eupatorium*typically contain high levels of PAs. Humans are exposed to PAs through the accidental contamination of foodstuffs and intentional ingestion of PA-containing vegetables and herbal medicines. Serious incidences of illness have been reported in people consuming cereal grains that are contaminated with the seeds of PA-containing plants. PAs are also present in milk from cows and goats and in honey.

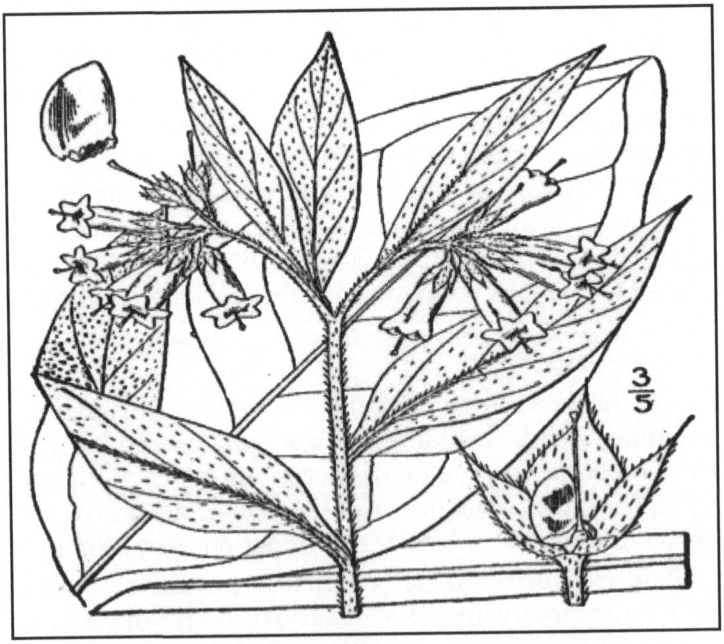

Fig. 6.2: **Comfrey (*Symphytum officianale* L.)**

The pyrrolizidine structure is based on two fused, five-membered rings that share a bridgehead nitrogen atom, forming a tertiary alkaloid. The rings contain a hydroxymethylene group at the C-1 position and a hydroxyl group at the C-7 position, forming a necine base. Several PAs that contain unsaturated necine rings are hepatotoxic, mutagenic, teratogenic and/or carcinogenic. Toxicity is thought to be due to enzymatic conversion of PAs to pyrroles, which act as alkylating agents. Pyrroles formed in the liver can travel to the lungs, causing thickening of the pulmonary vasculature and pulmonary hypertension.

Rhubarb and oxalic acid

Oxalic acid (oxalate) is generally found in rhubarb (0.2-1.3%), tea (0.3-2.0%), spinach (0.3-1.3%), parsley (1.7%) and purslane (1.3%), but may also be found in asparagus, broccoli, Brussels sprouts, collards, lettuce, celery, cabbage, cauliflower, turnips, beets, peas, coffee, cocoa, beans, potatoes, berries, and carrots.

Oxalic acid is an organic acid that can bind calcium and other minerals, making them insoluble and decreasing their bioavailability. Ingestion of foods containing high concentrations of oxalates may cause decreased bone growth, kidney stones, renal toxicity, vomiting, diarrhoea, convulsions, coma and impaired blood clotting. The significant role oxalate plays in kidney stone development is exemplified by the fact that approximately 65 per cent of kidney stones consist of calcium oxalate.

Using the oral LD_{50} value of 375 mg/kg in rats, it has been estimated that ingestion of approximately 22 g of oxalic acid could be lethal to a 59 kg human. Because approximately 4.5 kg of rhubarb leaves would have to be ingested in order to achieve a lethal dose, it has been hypothesized that documented cases of fatal rhubarb poisoning in humans were due to consumption of some other substance than oxalic acid.

Because cooking does not remove oxalate, and mineral complexes with oxalate are insoluble in water, oxalates are somewhat difficult to remove from foods. Therefore, diets rich in oxalate-containing foods should be supplemented with minerals such as: calcium or potassium to prevent deficiencies. Limits on oxalic acid have been cited in ferric ammonium ferrocyanide and ferric ferrocyanide when used as color additives (21 CFR 73.1298 and 21 CFR 73.1299) with oxalic acid or its salts at not more than 0.1 per cent of the colorant.

Zucchini and cucurbitacins

Members of the *Cucurbitacea* family (zucchini, cucumbers, pumpkins, squash, melons and gourds) produce cucurbitacins (oxygenated tetracyclic terpenes) that act as movement arresters and compulsive feeding stimulants for Diabriticine beetles (corn rootworms and cucumber beetles). Cucurbitacins are among the most bitter compounds known, and in nanogram quantities they deter most non-Diabrotic herbivores.

Because cucurbitacins act as feeding stimulants, they are added to insecticidal baits to increase efficacy. Therefore, dietary exposure to cucurbitacins could occur through ingesting plants that normally contain them or by ingesting plants to which cucurbitacin-containing pesticides have been applied.

Under normal circumstances, cucubitacins are produced at low enough concentrations that are not perceived as being bitter by humans. In response to stresses such as: high temperatures, drought, low soil fertility and low soil pH, concentrations in fruits such as: cucumbers may increase and cause the fruits to have a bitter taste. Occasional cases of stomach cramps and diarrhea have occurred in people ingesting bitter zucchini. Twenty-two cases of human poisoning from ingestion of as little as 3 grams of bitter zucchini were reported in Australia from 1981 to 1982, and in Alabama and California in 1984. The cultivar implicated in the Australia poisonings was 'Blackjack'. There are no FDA regulations or guidelines specific to the presence of cucurbitacins in food.

Coumarins (tonka bean, woodruff, clover)

Coumarin (2H-1-benzopyran-2-one) is found in herb teas made from tonka beans (*Dipteryx odorata*), melilot (*Melilotus officinalis* or *Melilotus arvensis*) and woodruff (*Asperula odorata*), the flavoring oil of bergamot (from *Citrus bergamia*) and the spice cassia (*Cinnamomum cassia*; sometimes sold as cinnamon). Coumarin is liberated from the glycoside melilotoside (an ether of glucose bonded with an ester bond to coumarin) on drying coumarin-containing herb material.

Molds present in spoiled sweet (Melilotus) clover and other hay products can metabolize coumarin to dicoumarol, which is similar in structure to vitamin K. Vitamin K is necessary to activate prothrombin, which is converted to the blood clotting substance thrombin. By inhibiting vitamin K, dicoumarol promotes bleeding. Concentrations of dicoumarol in fodder >10 ppm have been responsible for fatalities by hemorrhaging in cattle.

The addition of coumarin to food in the United States was banned in 1954, based on reports of hepatoxicity in rats. However, because a number of foods contain coumarin, humans ingest approximately 0.02 mg coumarin/kg bw/day. The chronic administration of high doses of coumarin causes liver tumors in the rat and liver and lung tumors in the mouse. Overall, available data indicate that coumarin is not genotoxic. It is thought that the carcinogenicity of coumarin is caused by metabolism to toxic epoxides. Because doses of coumarin that cause toxicity and carcinogenicity in the lung and liver of experimental animals are more than 100 times the maximum human intake, exposure to coumarin from food poses no health risk to humans.

Phytates and phytic acid

Phytic acid (also referred to as phytate) is found in bran and germ of many plant seeds and in grains, legumes and nuts. Phytic acid is a simple sugar (myo-inositol) containing six phosphate sidechains, and as such, is a dietary source of phosphorus and an effective chelator of divalent cations such as: zinc, copper, iron, magnesium and calcium. Studies indicate that phytate-mineral complexes are insoluble in the intestinal tract, reducing mineral bioavailability. Phytate also has been shown to inhibit digestive enzymes such as: trypsin, pepsin, α-amylase and β-glucosidase. Therefore, ingestion of foods containing high amounts of phytate could theoretically cause mineral deficiencies or decreased protein and starch digestibility. Vegetarians that consume large amounts of tofu and bean curd are particularly at risk of mineral deficiencies due to phytate consumption.

Because phytate-rich foods are digested at a slower rate and produce lower blood glucose responses than foods that do not contain phytate, it has been hypothesized that phytate could have a therapeutic role in management of diabetes. It also may have utility as an antioxidant. However, because the beneficial effects of phytate are outweighed by its ability to cause essential mineral deficiencies, consumption of a diet containing high amounts of phytate is not recommended. Food manufacturers are developing methods to reduce phytate in foods, such as: addition of the microbial phytase, which releases phosphates from the inositol backbone of phytate.

Phytate is fairly heat stable, but can be removed by soaking or fermentation. The soybean has one of the highest phytate levels of any grain or legume, and requires a long period of fermentation for reduction. In people who consume large amounts of soy products, mineral deficiencies can be prevented by consumption of meat or dairy products or use of supplemental vitamins. There are no FDA regulations or guidelines restricting the presence of phytates in food.

Hypoglycin in ackee

Ackee (*Blighia sapida*; Figure 6.3) is the national fruit of Jamaica and is also found in other Caribbean nations, Central America, South American and southern Florida. Consumers of the unripe fruit sometimes suffer from 'Jamaican vomiting sickness syndrome' allegedly caused by the alkaloids hypoglycin A (HGA) and B. Levels of HGA in the opened, ripe fruit are undetectable, making opened fruit safe for consumption.

The hypoglycin toxin (L-methylenecyclopropylalanine) inactivates several flavoprotein acyl-CoA dehydrogenases, causing disturbances of the oxidation of fatty acids and amino acids. This leads to a secondary inhibition of gluconeogenesis which can precipitate an extreme, dangerous drop in blood-glucose levels (hypoglycemia) that can be fatal. Symptoms of poisoning from unripe ackee fruit occur within 6 to 48 hours of ingestion and include drowsiness, repeated vomiting, thirst, delirium, fever or loose bowels. Exhaustion of the muscular and nervous systems, collapse, coma, and death may ensue.

Fig. 6.3: **Unripe Ackee Fruit (left panel) and ripe Ackee Fruit (right panel)**

Dietary exposure to hypoglycin in Jamaicans ranges from 1.21-89.28 micrograms/gram ackee. Ingestion of one 100 gram fruit could therefore result in a dose of approximately 300 micrograms/kg bw in a 30 kg child. This dose is approximately one-fifth of the maximum tolerated dose of HGA in male and female rats of 1500 micrograms/kg bw/day, indicating that normal use levels of ackee do not have a large margin of safety.

The importation of canned ackee fruit into the United States is restricted to certain manufacturers to insure that only properly ripened ackees are used for canning, and the FDA routinely analyzes incoming shipments of ackee for hypoglycin levels that could be a health concern, having issued a recall of canned ackee fruit for this very reason in 2005. If hypoglycin poisoning is expected, glucose, fluids and electrolytes should be administered. Antiemetics may be used to control vomiting and benzodiazepines to control seizures. Endotracheal intubation should be performed in people exhibiting seizures or coma.

Safrole

Safrole (1-allyl-3,4-methylenedioxybenzene) is found in aromatic oils of nutmeg (*Myristica fragrans*), cinnamon (*Cinnamomum verum*) and camphor (*Cinnamomum camphora*) and is a major constituent of oil of sassafras (*Sassafras albidum*). Prior to being banned as a food additive in the United States in 1960, safrole was commonly used to flavor root beer and other foods. Most commercial 'sassafras teas' and root beers are now artificially flavored as a result of the FDA ban.

At a concentration of 1 per cent in the diet, safrole produces weight loss, testicular atrophy, bone marrow depletion and malignant liver tumors in rats. Based on sufficient evidence of carcinogenicity in experimental animals, safrole is reasonably anticipated to be a human carcinogen. The mechanism of carcinogenicity is thought to involve cytochrome P450 catalyzed hydroxylation of safrole to 1'-hydroxysafrole, and its subsequent metabolism to highly reactive electrophiles that bind to DNA.

Myristicin

Myristicin (Figure 6.4) is a naturally occurring insecticide and acaracide that is found in nutmeg and mace (*Myristica* spp.,) at concentrations of 1.3 per cent and 2.7 per cent, respectively. It is also present in black pepper, carrot, celery parsley and dill. It is estimated that the average total intake of myristicin from dietary sources is 'in the order of a few mg per person per day'.

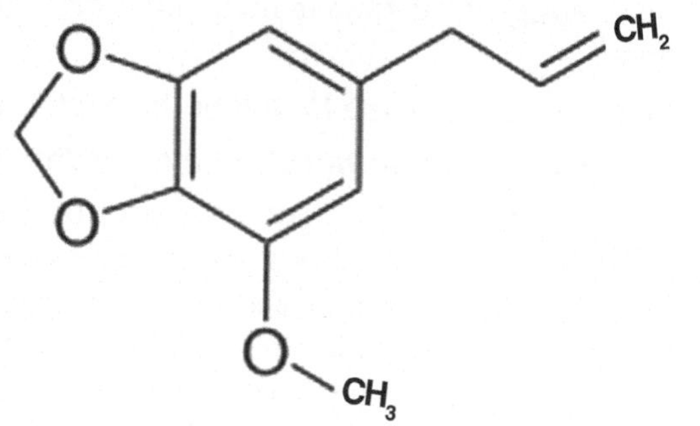

Fig. 6.4: **Structure of myristicin**

Myristicin is a weak inhibitor of monoamine oxidase, and is structurally related to mescaline. At a dose level of 6-7 mg/kg bw, it may cause psychotropic effects in man, such as: increased alertness, and a feeling of irresponsibility, freedom and euphoria. Unpleasant symptoms, such as: nausea, tremor, tachycardia, anxiety and fear have also been reported in humans ingesting this dose. Although the metabolism of myristicin resembles that of safrole, there is no evidence to suggest that myristicin is carcinogenic. There are no FDA regulations or guidelines specific to the presence of myristicin in food.

At the concentrations normally present in spices or food, the likelihood of toxicity arising from myristicin is low. However, ingestion of greater than 5 grams of nutmeg (corresponding to 1-2 mg/kg bw myristicin) has produced toxicological symptoms in humans that are similar to alcohol intoxication. Because the myristicin content of nutmeg is approximately 1-3 per cent, it is likely that components of nutmeg in addition to myristicin contribute to nutmeg toxicity.

Tomatine in tomatoes

The leaves, stems and unripe fruit of the tomato plant contain α-tomatine, a steroidal alkaloid containing D-xylose, D-galactose, and two molecules of D-glucose. Tomatine is toxic to a number of different fungi, thereby acting as a natural fungicide. It has been hypothesized that the toxic effects of tomatine on fungi are due to the ability of tomatine to complex with membrane sterols, causing membrane disruption.

Currently, there is no evidence to suggest that tomatine is a substance of concern. There are no reports of acute toxicity in humans due to ingestion of green tomatoes and there are no FDA regulations or guidelines specific to the presence of tomatine in food. Ingestion of a rare variety of ripe tomato (*Lycopersicon esculentum* var. cerasiforme) that contains up to 5 mg tomatine/g of dry weight has no adverse effects on natives who commonly ingest the M.

Concentrations of tomatine decrease as tomatoes ripen, and ripe fruit contains approximately 36 mg per a 100 gram tomato. Microwaving or frying does not reduce content of tomatine, and delayed-ripening varieties of tomatoes contain similar concentrations of tomatine as other tomatoes. At this time, there is no evidence to suggest that a diet high in green tomatoes would be injurious to human health. Tomatine forms strong, insoluble complexes with cholesterol *in vitro*, and has been shown to lower plasma LDL cholesterol in hamsters, suggesting that it may have beneficial effects on blood lipids of humans.

Substances Formed as the Result of Product Abuse

Glycoalkaloids (solanine and chaconine) in Potatoes

The glycoalkaloids α-solanine and α-chaconine are natural pesticides that are produced in potatoes. α-Solanine is also found in eggplant, apples, bell peppers, cherries, sugar beets and tomatoes. The only difference between α-solanine and α-chaconine is the sugars in the trisaccharide potion of the molecule, *i.e.*, glucose with two rhamnoses for α-solanine and a glucose, galactose and a rhamnose for α-chaconine.

Depending on variety and storage conditions, concentrations of α-chaconine and α-solanine in potato tubers vary between 0.5-635 ppm (0.0005-0.64 mg/g potato) and 5-125,100 molecule ppm (0.005-25.1 mg/g potato), respectively. Although glycoalkaloids are found throughout the potato tuber, the greatest concentrations are in the sprouts, peels and sun-greened areas. The FDA considers the maximum acceptable glycoalkaloid content to be 20-25 mg/100 g fresh potato weight (or 200-250 ppm). Under current FDA regulations, 20 milligrams of solanine per 100 grams (a small potato) can render it unfit to eat.

Synthesis of α-chaconine and α-solanine is stimulated by light, mechanical injury, aging and potato beetle infestation. Exposure of potatoes to light in the field or marketplace can lead to glycoalkaloid concentrations that are unsafe for human consumption. Concentrations of solanine in green or blighted potatoes have been shown to increase by seven fold.

The symptoms of acute toxicity to α-solanine and α-chaconine are due to their ability to act as inhibitors of acetylcholinesterase and disruptors of cell membranes. Glycoalkaloid doses of 1 to 5 mg/kg have been shown to be acutely toxic to humans, and doses of 3 to 6 mg/kg have resulted in death. Symptoms of glycoalkaloid toxicity in humans include drowsiness, itchiness in the neck region, increased sensitivity (hyperesthesia), labored breathing and gastrointestinal symptoms (abdominal pain, nausea, vomiting and diarrhoea).

α-Solanine and α-chaconine are not mutagenic or only weakly mutagenic *in vitro*, are not genotoxic *in vivo*, and are embryotoxic and teratogenic to experimental animals. Teratogenic effects in mammals include central nervous system abnormalities (*e.g.*, exencephaly, cranial bleb, encephalocele, and anophthalmia), mild hydronephrosis, hydroureter, and irregular or fused ribs. Although one human case study reported a correlation between the severity of potato late-blight and the incidence of spina bifida, no other studies in humans have found a correlation between the consumption of potatoes and birth defects . There is no evidence that α-solanine and α-chaconine are carcinogenic in animals or humans.

In 1993, the National Institute of Environmental Health Sciences determined that the average consumption of glycoalkaloids from potatoes was 12.75 mg glycoalkaloids/person/day (0.18 mg/kg bw based on a bw of 70 kg), which is approximately one-fifth of the lowest dose that has been shown to produce acute toxicity in humans (1 mg/kg bw).

Substances formed as the Result of Processing

Heterocyclic Aromatic Amines

There are two major classes of heterocyclic aromatic amines (HAAs). Pyrolytic HAAs are formed from the pyrolysis of amino acids or proteins at high temperature and aminoimidazoarenes (AIAs) are formed from creatine, free amino acids and monosaccharides, via the Maillard reaction. HAAs are present in many protein-rich foods of animal origin including: cooked meat, fish, poultry and gravies and sauces derived from pan residues and scrapings of cooked meats. The formation and yield of HAAs are dependent on cooking temperature and time (concentrations increase with higher temperatures and longer cooking times), cooking technique and equipment (concentrations of HAAs in meat are generally higher after grilling and panfrying than broiling or roasting), and the ability of HAA precursors to migrate to the surface.

The AIAs 2-amino-3-methylimidazo-[4,5-f]quinoline (IQ), 2-amino-3,4-dimethylimidazo[4,5-f]quinoline (MeIQ) and 2-amino-3,8, dimethylimidazo [4,5-f]quinoxaline (MeIQx) are among the most potent mutagens ever tested in the Ames assay. The pyroltic AIA 2-amino-1-methyl-6-phenylimidazol(4,5-b)pyridine (PhIP) and the HAAs 2-amino-1,4-dimethyl-5H-pyrido[4,3-b]indole (Trp-P-1), 2-amino-4-methyl-5H-pyrido[4,3-b]indole (Trp-P-2), 2-amino-9H-pyrido[2,3-b]indole (AαC), 2-amino-3-methyl-9H-pyrido[2,3-b]indole (MeAαC) are also mutagenic. PhIP accounts for 75 per cent of the mass of genotoxic material that has been attributed to HAAs in fried ground beef. Therefore, the potential for genotoxicity due to PhIP may be higher than that of more genotoxic HAAs in meat consumers.

Several HAAs are carcinogenic in rodents after long-term dietary administration. The doses required to induce tumors at a 50 per cent rate (TD_{50}) vary for each HAA, and range from 0.1 to 64.6 mg/kg bw/day .Four HAAs (IQ, MeIQ, MeIQx and PhIP) are 'reasonably anticipated to be human carcinogens'. Due to the fact that exposure to HAAs in cooked meats is highly variable (concentrations in cooked meat may range from <1 to 500 ng/g), it has been estimated that the risk of developing cancer from exposure to HAAs in food is anywhere from 50 in one million to one in a thousand. Currently, no tolerable upper limit of exposure to HAAs has been established.

Polycyclic Aromatic Hydrocarbons

Polycyclic aromatic hydrocarbons (PAHs) are known carcinogens that are formed from the incomplete combustion of fossil fuels such as: wood, coal and oil. PAHs can enter the food chain from environmental contamination or from food processing. Foods containing the highest concentrations of PAHs include: cooked or smoked meat or fish, smoked or cured cheese, tea and roasted coffee. Grilling or broiling of meat, fish or other foods over intense heat or direct contact with flames promotes production of PAHs. In general, concentrations of PAHs in meat are highest after charcoal grilling, followed by smoking, roasting and steaming. Concentrations of PAHs in smoked foods are influenced by temperature, type of wood, oxygen concentration and type of smoker. Concentrations of PAHs in tea dried over burning wood, oil or coal are generally higher than in tea dried over air, and coffee beans that are roasted over a direct fire contain higher concentrations than beans that do not come in contact with flames.

The European Commission's (EC) Scientific Committee on Food and the Joint FAO/WHO Expert Committee on Food Additives (JECFA) has concluded that thirteen different PAHs are genotoxic and carcinogenic benz[a]anthracene, benzo[b]fluoranthene, benzo[j]fluoranthene, benzo[k]fluoranthene, benzo[a]pyrene, chrysene, dibenz[a,h]anthracene, dibenzo[a,e]pyrene, dibenzo[a,h]pyrene, dibenzo[a,i]pyrene, dibenzo[a,l]pyrene, indeno[1,2,3-cd]pyrene and 5-methylchrysene. Three of the four PAHs that have been tested for carcinogenicity in rats after oral exposure (benz[a]anthracene, benzo[a]pyrene and dibenz[a,h]anthracene) are carcinogenic. The estimated high and safe levels of intake of the benchmark PAH benzo[a]pyrene are 0.01 and 100 µg benzo[a]pyrene/kg bw/day, respectively, indicating that the estimated intake of PAHs in food is 10,000-fold lower than the level that is expected to cause toxicity in humans. Currently, no tolerable upper limit of exposure to PAHs has been established by the FDA.

Acrylamide

Acrylamide (Figure 6.5) is found in a number of starch-based foods that are fried or baked at temperatures greater than 120°C (248°F), including bread, bakery products, breakfast cereal, and potato products (*e.g.*, chips, french fries). It also is found in cocoa-based products and coffee. Acrylamide is formed via a Maillard reaction, a reaction between the carbonyl group of a reducing sugar and the nucleophilic group of an amino acid. Although a number of carbohydrates can be used as the source of the carbonyl group, the amino acid required for the formation of acrylamide is asparagine.

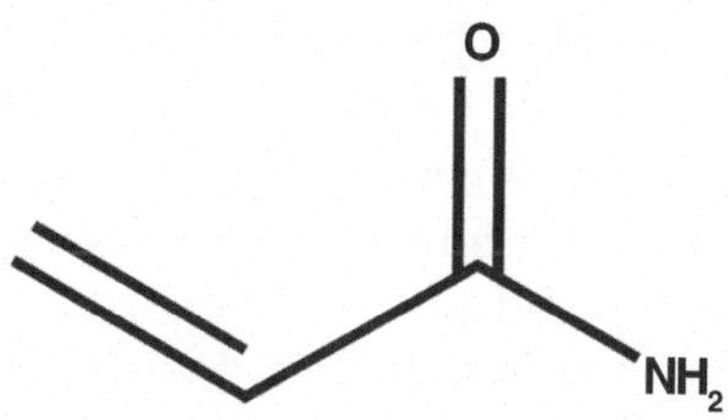

Fig. 6.5: **Structure of acrylamide**

Acrylamide is mutagenic and has been shown to be a neurotoxicant, reproductive toxicant and carcinogen in experimental animals and is classified by IARC as a probable human carcinogen. The main metabolite, glycidamide (an epoxide) is thought to be responsible for genotoxicity. In humans, the only toxicological effect that has been linked to acrylamide is neurotoxicity in individuals occupationally exposed to high levels. Epidemiological studies have failed to show an increased risk of cancer from either occupational or dietary exposure to acrylamide and reproductive toxicity has not been reported in humans exposed to acrylamide. Acrylamide is a unique substance that exemplifies the concept that the structure of the substance greatly influences the toxicity, as acrylamide is an animal feed ingredient (thickener and suspending agent) only when a part of a long-chain polymer having a minimum molecular weight of 3 million and a viscosity range of 3,000 to 6,000 centipoises at 77°F. The residual acrylamide cannot be more than 0.05 per cent.

In 2005, JECFA estimated that average and high intake consumers ingest 1 or 4 μg/kg bw/day acrylamide from food, respectively. Using a NOAEL for neurotoxicity of 200 μg/kg bw/day in animals, margins of safety of 200 and 50 for the average and high intake groups were derived, respectively. Utilizing a benchmark dose of 0.3 mg/kg bw/day and a NOAEL of 2 mg/kg bw/day for development of mammary tumors or reproductive in rats (respectively), higher margins of safety were calculated for carcinogenicity (300 and 75, respectively) and reproductive toxicity (200 and 50, respectively).

Exposure to acrylamide can be reduced by avoiding deep-fried foods, soaking potato slices before cooking, cooking french fries at lower temperatures and to a lighter color, and toasting bread to a lighter color.

Chloropropanols

Chloropropanols are formed in hydrolyzed vegetable proteins (HVP) produced by hydrochloric acid (HCl) hydrolysis of proteinaceous by-products from edible oil extraction, such as: soybean meal, rapeseed meal and maize gluten. The chloropropanol most commonly found in food is 3-MCPD (3-monochloropropane-1,2-diol), although others may also be present, including: 2-MCPD (2-monochloropropane-1,3-diol), 1,3-DCP (1,3-dichloro-2-propanol), and 2,3-DCP (2,3-dichloro-1-propanol). The two most widely studied chloropropanols are 3-MCPD and 1,3-DCP. It is thought that 3-MCPD is formed as a result of a reaction between a source of chlorine (chlorinated water or sodium chloride) in a food or a food contact material and a lipid. Two basic pathways have been proposed: thermally driven and enzyme-catalysed (generally lipase) reactions. Direct precursors are thought to be glycerol and chloride. Recent work has also suggested glycidol (2,3-epoxy-1-propanol) as a precursor. 1,3-DCP is thought to arise from 3-MCPD.

High concentrations of 3-MCPD have been found in acid hydrolyzed HVP (acid-HVP), and soy or oyster sauce produced using an acid hydrolysis process. Other foods that may contain 3-MCPD are cereal, toasted bread, coffee, cheese, licorice, baked goods, processed garlic, liquid smokes, malts, cured or smoked meat or fish or foods containing acid-HVP as a savory ingredient (soups, prepared meals, savory snacks, gravy mixes and stick cubes. Foods containing 1,3-DCP include raw meat and soy sauce produced using an acid hydrolysis process.

In rats and mice, 3-MCPD is toxic to the kidney, producing renal tubule hyperplasia. It is also carcinogenic in rats when given in high doses over prolonged periods. Although 3-MCPD is genotoxic *in vitro*, it is not *in vivo*. The UK Committee on Carcinogenicity of Chemicals in Food, Consumer Products and the Environment (COC) has concluded that 3-MCPD is unlikely to present a carcinogenic risk to man, provided the exposure is 1000 times lower than the no observed effect level (NOEL) of 1.1 mg/kg bw/day for tumorigenicity. JECFA set a tolerable daily intake (TDI) of 2 μg 3-MCPD/kg of body weight in 2001 and a maximum allowable content of free 3-MCPD in liquid condiments at 0.4 mg/kg (400 μg/kg) in 2008 [130]. Assuming 400 μg/kg 3-MCPD is present in soy sauce, a 60 kg human would have to ingest 300 g of soy sauce (approximately two-thirds of a 444 mL bottle) per day to achieve the TDI. The FDA has provided a policy statement stating that acid-H[V]P or Asian sauces that contain 3-MCPD at levels greater than 1 ppm are not Generally Recognized As Safe (GRAS); therefore, these ingredients are unapproved food additives.

1,3-DCP is hepatotoxic, genotoxic and induces a variety of different types of tumors in rats. Therefore, 1,3-DCP is considered to be a potential carcinogen in humans. In 1993, FAO/WHO and JECFA concluded in that 1,3-DCP is an undesirable contaminant in food and that levels should be reduced to as low as 'technologically achievable'.

Furan

Furan (Figure 6.6) is a by-product of high-energy and thermal treatment of carbohydrate. Meat and vegetable containing foods that are heat processed in cans and jars (such as: soups, pastas, sauces, gravy and baby food) and brewed coffee, typically contain the highest concentrations. Concentrations of furan present in food and coffee range from undetectable to approximately 175 μg/kg. Coffee powders may contain up to 5000 μg/kg on a dry weight basis. Although the mechanism of formation of furan in food is not completely understood, it can be synthesized from vitamin C, amino acids, reducing sugars, organic acids, carotenes and polyunsaturated fatty acids in the presence of heat.

Furan is mutagenic and clastogenic in a number of *in vitro* mammalian cell assays, causes damage to chromosomes in mice, and is carcinogenic in both rats and mice after oral administration Furan is classified by IARC as possibly carcinogenic to humans.

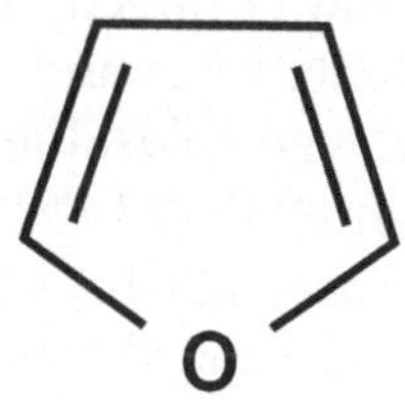

Fig 6.6: **Structure of Furan**

Mitigation of furan in foods is difficult because the mechanism for its formation in food is unclear. Due to the fact that furan is volatile, it is thought that concentrations can be reduced by heating food in open containers or leaving ready-to-eat foods open to air after preparation. However, the effectiveness of this strategy in reducing exposure to furan has yet to be demonstrated. Currently, there are no FDA regulations specific to the level of furan in food.

Trans Fatty Acids

Trans fatty acids (also known as trans fat) are the sum of all unsaturated fatty acids that contain one or more isolated double bonds in a trans configuration. Trans fatty acids more closely resemble saturated fatty acids than cis unsaturated fatty acids because their trans configuration makes them rigid. Trans fatty acids in the diet originate from two sources. The first is from bacterial hydrogenation in the forestomach of ruminants, which produces trans fatty acids that are found in beef and mutton fat, milk and butter. Trans fatty acids are also produced from the hydrogenation of liquid oils (mainly of vegetable origin). This produces solid fats and partially hydrogenated oils such as: margarines, spreads, shortenings and frying oil, which are more stable than liquid oils.

Biochemically, trans-fatty acids act similarly to saturated fatty acids, raising low density lipoprotein (LDL) cholesterol and decreasing high-density lipoprotein (HDL) cholesterol levels High intakes of trans fatty acids have been associated with an increased risk of coronary heart disease (CHD) independent of other risk factors in large epidemiological studies. A tolerable upper limit of trans fatty acids has not been set because any incremental increase in the intake of trans fatty acids increases the risk of coronary heart disease.

Due to increased efforts by food manufacturers to reduce or eliminate the use of partially hydrogenated vegetable fat in food production, it is estimated that trans fatty acid content of processed foods has decreased over the last decade.

Nitrosamines formed during Drying, Curing and Preserving

Nitrosamines are formed from the interaction of nitrites or other nitrosating agents with amines in food (or *in vivo*), under acidic conditions.

Nitrites may be directly added to food or can be formed from bacterial reduction of nitrate. Nitrites and nitrates may occur naturally in water or foods such as: leafy vegetables due to the use of fertilizer, or may be added to foods to prevent growth of *Clostridium botulinum*, or to add color or flavour.

Nitrosamines have been found in a variety of different foods such as: cheese, soybean oil, canned fruit, meat products, cured or smoked meats, fish and fish products, spices used for meat curing, and beer and other alcoholic beverages. Beer, meat products and fish are considered the main sources of exposure. Drying, kilning, salting, smoking or curing promotes formation of nitrosamines.

The nitrosamines most frequently found in food are nitrosodimethylamine (NDMA), *N*-nitrosopyrrolidine (NPYR), *N*-nitrosopiperidine (NPIP), and *N*-nitrosothiazolidine (NTHZ). NDMA, NPYR, NPIP are reasonably anticipated to be human carcinogens based on evidence of carcinogenicity in experimental animals. Evidence from case-control studies supports an association between nitrosamine intake with gastric cancer, but not esophageal cancer in humans.

Levels of nitrosamines have been declining during the past three decades, concurrent with a lowering of the nitrite used in food, use of inhibitors such as: ascorbic acid and use of lower operating temperatures and indirect heating during food processing. Based on an estimated exposure level of 3.3-5.0 ng/kg bw/day, the and the benchmark lower limit of 60 μg/kg bw/day, a margin of error associated with a low level of concern (12,000-18,2000) has been derived for NDMA, the most common nitrosamine in food.

Although current FDA regulations do not limit nitrosamine levels in foods, the FDA has provided an action level of 10 ppb for individual nitrosamines in both consumer and hospital rubber baby bottle nipples, while the FDA limits the approval of nitrites in curing mixes to the FDA-regulated food additive process (21 CFR 170.60), with the approval of sodium nitrite as a food additive (food preservative) (21 CFR 172.175). The USDA monitors finished meat products to insure that nitrite is not present in amounts exceeding 200 ppm (9 CFR 424.21).

Biogenic Amines

Biogenic amines are normally formed in humans by normal cellular metabolism. In food, biogenic amines are mainly formed from microbial decarboxylation of amino acids. They are commonly found in fermented meat, beverages and dairy products, sauerkraut, and spoiled fish. The main biogenic amines in food are histamine, tyramine cadaverine, putrescine, spermidine and spermine. The two biogenic amines that have been associated with acute toxicity are histamine and tyramine. Putresine, spermine, sperimidine and cadaverine are not toxic in and of themselves, but may react with nitrite or nitrate to form nitrosamines (see Section 4.4.7 above).

Scombrotoxicosis is a common seafood-borne disease associated with the consumption of toxic levels of histamine in spoiled scombroid fish such as: tuna (*Thunnus* spp.), mackerel (*Scomber* spp.), saury (*Cololabis*saira) and bonito (*Sarda* spp.). Red wine may also contain relatively high levels of histamine. Symptoms of histamine intoxication from food are similar to allergies to other substances and include: sneezing, nose congestion, breathing difficulties and urticaria.

Consumption of tyramine may precipitate migraine headache or a hypertensive crisis. The most serious case reports of tyramine toxicity have occurred in people consuming aged cheese. Because monoamine oxidase inhibitor (MAOI) drugs inhibit metabolism of amines, people taking these drugs may be particularly susceptible to tyramine toxicity. Whereas 200-800 mg of dietary tyramine induces only a mild rise in blood pressure in unmedicated adults, 10-25 mg may produce a serious adverse event in those taking MAOI drugs. Other potentiating factors for tyramine toxicity include: alcohol consumption, gastrointestinal distress and exposure to other amines.

Efforts taken by food manufacturers to reduce biogenic amine concentrations in fermented foods include using amine-negative starter cultures, adding probiotic bacterial strains alone or in combination with starter cultures, high pressure processing or low-dose gamma radiation. FDA guidelines specify 50 mg/100 g as the toxic concentration of histamine in scombroid fish and the agency has published guidance on how to control levels.

Substances Passed from Animals to Humans

Toxins in Seafood

Consumption of seafood contaminated with algal toxins results in five different syndromes, paralytic, neurotoxic, amnesic, or diarrhetic shellfish poisoning and ciguatera fish poisoning.

Paralytic shellfish poisoning

Paralytic shellfish poisoning (PSP) is caused by the consumption of molluscan shellfish contaminated with heterocyclic guanidines called saxitoxins. Currently, over 21 known saxitoxins are produced by dinoflagellate species from three genera: *Alexandrium, Gymnodium* and *Pyrodinium*. Toxicity is caused by binding of saxitoxins to voltage-dependent sodium channels, which blocks neuronal activity. The primary site of action in humans is the peripheral nervous system. Symptoms of toxicity include: tingling and numbness of the perioral area and extremities, loss of motor control, drowsiness, and incoherence. Ingestion of 1-4 mg saxitoxin has resulted in death from respiratory paralysis.

Outbreaks of PSP have occurred worldwide, due to the fact that saxitoxin-producing species of dinoflagellates can live in either temperate or tropical waters. Saxitoxins are not inactivated by cooking, and must be mitigated at their source to prevent ingestion. PSP is prevented by large-scale, proactive monitoring programmes and rapid closures of harvest in areas containing dinoflagellate algal blooms. In the United States, the permissible level of saxitoxin equivalents in shellfish is 80 micrograms/100 grams.

Neurotoxic shellfish poisoning

The dinoflagellate *Karenia brevis* produces brevetoxins that are lethal to fish, but not to mollusks such as: oysters, clams and mussels. Consequently, they can accumulate in healthy-appearing mollusks to concentrations that are toxic to humans who ingest them. *Karenia brevis* brevitoxins cause the syndrome known as neurotoxic shellfish poisoning (NSP), which affects sodium transport in the autonomic nervous system and causes inhibition of neuromuscular transmission in skeletal muscle.

NSP is usually a relatively mild illness and should not be confused with the more serious condition of PSP. NSP symptoms usually occur within three hours of ingesting contaminated shellfish and may include: abdominal pain, nausea and vomiting, vertigo, malaise, generalized muscle weakness, ataxia, incoordination, chills, headache, myalgia, a reversal of hot/cold temperature sensation and progressive parasthesias. Dilated pupils, bradycardia and convulsions may occur in cases of severe poisoning. Unlike PSP, no deaths have been reported from NSP.

K. brevis is the organism that is usually responsible for the red tides in the Gulf of Mexico and along the southern Atlantic coast of North America. Blooms along the west coast of Florida occur regularly. Biotoxin control plans that are implemented during period of red tide are generally effective in preventing NSP, but have not eliminated NSP entirely.

The FDA has established an action level of 0.8 ppm (20 mouse units/ 100g) brevetoxin-2 equivalents.

Amnesic shellfish poisoning (domoic acid)

Amnesic shellfish poisoning (ASP) is caused by domoic acid produced by diatoms of the genus *Pseudo-nitzchia* (Figure 6.6-6.7), which are consumed by mussels, scallops, clams and crabs. Domoic acid is a water-soluble, tricarboxylic amino acid that is a structural analog of the neurotransmitter glutamate and is a glutamate receptor agonist. Persistent activation of the kainite glutamate receptor causes an increase in intracellular calcium, which can cause neuronal cell death and lesions of the brain where glutamineric pathways are concentrated. Areas of the brain involved in learning and memory processing are particularly susceptible. The symptoms of ASP are gastroenteritis, dizziness, disorientation, lethargy, seizures and loss of short-term memory. Respiratory difficulty, coma and death may ensue. Human toxicity has occurred after ingestion of 1-5 mg/kg domoic acid.

In 1987, approximately 100 people became ill and died in Prince Edward Island, Canada, after eating contaminated mussels. In 1991, domoic acid poisoning caused the deaths of numerous pelicans and cormorants in

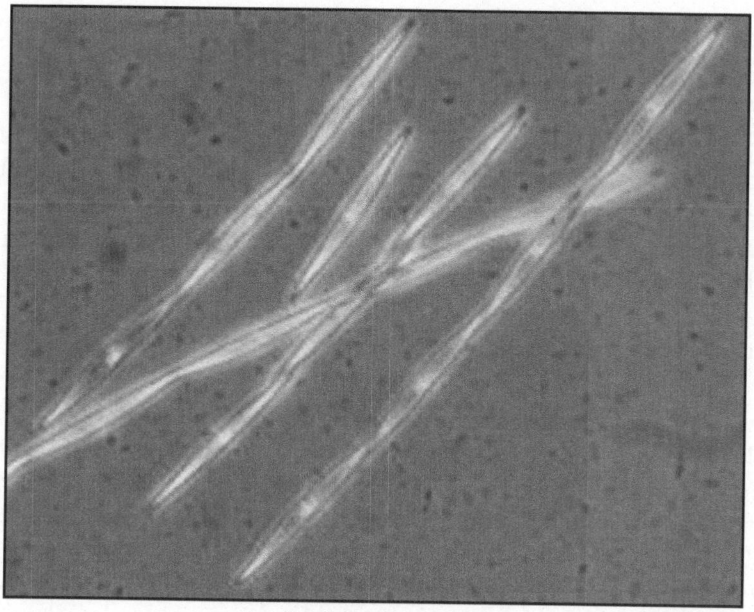

Fig. 6.7: **Pseudo-nitzchia**

Monterey Bay that ingested sardines and anchovies. Domoic acid also was responsible for a massive sea lion kill in Monterey Bay in 1998. *Pseudo-nitzchia* and domoic acid are now closely monitored throughout the world. The FDA has established an action level of 20 ppm for domoic acid, except in the viscera of Dungeness crab, where 30 ppm is permitted. Regulatory guidance has been effective in preventing ASP in humans, since no human outbreaks of ASP have occurred since 1987.

Diarrhoetic shellfish poisoning

Diarrhoetic shellfish poisoning (DSP) is caused by the production of okadaic acid and dinophysistoxins in the dinoflagellates *Dinophysis fortii* or *Prorocentrum lima,* which are consumed by mollusks. Okadaic acid and dinophysistoxins are inhibitors of serine/threonine phosphatases, critical components of signaling cascades that regulate a number of cellular processes involved in metabolism, ion balance, neurotransmission and cell cycle regulation.

Compared to other types of shellfish poisoning, symptoms of DSP are relatively mild, and generally consist of diarrhoea, abdominal cramps, nausea, chills or vomiting within 30 minutes to a few hours after consumption of DSP toxins. Symptoms generally resolve within 2-3 days, with or without medical treatment. Diarrhoea is most likely due to the hyperphosphorylation of proteins (including: ion channels) in the intestinal epithelia, resulting in impaired water balance and fluid loss. The long-term consequences of low level exposure to DSP toxins may be more serious, as they have been shown to be tumor promoters. The FDA has established an action level of 0.2 ppm okadaic acid plus 35-methyl okadaic acid (DXT 1).

Ciguatera Poisoning

Ciguatera fish poisoning (CFP) is caused by the dinoflagellate *Gambierdiscus toxicus*, which grows on filamentous macroalgae associated with coral reefs. The lipophilic precursors to ciguatoxin are biotransformed to ciguatoxins in herbivorous fish and invertebrates that consume the macroalgae, and bioaccumulate in large carnivorous fishes associated with coral reefs. High ciguatoxin concentrations may be found in barracuda, snapper, grouper and jacks.

Ciguatoxins are structurally related to the brevetoxins and compete with brevetoxin for binding to the same site on the voltage-dependent sodium channel. However, because ciguatoxin has a higher binding affinity for the site than brevetoxin, the toxic potency of ciguatoxin is higher than that of brevetoxin. The threshold level for toxicity in humans is estimated to be 0.5 ng/g.

CFP is estimated to affect over 50,000 people worldwide each year. The symptoms of CFP generally include: gastrointestinal disturbances (nausea, vomiting and diarrhoea) within 2-6 hours, followed by neurologic symptoms such as: numbness of the perioral area and extremities, a reversal of hot/cold temperature sensation, muscle and joint aches, headache, itching, tachycardia, hypertension, blurred vision and paralysis. In rare cases, CFP is fatal.

Inasmuch as ciguatoxin is produced by organisms that live beneath the surface and is not routinely monitored for concentration in seafood, the only way to prevent consumption is to completely abstain from ingesting tropical reef fish, as the occurrence of toxic fish is sporadic, and not all fish of a given species or from a given locality will be toxic. Currently, there are no FDA regulations limiting levels of ciguatoxins in fish, although a recent publication suggests an advisory level of 0.1 ppb pacific ciguatoxin equivalent (P-CTX-1) toxicity values in fish from the tropical Atlantic, Gulf of Mexico, Caribbean, and 0.01 ppb P-CTX-1 equivalent toxicity in fish from Pacific regions.

Conclusion

Given the state of the science, the pressure on the food supply and the development of new products, the FDA has performed admirably in protecting the consumer from exposure to toxins in food with its judicious use of warning labels, action levels, tolerances, specifications, prohibitions and the ability conferred by Congress to declare substances 'unsafe' or 'unfit for food.' However, the FDA cannot protect consumers absolutely from exposure to toxins normally present in foods. At normal levels of food consumption, there is little potential for toxicity from natural food toxins. Nevertheless, there is always the possibility of an idiosyncratic response or undetected contamination.

REFERENCES

1. Institute of Medicine (IOM) Dietary Reference Intakes for Vitamin A., Vitamin K., Arsenic, Boron, Chromium, Copper, Iodine, Iron, Manganese, Molybdenum, Nickel, Silicon, Vanadium and Zinc. National Academies Press; Washington, DC, USA: 2001.
2. Burton G.W., Ingold K.U. beta-Carotene: An Unusual Type of Lipid Antioxidant. Science. 1984;224:569-573.
3. Bannister B., Gibsburg G., Shneerson T. Cardiac Arrest due to Liquorice Induced Hypokalaemia. *Br. Med. J.* 1977; 2:738-739.
4. Isbrucker R.A., Burdock G.A. Risk and Safety Assessment on the Consumption of licorice root (*Glycyrrhiza* sp.), its Extract and Powder as a Food Ingredient, with Emphasis on the Pharmacology and Toxicology of glycyrrhizin. *Regul. Toxicol. Pharmacol.* 2006;46:167-192. doi: 10.1016/j.yrtph.2006.06.002.
5. United States Government Accountability Office (GAO) Food safety. FDA should Strengthen its Oversight of Food Ingredients Determined to be Generally Recognized as Safe (GRAS) GAO-10-246. Feb, 2010. [(accessed on 21 July 2010)]. Available online: http://www.gao.gov/new.items/d10246.pdf.
6. Food and Drug Law Institute. FDCA Statutory Supplement Including FDA Amendments Act of 2007 and Related Sections of Additional Statutes. Food and Drug Law Institute; Washington, DC, USA: 2008. Sec. 201. [321] Definitions; pp. 1-2.
7. Food and Drug Law Institute . FDCA Statutory Supplement Including FDA Amendments Act of 2007 and Related Sections of Additional Statutes. Food and Drug Law Institute; Washington, DC, USA: 2008. Sec. 402. [342] Adulterated Food; p. 31.
8. Food and Drug Law Institute. FDCA Statutory Supplement Including FDA Amendments Act of 2007 and Related Sections of Additional Statutes. Washington, DC, USA. Food and Drug Law Institute; 2008. Sec. 406. [346] Tolerances for Poisonous Ingredients in Food; p. 31.
9. Kracov D.A. The Regulation of Foods and Food Additives. In: Piña K.R., Pines W.L., editors. A Practical Guide to Food and Drug Law Regulation. 2nd. Food and Drug Law Institute; Washington, DC, USA: 2002. pp. 159-214.
10. Tullo A. Newscripts: Vile weed or Essential Ingredient? Chem. Eng. News. 2010;88:72.
11. Fischer R., Griffin F., Kaplan A.R. Taste Thresholds, Cigarette Smoking, and Food Dislikes. *Med. Exp. Int. J. Exp. Med.* 1963; 9: 151-167.
12. Goff S.A., Klee H.J. Plant Volatile Compounds: Sensory clues for Health and Nutritional Value? Science. 2006;311:815-819.
13. National Organization for Rare Disorders (NORD) 2010. [(accessed on 21 July 2010)]. Available online: http://www.rarediseases.org.
14. Carabin I.G., Magnuson B.A. New Labeling Requirements for Food Allergens. Nutritional Outlook.Apr, 2006. [(accessed on 21 July 2010)]. Available online: http://www.nutritionaloutlook.com/article.php?ArticleID=2096.
15. Kotsonis F.N., Burdock G.A. Food Toxicology. In: Klaassen C.D., editor. Casarett and Doull's Toxicology: The Basic Science of Poisons. 7th. McGraw-Hill; New York, NY, USA: 2008. pp. 1191-1236.
16. Sors T.G., Ellis D.R., Salt D.E. Selenium uptake, translocation, Assimilation and Metabolic Fate in Plants. *Photosynth. Res.* 2005; 86:373-389.

17. Yang G., Wang S., Zhou R., Sun S. Endemic Selenium Intoxication of Humans in China. *Am. J. Clin. Nutr*. 1983;37:872-881.
18. Reilly C. Selenium: Physiology, Dietary Sources and Requirements. In: Sadler M.J., editor. Encyclopaedia of Human Nutrition. Academic; San Diego, CA, USA: 1998. pp. 1752-1758.
19. United States Environmental Protection Agency (EPA) Selenium and Compounds (CASRN 7782-49-2) Mar 1, 1991. [(accessed on 21 July 2010)]. Available online: http://www.epa.gov/iris/subst/0472.htm.
20. Waldron H.A. Did the Mad Hatter have Mercury Poisoning? *Br. Med. J*. 1983; 287:1961. doi: 10.1136/bmj.287.6409.1961.
21. Carrington C., Bolger M. An Exposure Assessment for Methylmercury from Seafood for Consumers in the United States. [(accessed on 21 July 2010)]. Available online: http://www.fda.gov/downloads/Food/FoodSafety/Product-SpecificInformation/Seafood/FoodbornePathogensContaminants/Methylmercury/UCM114740.pdf.
22. United States Food and Drug Administration (FDA) Chapter 10: Methyl Mercury. Fish and Fisheries Products Hazards and Controls Guidance. 3rd. Jun, 2001. [(accessed on 21 July 2010)].
23. Hutt P.B., Merrill R.A., Grossman L.W. Food and Drug Law. 3rd. Foundation Press; New York, NY, USA: 2007. p. 369.
24. European Commission. Scientific Committee on Food Opinion of the Scientific Committee on Food on thujone. Feb 6, 2003. [(accessed on 21 July 2010)]. Available online:http://ec.europa.eu/food/fs/sc/scf/out162_en.pdf.
25. United States Food and Drug Administration . Code of Federal Regulations (CFR) 21 172.510. U.S. Government Printing Office; Washington, DC, USA: 2006. pp. 55-57.
26. Galli C.L., Galli G., Tragni E., Caruso D., Fiecchi A. Quantitative Analysis of alpha, beta-thujone, pulegone, safrole, coumarin and beta-asarone in alcoholic beverages by selected-ion monitoring. *J. Appl. Toxicol*. 1984;4:273-276. doi: 10.1002/jat.2550040514.
27. Lawrence B.M. Essential Oils: 2001-04. Allured Publishing; Carol Stream, IL, USA: 2006. Progress in Essential Oils. Sage Oil; pp. 25-30.
28. Ben Farhat M., Jordán M.J., Chaouech-Hamada R., Landoulsi A., Sotomayor J.A. Variations in Essential Oil, phenolic Compounds, and Antioxidant Activity of Tunisian Cultivated *Salvia officinalis* L. *J. Agric. Food Chem*. 2009; 57: 10349-10356.
29. Patocka J., Plucar B. Pharmacology and Toxicology of absinthe. *J. Appl. Biomed*. 2003;1:199-205.
30. Millet Y., Jouglard J., Steinmetz M.D., Tognetti P., Joanny P., Arditti J. Toxicity of some Essential Plant Oils. Clinical and Experimental Study. Clin. Toxicol. 1981;18: 1485-1498. doi: 10.3109/15563658108990357.

Page 133-150

AGRICULTURAL PRACTICES AND CROP DISEASE CONTROL
Edited by **: Dr. Alka Chauhan** and **Dr. Anubhuti Sharma**
Edition **: 2017**
ISBN : 978-93-5056-859-0
Published by **: Discovery Publishing House Pvt. Ltd., New Delhi (India)**

7

Impact of Climate Change on Insect Pests

Approaches to Combat its Impact

Arti Katiyar[1*]
S.K. Singh[2]
Sandeep Sharma[3]

ABSTRACT

Climate change has become a major alarm to agricultural development in entirety. Among the changes expected in the new climate, all prediction models forecast about 2-4°C amplification in temperature over the next century. Insects are poikilothermic creature which cannot thermo-regulate the body temperature to their surroundings. Temperature is probably the single most important environmental factor influencing their behaviour, distribution, development, survival, and reproduction. Global warming and climate change will trigger major changes in diversity and abundance of arthropods, geographical distribution of insect pests, population dynamics, insect biotypes, activity and abundance of natural enemies, species extinction, and efficacy of crop protection technologies. Changes in temperature and relative humidity are likely having a reflective effect on geographical distribution and incidence of insect pests. Temperature increases associated with climate changes could result in a geographical expansion of pests, changes viz; aestivation/hibernation, population growth rates, loss of resistance in cultivars containing temperature-sensitive genes,

1. Senior Research Fellow, Division of Crop Protection, ICAR-Indian Institute of Pulses Research, Kanpur - 208 024, U.P., (India).
2. Principal Scientist Entomology, Division of Crop Protection, ICAR-Indian Institute of Pulses Research, Kanpur - 208 024, U.P., (India).
3. Senior Research Fellow, Division of Social Sciences, ICAR-Indian Institute of Pulses Research, Kanpur - 208 024, U.P., (India).

crop-pest synchrony, natural enemy-insect-host interactions and changes in the diversity of natural enemy complex as well. Pest outbreaks are more likely to occur with stressed plants because, under such circumstances, the plant defensive system is compromised and the resistance to pest infestation is lowered as well. Low temperature are often more important than high temperature in determining global geographical distribution of insect pests. Eventually, species which are currently limited by low temperature, increasing temperature may result in greater ability to overwinter at higher latitudes and may increase a pest's chance to extending its range.

INTRODUCTION

Agriculture, particularly in India with nearly 60 per cent rainfed area, has been a highly risky venture with vagaries of monsoon besides the interplay of other abiotic and biotic factors. Climate change is set to compound the daunting complex challenges already being faced by agriculture. Therefore, concerted efforts are required for mitigation and adaptation to reduce the vulnerability of Indian agriculture to the adverse impacts of climate change and making it more resilient. However, there are lot of uncertainties about the assessment of impact, adaptation and mitigation of climate change in agriculture. There is a need to develop and apply a standard methodology across the board for various studies related to climate change and agriculture. Climate change refers to a change of climate that is attributed directly or indirectly by human (anthropogenic) activity that alters the composition of the global atmosphere and climate variability observed over comparable time periods. Climate encompasses the long-run pattern of numerous meteorological factors (*e.g.* Temperature, humidity, atmospheric pressure, wind, rainfall, sunshine etc.,) in a given location or larger region. Past some decades, the gaseous composition of earth's atmosphere is undergoing a significant change, largely through increased emissions from – energy sector, Industry sector, agriculture sectors, widespread deforestation, fast changes in land use, land management practices. These anthropogenic activities are resulting in an increased emission of active gases, *viz;* carbon dioxide (CO,), methane (CH,) and nitrous oxide (N, O), chloroflourocarbons (CFC_S) popularly known as the 'greenhouse gases' (GHGs). According to inter-governmental Panel on climate change (IPCC), the global mean surface air temperature has increased by nearly 1°C over the past centuary, and it is expected to continue to increase by 1-3°C by the middle to end of 21st Century (IPCC, 2007) in response to two-folds increase in atmospheric carbon dioxide and other GHG_S (Table 7.1). The global warming is expected to lead to other regional and global changes in the climate-related parameters such as: rainfall, soil moisture, and sea level. (IPCC, 2001). Climate change also influences the ecology of weeds, pests and disease, with possible implications for crop protection and pesticide use. Therefore, it is highly expected that, the major drivers of climate change *i.e.*, elevated CO_2, increased temperature and depleted soil moisture can impact population dynamics of insect-pests. The occurrence of climate changes is evident from increase in global average temperature, changes in the rainfall pattern and extreme climatic events. These seasonal and long-term changes would affect the fauna, flora and population dynamics of insect pests (Srivastava *et al.* 2010, Pandey 2008). The abiotic parameters are known to have direct impact on insect population dynamics through modulation of developmental rates, survival, fecundity, voltinism and dispersal. Additionally, changes in the distribution of insect pests will be greatly influenced by changes in the range of host crops because of distribution of a pest is also dependant on the availability of a host. Undeniably, whether or not a pest would move with a crop in to a new area would depend on other environmental conditions *i.e.,* presence of overwintering sites, soil type and moisture. In this episode population of pod borers, *Helicoverpa armigera* and *Maruca vitrata,* might move to the temperate regions and attain higher densities in the tropics, leading to greater damage to pulses and other crops. The pod wasp, *Tanaostigmodes cajaninae,* podfly, *Melanagromyza obtusa,* pod borer weevil, *Apion clavipes,* pod bug *Clavigralla* spp., are becoming major pests infesting pulses. For all the pest species, higher temperatures below the species' upper lethal limit could result in faster development rates and therefore more rapid increase of pest populations at the time to reproductive maturity is reduced. Over and above to the direct effect of temperature changes on development rates, increase in food quality as a result of plant stress may result in dramatic increases in the development rate of pest populations. On the other hands, changes in the climate variability and increase in temperature will modify the pest distribution and how theses need to be managed, having consequences on the economics of pest control measures and the economic thresholds.

Causes of Climate Change

There are several causes of climate change. Among them some are as following:

(A) Natural Causes

- Continental drift.
- Volcanoes.
- The Earth's Tilts.
- Ocean Currents.
- Intensity of Solar Radiation.

(B) Anthropogenic Causes

- Green Houses Gases.
- Carbon dioxide (CO_2).
- Methane (CH_4).
- Nitrous oxide (NO_2).

- Chloro floro carbons (CFCs).
- Ozone (O_3).
- Water Vapors (H_2O).
- Land Use Change.
- Deforestation.
- Urbanization.

Table 7.1: Abundance and lifetime of greenhouse gases in the atmosphere

Parameters	CO_2	CH_4	N_2O	Chlorofluorocarbons
Average concentration 100 years ago (ppbV)	290,000	900	270	0
Current concentration (ppbV) (2007)	380,000	1,774	319	3-5
Projected concentration in the year 2030 (ppbV)	400,000-500,000	2,800-3,000	400-500	3-6
Atmospheric lifetime (year)	5-200	9-15	114	75
Global warming potential (100 years relative to CO_2)	1	25	298	4750-10900

Source: IPCC (2007).

Elevated CO_2 Levels and Insects

The climate change impacts on pests may include shifts in species distributions with species shifting their ranges to higher latitudes and elevations, changes in phenology with life cycles beginning earlier in spring and continuing later in autumn, increase in population growth rates and number of generations, change in migratory behaviour, alterations in crop pest synchrony and natural enemy-pest interaction, and changes in interspecific interactions (Sutherst, 1996; Root *et al.* 2003). Changes in community structure and extinction of some species are also expected (Thomas *et al.* 2004).

Impact of CO_2 on insect population via host plants can be studied through open top chambers (OTCs) and free air carbon dioxide enrichment (FACE) Ainsworth and Long (2005). OTCs are essentially plastic enclosures placed around a sample of an ecosystem. Air is drawn into a box by a fan, enriched with CO_2, and blown through the chamber. Open-top chambers are relatively inexpensive to build because they consist simply of an aluminium frame covered by panels of polyvinyl chloride plastic film. The FACE technology facilitates modification of the environment around growing plants to future concentrations of atmospheric CO2 under natural conditions of temperature, precipitation, pollination, wind, humidity, and sunlight. FACE field data represent plant responses to concentrations of atmospheric CO_2 in a natural setting. Global atmospheric carbon dioxide (CO_2) levels continue to increase rapidly, mainly because of the burning of fossil fuels. The atmospheric concentration of CO_2 has increased from a preindustrial level (1750) of 270 ppm to a current level of 394 ppm, an increase of 124 ppm, or 45 per cent (Global Carbon Budget.org). Most studies indicate that CO_2 levels will at least double from pre-industrial levels over the next five to ten decades. This increase represents one of the most large-scale and wide-reaching perturbations to the environment ((IPCC. 1990a, IPCC. 1990b, IPCC, 2007). Over the past 20 years of research carried out by many of authors across the globe generated general understanding of the direct effects of increasing CO_2 concentration on plant growth and function (Table 7.2). The most commonly observed effects of elevated CO2 on insects' are indirect (Murray *et al.* 2013). These indirect effects occur as a result of changes in plant physiology and biochemistry (Fig. 7.1). Elevated CO_2 levels generally lead to the accumulation of carbohydrates in the leaf tissue of plants through increased photosynthetic rates, causing an increase in leaf carbon (C) to nitrogen (N) ratio (Rao *et al.* 2009, Chander *et al.* 2003, Coley and Markham 1998 Collier, *et al.* 1991 Corlett and LaFrankie 1998). Since N is considered a limiting nutrient for insects this dilution of N reduces the nutritional quality of the leaves.

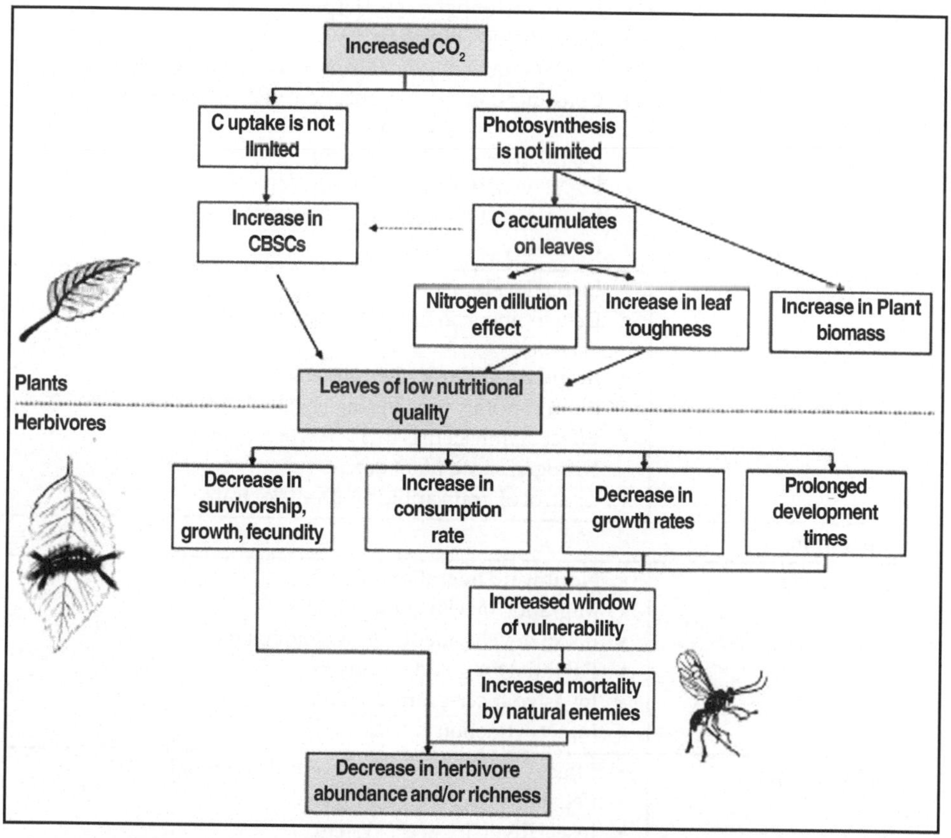

Fig. 7.1: **Predicted effects of elevated CO_2 conditions on plants and insect herbivores (C: carbon, CBSCs, carbon-based secondary compounds).**

Environmental change is anticipated to negatively, affecting both plant and insect populations. Herbivores are primary consumers and get energy from plants or plant products. The impact of climate change on herbivorous insects can have far-reaching consequences for ecosystem processes and may alter significantly. In many cases, the changes caused by enriched CO2 bring about a reduction in its quality as a food source to herbivores, which affects herbivore performance. As herbivores are affected, so are high ertrophic levels organisms (secondary consumers) are also get affected. While the effects of elevated CO_2 on interactions between individual herbivore species and their host plants are becoming better understood, little is known about how these effects may flow on to secondary consumers (predators and parasitoids) and thus affect whole food webs. Atmospheric CO2 levels may affect the performance of natural enemies and/or susceptibility of prey directly or indirectly.

Table 7.2: Showing direct Impact of CO_2 and temperature on Insect-pest

CO_2	Effect on Insect-pests
(A) Increasing	• Food consumption by caterpillars • Reproduction of aphids • Effect of foliar application of *Bacillus thuringiensis* • Consumption and N utilization efficiency in pine saw fly and Gypsy moth • Larval growth in pine saw fly • Pupal weight in blue butterfly • Feeding and growth rate in tobacco caterpillar • Fecundity of aphids on cotton
(B) Decreasing	• Insect development rates • Development and pupal weight in *Chrysanthemum leaf miner* • Response to alarm pheromones by aphids • Lipid concentration in small heath Parasitism • Effect of transgenics to *Bacillus thuringiensis* • Nitrogen based plant defence • Control of grain aphids with sticky traps
Temperature	
(A) Increasing	• Northward migration • Migration up elevation gradient • Insect development rate and ovipositions • Potential for insect outbreaks • Invasive species introductions • Insect extinction
(B) Decreasing	• Effectiveness of insect bio-control buy fungi • Reliability of economic threshold levels • Insect diversity in ecosystem • Parasitism

Source: Das *et al*. 2011; Parmesan, 2006; Bale *et al*. 2002; Thomas *et al*. 2004.

Impacts of Climate Change on Insect-Pest

Insects are the most diverse group of animals on Earth an estimated 6-10 million. The major predictions about impacts of climate change on insect-pests are compiled and presented below:

Loss of Ecological Biodiversity

The biodiversity signifies the biological wealth of habitat by means of species richness in an ecosystem. For sustainable agriculture development in any given country, biodiversity is of paramount. South Asia in general and India in particular is blessed with ecologically rich natural and crop-related biodiversity due to its unique geographic location and diversified climatic conditions (Fig. 7.2). India is one of the 12 mega-biodiversity centers with three out of 34 biodiversity hotspots in the world. Due to change in the climate pattern in recent decades owing to increasing industrialization and over-exploitation of natural resources for various anthropogenic developmental activities, many species of plants, animals and insects are decreasing at an alarming (Porter *et al.* 1991, Lange *et al.* 2006 Kiritani 2006). The loss of biological diversity is still accelerating which may reduce the ecosystem's resilience to the climatic changes. Insects comprise the largest group of animal kingdom and play vital role in providing various ecosystem services (Altieri 1994). The insect diversity in a habitat indicates the health status of an ecosystem as they are very good indicators of environmental change, play an important role in food chains, are excellent pollinators for many of the economically important and contribute directly to the human economies through valuable products like: silk, lac, honey and wax. The climatc change may affect the relative abundance of different insect species and the species unable to adapt the changes may be lost in the due course of time. The loss of biodiversity may impact negatively the structure, composition and functioning of ecosystems and wildlife habitat leading to outbreaks of destructive insect-pests and disease.

Increased Overwintering Survival

Being poikilotherms, insects have limited ability of homeostasis with external temperature changes. Hence they have developed a range of strategies such as: behavioural avoidance through migration and physiological adaptations like diapause to support life under thermally stressful environments. Diapause is a period of suspended developmental activities, the manifestation of which is governed by environmental factors like: temperature, humidity and photoperiod. As an adaptive trait, diapause plays vital role in seasonal regulation of insect life cycles because of which the insects have better advantage to survive great deal of environmental adversities. There are two main types of insect diapause; aestivation and hibernation to sustain life under high and low temperature extremes respectively. Global warming is occurring notably in winter than in summer and is greatest at high latitudes Looking at the past 100 years climate profile of India, warming was more pronounced

Fig. 7.2: **Showing the indirect effects of climate change are affiliated with host plants, competitors and natural enemies**

during winter season and it was the minimum and not the maximum temperature where significant increase was observed. The temperature in India is expected to increase by 1-5°C within next 100 years. Thus, insects undergoing a winter diapause are likely to experience the most significant changes in their thermal environment. Accelerated metabolic rates at higher temperatures shorten the duration of insect diapause due to faster depletion of stored nutrient. Warming in winter may cause delay in onset and early summer may lead to faster termination of diapause in insects, which can then resume their active growth and development.

Increase in Number of Generations

Temperature being the single most important regulating factor for global increase in temperature within certain favourable range may accelerate the rates of development, reproduction and survival in tropical and subtropical insects (Fig. 7.3). Consequently, insects will be capable of completing more number of generations per year and ultimately it will result in more crops.

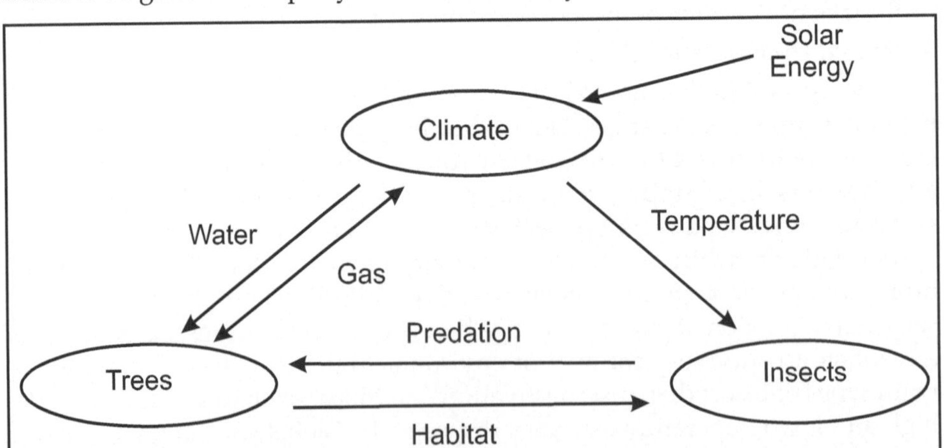

Fig. 7.3: **Showing the interaction between insect-pests and climate change**

Risk of Introducing Invasive Alien Species

Even though the causes of biological invasions are manifold and multifaceted, changes in abiotic and/or biotic components of the environment (climate change, biological control) are recognised as primary drivers of species invasion. Globalization and liberalization of world agricultural trade coupled with the rapid transport and communication means now-a-days, have substantially and plausibly increased the chances of exotic introductions.

Reduced Effectiveness of Biological Control Agents

Biological control of insect-pests is one of the important components of integrated pest management, safeguarding the ecosystem. Natural enemies of crop pests *viz;* predators, parasitoids and pathogens are prompt density responsive in their action subjected to the action of abiotic components. Being tiny and delicate, natural enemies of the insect-pests are more sensitive to the climatic extremes like: heat, cold, wind and rains. Precipitation changes can also affect predators, parasites and pathogens of insect-pests resulting in a complex dynamics. With changing climate, incidence of entomopathogenic fungi might be favoured by prolonged humidity conditions and obstinately be reduced by drier conditions. Natural enemy and host insect populations may respond differently to changes in climate. Hosts may pass though vulnerable life stages more quickly at higher temperatures, reducing the window of opportunity for parasitism which may give great set back to the survival and multiplication of parasitoids.

Effect of Climate on Pest Population via Natural Enemies

Shifts in climate can differentially affect the development rates of pest and natural enemy population. Hence, in biological control systems of insect pests, utilizing parasitoids, the temperature response of the parasitoids determines their success in controlling the pest population. The egg predator *Cyrtorhinus lividipennis* of brown plant hopper (BPH) had increased instantaneous attack rates and decreased handling times with increasing temperatures until 32°C. At 35°C, the attack rate and handling time decreased drastically. This implies that predator activity is likely to increase with increasing temperatures up to a critical temperature of about 35°C (Kobayashi *et al.* 2006).

Effect of Rainfall

Distribution and frequency of rainfall may also affect the incidence of pests directly as well as through changes in humidity levels. It is being predicted that under the climate change, frequency of rainfall would decline while its intensity would increase. This would lead to heavy showers and floods on one hand and drought spells on the other. Lever (1969) had analysed the relationship between outbreaks of armyworm and to a lesser extent *Spodoptera mauritia* (Boisd.) and rainfall from 1938 to 1965 and observed that all but three outbreaks occurred when rainfall exceeded the average 89 cm. The effect of rainfall on pests can be studied by simulating various rainfall intensities through sprinklers. Aphid population on wheat and other crops was adversely affected by rainfall and sprinkler irrigation (Daebeler and Hinz, 1977; Chander, 1998, 2009). Masters *et al.* (1998) have carried out novel manipulations of local climate to investigate how warmer winters with either wetter or drier summers would affect the homopteran insects – a major component of the insect fauna of grasslands.

Effect of Global Warming on the Activity and Abundance of Natural Enemies

Relationships between insect pests and their natural enemies will change as a result of global warming, resulting in both increases and decreases in the status of individual pest species. Changes in temperature will also alter the timing of diurnal activity patterns of different groups of insects (Young, 1982), and changes in interspecific interactions could also alter the effectiveness of natural enemies for pest management (Hill and Dymock 1989). Quantifying the effect of climate change on the activity and effectiveness of natural enemies for pest management will be a major concern in future pest management programmes. The majority of insects are benign to agro-ecosystems, and there is considerable evidence to suggest that this is due to population control through interspecific interactions among insect pests and their natural enemies – pathogens, parasites, and predators (Price 1987). Oriental armyworm, *Mythimna separata* (Walk.) populations increase during extended periods of drought (which is detrimental to the natural enemies), followed by heavy rainfall because of the adverse effects of drought on the activity and abundance of the natural enemies of this pest (Sharma *et al.* 2002). Aphid abundance increases with an increase in CO_2 and temperature, however, the parasitism rates remain unchanged in elevated CO_2. Temperatures up to 25°C will enhance the control of aphids by coccinellids (Freier and Triltsch 1996). Temperature not only affects the rate of insect development, but also has a profound effect on fecundity and sex ratio of parasitoids (Dhillon and Sharma, 2008, 2009). The interactions between insect pests and their natural enemies need to be studied carefully to devise appropriate methods for using natural enemies in pest management.

Impact of Climate Change on Geographic Distribution and Population Dynamics of Insect Pests

Climate change will have am major effect on geographic distribution of insect pests, and low temperatures are often more important than high temperatures in determining geographical distribution of insect pests (Hill 1987). Increasing temperatures may result in a greater ability to overwinter in insect species limited by low temperatures at higher latitudes, extending their geographical range (EPA 1989; Hill and Dymock 1989; Elphinstone and Toth 2008), and sudden outbreaks of insect pests can wipe out certain crop species, and also encourage the invasion by exotic species. Spatial shifts in distribution of crops under changing climatic conditions will also influence the distribution of insect pests in a geographical region (Parry and Carter 1989). Some plant species may be unable to follow the climate change, resulting in extinction of species that are specific to particular hosts (Thomas *et al.* 2004). However, whether or not an insect pest would move with a crop into a new habitat will depend on other environmental conditions such as: the presence of overwintering sites, soil type, and moisture, *e.g.*, populations of the corn earworm, *Heliothis zea* (Boddie) in the North America might move to higher latitudes/altitudes, leading to greater damage in maize and other crops (EPA 1989). For all the insect species, higher temperatures, below the species upper threshold limit, will result in faster development and rapid increase in pest populations as the time to reproductive maturity will be reduced considerably. In addition to the direct effects of temperature changes on development rates, improvement in food quality due to abiotic stress may result in dramatic increases in growth of some insect species (White 1984), while the growth of certain insect pests may be adversely affected (Maffei *et al.* 2007). Pest outbreaks are more likely to occur with stressed plants as a result of weakening of plants' defensive system, and thus, increasing the level of susceptibility to insect pests (Rhoades 1985).

Overwintering of insect pests will increase as a result of climate change, producing larger spring populations as a base for a build-up in numbers in the following season. These may be vulnerable to parasitoids and predators if the latter also overwinter more readily. Diamond back moth, *Plutella xylostella* L. overwintered in Alberta in 1994 (Dosdall 1994), and if overwintering becomes common, the status of this insect as a pest in North America will increase dramatically. There may also be increased dispersal of airborne insect species in response to atmospheric disturbances. Many insects such as: *Helicoverpa* spp., are migratory, and therefore, may be well adapted to exploit new opportunities by moving rapidly into new areas as a result of climate change (Sharma 2005, 2010).

Approaches for Mitigation and Adaptation to Combat Adverse Impacts of Climate Change

The global climate change and extreme weather fluctuations are the most threatening challenges of this century to agriculture and allied activities. Impact of climate change due to increased intensity and frequency of storms, drought and flooding, precipitation variance, and increase in temperature and CO_2 have serious implications for global food production and food security (Chattopadhyay and Hulme 1997, IPCC 2007). Agriculture in India will be under severe constraints as the productivity of crops is predicted to depress by 10-40 per cent by 2080-2100. This will not only put a severe strain on national economy but will also pose a formidable challenge to achieving food security at the national level. Most of the standard climate models predict rise in temperature across the regions where pulses are grown. With rising temperature, the host of biotic and abiotic stresses is predicted to become more severe in terms of their scope and spectrum, and adversely impacting productivity and stability of production of pulse crops (Fig. 7.4). Such a scenario emanating from the climate change presents a veritable challenge to food and feed economy of the country as large population of India is heavily dependent on agriculture for food and income. To meet these emerging challenges of climate change, there is an urgent need for developing policy framework for implementing approaches for mitigation and adaptation to combat adverse impacts of climate change and climate variability on Indian agriculture especially dryland areas which account for 40 per cent of the total food production of the country and therefore, there is a need to:

- Assist farmers in coping with current climatic risks by providing value-added weather services to farmers. Farmers can adapt to climate changes to some degree by shifting planting dates, choosing varieties with different growth duration, or changing crop rotations (Aggarwal 2009, Bhatia 2005).

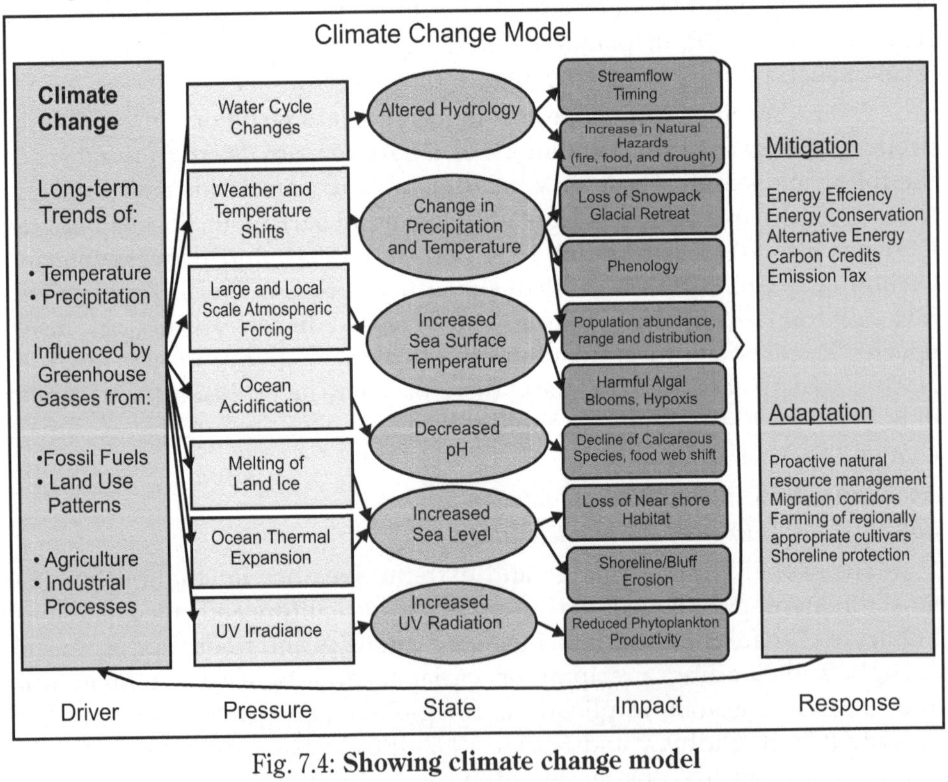

Fig. 7.4: **Showing climate change model**

- An Early warning system should be put in place to monitor changes in pest and disease outbreaks. The overall pest control strategy should be based on integrated pest management because it takes care of multiple pests in a given climatic scenario.

- Participatory and formal plant breeding to develop climate-resilient crop varieties that can tolerate higher temperatures, drought and salinity.
- Developing short-duration crop varieties that can mature before the peak heat phase set.
- Selecting genotype in crops that have a higher per day yield potential to counter yield loss from heat-induced reduction in growing periods.
- Preventive measures for drought that include on-farm reservoirs in medium lands, growing of pulses and oilseeds instead of rice in uplands, ridges and furrow system in cotton crops, growing of intercrops in place of pure crops in uplands, land grading and leveling, stabilization of field bunds by stone and grasses, graded line bunds, contour trenching for runoff collection, conservation furrows, mulching and more application of Farm yard manure (FYM).
- Efficient water use such as: frequent but shallow irrigation, drip and sprinkler irrigation for high value crops, irrigation at critical stages.
- Efficient fertilizer use such as: optimum fertilizer dose, split application of nitrogenous and potassium fertilizers, deep placement, use of *neem, karanja* products and other such nitrification inhibitors, liming of acid soils, use of micronutrients such as: zinc and boron, use of sulphur in oilseed crops, integrated nutrient management.
- Seasonal weather forecasts could be used as a supportive measure to optimize planting and irrigation patterns.
- Provide greater coverage of weather linked agriculture-insurance.
- Intensify the food production system by improving the technology and input delivery system.
- Adopt resource conservation technologies such as: no-tillage, laser land leveling, direct seeding of rice and crop diversification which will help in reducing in the global warming potential (Bohle *et al.* 1994, Chatterjee 1998). Crop diversification can be done by growing non-paddy crops in rain fed uplands to perform better under prolonged soil moisture stress in kharif.
- Develop a long-term land use plan for ensuring food security and climatic resilience.
- National grid grain storages at the household/community level to the district level must be established to ensure local food security and stabilize prices.
- Provide incentives to farmers for resource conservation and efficiency by providing credit to the farmers for transition to adaptation technologies.
- Provide technical, institutional and financial support for establishment of community banks of food, forage and seed.

- Provide more funds to strengthen research for enhancing adaptation and mitigation capacity of agriculture.
- Developing cultivars tolerant to heat and salinity stress.
- Resistant cultivars to flood and drought.
- Modifying crop management practices.
- Improving water management.
- Adopting new farm techniques such as: Resource Conserving Technologies (RCTs).
- Crop diversification.
- Improving pest management.
- Better weather forecasting.
- Crop insurance and harnessing the indigenous technical knowledge of farmers.
- Developing climate-ready crops.

Adaptation Strategies to Climate Change

- Diversification of crop and livestock varieties.
- Integrated pest management.
- Using available early warning system for insect pest.
- Biological control measures.
- Utilization of indigenous traditional knowledge base for Pest control.
- Soil solarization technique.
- Breeding for pest, disease and drought resistance varieties.
- Careful tracking of geographical distribution of pest.
- Phytosanitary regulations to prevent or limit the introduction to risky insect pest.

Conclusions

The greatest challenge facing humanity in the coming century will be the necessity to double our global food using less land area, less water, less soil nutrients, droughts from global warming. The exact impacts of climate change on insects and pathogens are rather uncertain. Global warming and climate change will have serious consequences on diversity and abundance of arthropods, and the extent of losses due to insect pests, which will impact both crop production and food security. Prediction of changes in geographical distribution and population dynamics of insect pests will be useful to adapt the pest management strategies to mitigate the adverse effects of climate change on crop production (Khan *et al.* 2009, Lal *et al.* 1998 and Priyadarshi 2009). Pest outbreaks might occur more frequently, particularly during extended periods of drought, followed by heavy rainfall. Some of the components of pest management such as: host plant resistance, biopesticides, natural enemies, and synthetic chemicals will be rendered less effective as a result of increase in temperatures and UV radiation, and decrease in relative humidity. The climate change, as realized through trends of temperature rise and increased CO_2 concentration, is a major concern. Effect of climate change is more in temperate areas; it can affect the range expansion, host and enemy synchrony and interspecific competition. Among the various abiotic factors, temperature is an important force to drive the natural enemy population. It can cause the direct effects like: survival, growth and development, voltinism, longevity, parasitism and dispersal of natural enemies. The CO_2 cause indirect effect through host nutrient alteration and it has both positive and negative effects.

Climate change will also alter the interactions between the insect pests and their host plants. As result, some of the cultivars that are resistant to insect pests, may exhibit susceptible reaction under global warming. Adverse effects of climate change on the activity and effectiveness of natural enemies will be a major concern in future pest management programmes. On the other hand, higher temperature would affect the change of agro-ecosystem in a region, and the cultural system and natural enemy population would also be changed following the global warming. Therefore, there is a need to have a concerted look at the likely effects of climate change on crop protection and long-term conservation bio control agents, which need greater attention to understand and address these issues through more research.

REFERENCES

Aggarwal, P.K. (2009). Executive Summary, in P.K. Aggarwal (ed.), *Global Climate Change and Indian Agriculture: Case Studies from the ICAR Network Project,* Indian Agricultural Research Institute Publication, New Delhi.

Ainsworth EA and Long SP (2005) What have we learned from 15 years of free air CO_2 Enrichment (FACE)? A Meta Analytic Review of the Responses of Photosynthesis, canopyproperties and Plant Production to Rising CO_2. *New Phytol.* 165: 351-372.

Altieri, M.A. (1994). Biodiversity and Pest Management in Agroecosystems. New York, USA: Haworth Press. 185 pp.

Bhatia, M.S. (2005). Viability of Rainfed Agriculture in Semi-Arid Regions, NABARD Occasional Paper no. 40, Department of Economic Analysis and Research, National Bank for Agriculture and Rural Development, Mumbai.

Bohle, Hans G., Downing, Thomas E., and Watts, Michael J. (1994). Climate Change and Social Vulnerability: Towards a Sociology and Geography of Food Insecurity, *Global Environmental Change,* 4, 1, pp. 37-48.

Chatterjee, A. (1998). Simulating the Impact of Increase in Temperature and CO_2 on Growth and Yield of Maize and Sorghum, M.Sc. thesis (unpublished), Indian Agricultural Research Institute, New Delhi; as cited in Mall, Singh, Gupta, Srinivasan and Rathore (2006).

Chattopadhyay, N., and Hulme, M. (1997). Evaporation and Potential Evapotranspiration in India under Conditions of Recent and Future Climate Change, *Agricultural and Forest Meteorology,* 87, pp. 55-73.

Chander S (1998). Infestation of Root and Foliage/Earhead Aphids on wheat in Relation Topredators. *Indian J. Agric. Sci.* 68(11): 754-755.

Chander S, Reji G and Aggarwal PK (2009). Assessing Impact of Climate Change on Rice Gundhi Bug using a Population Dynamics Simulation Model. In: *Global Climate Change and Indian Agriculture: Case Studies from the ICAR Network Project*. Ed: P.K. Aggarwal. ICAR, New Delhi, pp. 60-65.

Chander S., Singh VS and Kalra N (2003). Aphid Infestation on Barley in Relation to Climatic Variability. *Proc. National Symposium on Frontier Areas of Entomological Research*, 5-7 Nov. Entomology Division, Indian Agricultural Research Institute, New Delhi, pp. 37-38.

Coley, P.D. and Markham, A. (1998). Possible Effects of Climate Change on Plant/ herbivore Interactions in Moist Tropical Forests. *Climatic Change* 39:455-472.

Collier, R.H., Finch, S., Phelps, K., and Thompson, A.R. (1991). Possible Impact of Global Warming on Cabbage Root Fly (*Delia radicum*) Activity in the UK. *Annals of Applied Biology* 118: 261-271.

Corlett, T.T. and LaFrankie, Jr. J.V. (1998). Potential Impacts of Climate Change on Tropical Asian forests through and Influences on phenology. *Climate Change* 39: 439-454.

Daebeler F and Hinz B (1977). Compensation of Aphid Injury to Sugarbeet by Means of Supplementary Rain. *Arch Phytopathol. Pflanzenschutz*, 13(3): 199-205.

Dhaliwal, G.S., Arora, R., and Dhawan, A.K. (2004). Crop Losses due to Insect Pests in Indian Agriculture: An Update. *Indian Journal of Ecology* 31: 1-7.

Dhillon, M.K. and Sharma, H.C. (2007). Effect of Storage Temperature and duration on Viability of Eggs of *Helicoverpa armigera* (Lepidoptera: Noctuidae). *Bulletin of Entomological Research* 97: 55-59.

Dhillon, M.K. and Sharma, H.C. (2008). Temperature and *Helicoverpa armigera* Food Influence Survival and Development of the ichneumonid parasitoid, *Campoletis chlorideae*. *Indian Journal of Plant Protection* 36: 240-244.

Dhillon, M.K. and Sharma, H.C. (2009). Temperature Influences the Performance and Effectiveness of Field and Laboratory Strains of the ichneumonid parasitoid, *Campoletis chlorideae*. *BioControl* 54: 743-750.

Elphinstone, J. and Toth, I.K. (2008). *Erwinia chrysanthemi* (*Dikeya* spp.) - The Facts. Oxford, U.K: Potato Council.

Environment Protection Agency (EPA). (1989). *The Potential Effects of Global Climate Change on the United States*. Vol 2: National Studies. Review of the Report to Congress, US Environmental Protection Agency, Washington DC, 261 pp.

Freier, B. and Triltsch, H. (1996). Climate Chamber Experiments and Computer Simulations on the Influence of Increasing Temperature on wheat-aphid-predator interactions. *Aspects of Applied Biology* 45:293-298.

Hill, D.S. (1987). *Agricultural Insects Pests of Temperate Regions and Their Control*. Cambridge, UK: Cambridge University Press. 659 pp.

Hill, M.G. and Dymock, J.J. (1989). *Impact of Climate Change: Agricultural/Horticultural Systems*. SIR Entomology Division Submission to the New Zealand Climate Change Programme. Auckland, New Zealand: Department of Scientific and Industrial Research. 16 pp.

IPCC. 1990a. Climate Change: *The IPCC Scientific Assessment*. Intergovernmental Panel on Climate Change. Geneva and Nairobi, Kenya: World Meteorological Organization and UN Environment Programme. 365 pp.

IPCC. (1990b). *The Potential Impacts of Climate Change on Agriculture and Forestry.* Intergovernmental Panel on Climate Change. Geneva and Nairobi, Kenya: World Meteorological Organization and UN Environment Programme. 55 pp.

IPCC, (2001). Climate Change 2001: The Scientific Basis Contribution of Working Group I to the third Assessment Report of the Intergovernmental Panel on Climate Change (IPCC). Cambridge University Press, Cambridge http://www.grida.no/climate/ipcc_tar/.

IPCC (2007). In: Solomon, S., Qin, D., Manning, M., Chen, Z., Marquis, M., Averyt, K.B., Tignor, M., Miller, H. L. (eds.), 2007. Climate Change 2007: The Physical Science Basis. Contribution of *Climate Change and Its Impact on Groundwater Resources* 59 Working Group I to the Fourth Assessment Report of the Intergovernmental Panel on Climate Change, Cambridge University Press, Cambridge, UK and New York, NY, USA, 966 p.

Khan, S., Kumar, S., Hussain, M.Z., and Kalra, N. (2009). Climate Change, Climate Variability and Indian Agriculture: Impacts Vulnerability and Adaptation Strategies, in S.N. Singh (ed.), *Climate Change and Crops, Environmental Science and Engineering*, pp. 19-38.

Kiritani, K., (2006). Predicting Impacts of Global Warming on Population Dynamics and Distribution of Arthropods in Japan. *Popln. Ecol.*, 48: 5 12.

Kobayashi T., Ishiguro K., Nakajima T., Kim H.Y., Okada M. and Kobayashi K. (2006). Effects of Elevated Atmospheric CO_2 Concentration on the Infection of Rice Blast and Sheath Blight. *Phytopathology*, 96: 425-31.

Lal, M., Singh, K.K., Srinivasan, G., Rathore, L.S., and Saseendran, A.S. (1998). Vulnerability of Rice and Wheat Yields in NW-India to Future Change in Climate, *Agricultural and Forest Meteorology*, 89, pp. 101-14.

Lange, H., B. Okland and P. Krokene, (2006). Thresholds in the Life Cycle of the spruce bark beetle under Climate Change. *Int. J. for Complex Systems*, 1648: 1-10.

Lever RJW (1969). Do Armyworm follow the Rain? *Wild Crops*, 21: 351-352.

Maffei, M.E., Mithofer, A., and Boland, W. (2007). Insects Feeding on Plants: Rapid Signals and Responses Proceeding Induction of phytochemical Release. *Phytochemistry* 68: 2946-2959.

Masters G.J., Brown V.K., Clarke I.P., Whittaker J.B. and Hollier J.A. (1998). Direct and Indirect Effects.

Pandey, A.K. and C.P.M. Tripathi, (2008). Effect of Temperature on the Development, Fecundity, Progeny Sex Ratio and life-table 2 of *Campoletis chlorideae*, an endo-larval parasitoid of the pod borer, *Helicoverpa armigera*. Bio Control, 53: 461-471.

Parry, M.L. and Carter, T.R. (1989). An Assessment of the Effects of Climatic Change on Agriculture. *Climatic Change* 15: 95-116.

Price, P.W. (1987). The Role of Natural Enemies in Insect Populations. In: P. Barbosa and J.C. Schultz (Editors), *Insect Outbreaks*. San Diego, CA, USA: Academic Press. pp. 287-312.

Porter, J.H., M.L. Parry and T.R. Carter, (1991). The Potential Effects of Climatic Change on Agricultural Insect Pests. *Agrl and Forest Meteorol*, 57: 221-240.

Priyadarshi, Nitish., (2009). The Survival of Agriculture in a Destabilized Climate with Special Reference to India and its Jharkhand State.

Rao M.S., Srinivas K., Vanaja M., Rao GGSN, Venkateswarlu B and Ramakrishna, YS (2009). Host Plant (*Ricinus communis* Linn.) Mediated Effects of Elevated CO_2 on Growth Performance of two Insect folivores. *Curr. Sci.* 97(7): 1047-1054.

Rhoades, D.F. (1985). Offensive-defensive Interactions between Herbivores and Plants: Their Relevance in Herbivore Population Dynamics and Ecological Theory. *American Naturalist* 125: 205-238.

Root T.L., Price J.T., Hall K.R., Schneider S.H., Rozenzweig C and Pounds JA (2003). Fingerprints of Global Warming on Wild Animals and Plants. *Nature,* 421: 57-60. Roy DB and Sparks TH (2000). Phenology of British Butterflies and Climate Change. *Glob. Change Biol.* 6, 407-416.

Sharma, H.C., Dhillon, M.K., Kibuka, J., and Mukuru, S.Z. (2005). Plant Defense Responses to Sorghum Spotted Stem Borer, *Chilo partellus* under Irrigated and Drought Conditions. *International Sorghum and Millets Newsletter* 46: 49-52.

Sharma, H.C., Srivastava, C.P., Durairaj, C., and Gowda, C.L.L. (2010). Pest Management in Grain Legumes and Climate Change. In: *Climate Change and Management of Cool Season Grain Legume Crops* (Yadav, S.S., McNeil, D.L., Redden, R. and Patil, S.A., eds.). Dordrecht, The Netherlands: Springer Science + Business Media. pp. 115-140.

Sharma, H.C., Sullivan, D.J., and Bhatnagar, V.S. (2002). Population Dynamics of the Oriental Armyworm, *Mythimna separata* (Walker) (Lepidoptera: Noctuidae) in South-Central India. *Crop Protection* 21: 721-732.

Srivastava, C.P., N. Joshi and T.P. Trivedi, (2010). Forecasting of *Helicoverap armigera* Population and Impact of Climate Change. *Ind. J. Agrl. Sci.,* 80(1): 3-10.

Sutherst RW, Yonow T., Chakraborty S, O'Donnell C and White N (1996). A generic Approachto Defining Impacts of Climate Change on Pests, Weeds and Diseases in Australasia. In:*Greenhouse, Coping with Climate Change,* Ed: WJ Bouma, GI Pearman and MR Manning,CSIRO, Melbourne. pp. 281-307.

Thomas JA, Telfer MG, Roy DB, Preston CD, Greenwood JJD, Asher J and Fox R (2004). Comparative Losses of British Butterflies, Birds, and Plants and the Global Extinctioncrisis. *Science,* 303: 1879-1881.

White, T.C.R. (1984). The Abundance of Invertebrate Herbivores in Relation to the Availability of Nitrogen in Stressed Food Plants. *Oecologia* 63: 90-105.

Young, A.M. (1982). *Population Biology of Tropical Insects.* New York, USA: Plenum Press. 511 pp.

Page 151-170

AGRICULTURAL PRACTICES AND CROP DISEASE CONTROL
Edited by: **Dr. Alka Chauhan** and **Dr. Anubhuti Sharma**
Edition: **2017**
ISBN : 978-93-5056-859-0
Published by: **Discovery Publishing House Pvt. Ltd., New Delhi (India)**

8

Major Insect Pests and Diseases of Sugarcane in Indian Sub-tropics

Arti Katiyar[1*]
Shiva Kant Singh[2]
Sandeep Sharma[3]

ABSTRACT

Sugarcane, Saccharum officinarum Linnaeus is grown throughout the Tropics and Sub-tropics. It is one of the second largest major Industrial crops of India. It provides raw material to the sugar industries. Insect pests and disease are known to inflict considerable losses in sugarcane yield as well as sugar output. According to an estimate, sugarcane production declines by 20.0 and 19.0 per cent by insect pests and diseases respectively. As many as 288 insect pests and 76 non-insect pests are reported to harass this crop after sowing to till harvest and more than 50 diseases are reported in sugarcane. Sugarcane pests based on feeding habit may be grouped as sub-terranean pests-termites, white grubs, root aphid and mealy bugs, borers, sucking types-pyrilla, white flies, scale insects and mealy bugs defoliators-army worm, leaf rollers, skippers and gross hopper etc. The major diseases affecting sugarcane production are viz; Ret rot, mosaics, wilt, smut, ratoon stunting, grassy shoot disease and yellow leaf spots. To increase the crop productivity, management of insect-pests and diseases are of great significance. Due to diversity in agro-ecological conditions the importance of insect pests varies and therefore, management strategy should be adopted accordingly.

1. Senior Research Fellow, Division of Crop Protection, ICAR-Indian Institute of Pulses Research, Kanpur - 208 024, U.P., (India).
2. Principal Scientist Entomology, Division of Crop Protection, ICAR-Indian Institute of Pulses Research, Kanpur - 208 024, U.P., (India).
3. Senior Research Fellow, Division of Social Sciences, ICAR-Indian Institute of Pulses Research, Kanpur - 208 024, U.P., (India).

INTRODUCTION

Sugarcane, *Saccharum officinarum* L., is a perennial grass in the family *Poaceae* grown for its stem (cane) which is primarily used to produce sucrose. A mature stalk is typically composed of 11-16 per cent fiber, 12-16 per cent soluble sugars, 2-3 per cent non-sugars, and 63-73 per cent water. It is grown on about 5.3 million hectares, average yield 360 million tones and sugar production is about 252 million tones (Table 8.1). Brazil was the largest producer of sugar cane in the world. The next five major producers, in decreasing amounts of production, were India, China, Thailand, Pakistan and Mexico. The crop needs plenty of sun and water (min. 600mm of rain per annum, 1200 to 1800mm without irrigation, though water logging is not tolerated), pH of 6-7.5 is deemed as suitable soil. Some species of sugarcane are found to fix atmospheric nitrogen in the soil, in association with the bacterium *Acetobacter diazotrophicus*. Sugarcane is a main source of sugar to majority of human population; it is consumed in a variety of ways, ranging from direct chewing to extracted juice and from different forms of processed sugar to alcoholic beverages *i.e.*, rum, cachaca etc. A sugarcane crop is sensitive to the climate, soil type, irrigation, fertilizers, insect pests and diseases. It is attacked by a number of insect pests and diseases (Khanzada, 1993).

Sugarcane is cultivated in India in the tropical belt comprising the States of Maharashtra, Gujarat, Karnataka, Andhra Pradesh, Kerala and Tamil Nadu and the subtropical belt comprising the states of Punjab, Haryana, Uttar Pradesh, Bihar and Orissa. The planting season is from February to March in the subtropics and from January to February in the tropics. The soil in the subtropics is mostly alluvial and in the tropics clayey, loamy or sandy loam. In India sugarcane is cultivated on more than 3 million hectares for the manufacture of white sugar, Gur and Khandsari. Vegetative propagation encourages the accumulation and carry over of some pathogens in seed pieces. The factors that favour the prevalence of diseases are the continuous cultivation of sugarcane over large areas, the presence of the crop throughout the year, the genetic uniformity of the cane, the climate of tropical and subtropical regions and the unrestricted movement of seed material from one region to another. A conservative estimate of the total loss due to diseases of sugarcane ranged from 10 per cent to 15 per cent (Alexander 1982). However, total crop loss was seen in coastal Tamil Nadu due to a severe red rot outbreak recently. Though breeding strategies are being oriented toward development of disease resistant genotypes they have had limited success.

Table 8.1: Production, area under cultivation and yield of Sugarcane and Sugar in different marketing years

Crop/Marking Year	Area (Lakh Hectares)	Production (Lakh Tonnes)		Sugarcane Yield (Tonnes/Hectares)
		Sugarcane	Sugar	
2005-06	42.0	2811.7	193.2	66.92
2006-07	51.5	3555.2	282.0	69.02
2007-08	50.6	3481.9	263.0	68.88
2008-09	44.2	2850.3	146.8	64.55
2009-10	41.7	2923.0	188.0	70.02
2010-11	48.8	3423.8	243.5	70.09
2011-12	50.4	3610.4	263.4	71.67
2012-13	49.99	3412.0	258.5	68.25
2013-14	50.12	3521.4	245.5	69.84
2014-15	50.32	3565.61#	250.46	70.86

Source: Department of Food and Public Distribution (for Sugar Production) and Agricultural Statistics (for production and area of Sugarcane).

#: As per 3rd Advance Estimate (2014-15) of DAC released on 13/5/2015.

Major Insect Pests of Sugarcane

Sugarcane is infested by about 288 insects of which nearly two dozen causes heavy losses to the quality as well as quantity of the crop, as detail given below in (Table 8.2). The scenario of insect pests and diseases varies in sub-tropical and tropical belt of sugarcane. Top borer and stalk borer are found pre-dominantly in sub-tropical areas whereas internodes borer and early shoot borer and among disease rust and eye spot are prevalent in tropical region.

Early Shoot Borer (Chilo infescatellus)

- Attacks the crop during the early part of cane growth, before internode formation. It also attacks the cane stalks in the years of scanty rainfall.
- Larvae enter the cane laterally through one or more holes in the stalks (shoot) and bores downwards as well as upwards killing the growing point. Thus it cuts of the central leaf spindle, which eventually dries forming a dead heart. The dead heart can be easily pulled out. It emits an offensive odour (Duke and Eastwood 1997).
- Borer infestation during the germination phase kills the mother shoots resulting in the drying up of the entire clump. This leads to gaps in the field (Fig. 8.1).
- Causes heavy yield losses as it affects the plant stand/unit area. It also leads to canes of different age, which will be poor in juice quality, with less cane weight. When borer infects cane stalks, both yield and quality are reduced (Padmanabhan *et al*. 1992, Williams 1983 and Khanzada 1993).

Table 8.2: Showing major insect pests of sugarcane

Name of the Pest	Scientific Name	Plant Parts Infested	Peak Period of Activity
Termites	*Odentotermes obesus* Ramb.	Cane setts, shoots and canes.	Active in all seasons severe under drought conditions.
Shoot borer	*Chilo infuscatellus* Snellen.	Young Shoots and during drough the internodes.	March-June
Top borer	*Scirpophaga excerptalis* Wlk.	Shoot and grown up canes	June - December
Root borer	*Emmalocera depressella* Swinhoe	Young plants	April - June
Leaf hopper	*Pyrilla perpusilla* Wlk.	Leaf and leaf sheath	Summers with moderate to high humidity low rainfall or March-October
Lygaeid bug or black bug	*Cavelerius excavatus* Dist.	Leaf whorl mostly ratoons	Pre-mansoon period
Scale insect	*Melanaspis glomerata* (Green)	Internodes	May-December
Mealy bug	*Sacchariococcus sacchari* Cockerell.	Nodal region	Throughout the year but severe under drought
White fly	*Sacchariococcus sacchari* Cockerell.	Leaf	Well-manured and heavy crops or August-October
White grub	*Hilotrichia consanguinea* Blanch.	Roots, lower portion of stem covered by the soil	March to October (Mass emergence immediately after first heavy rain)

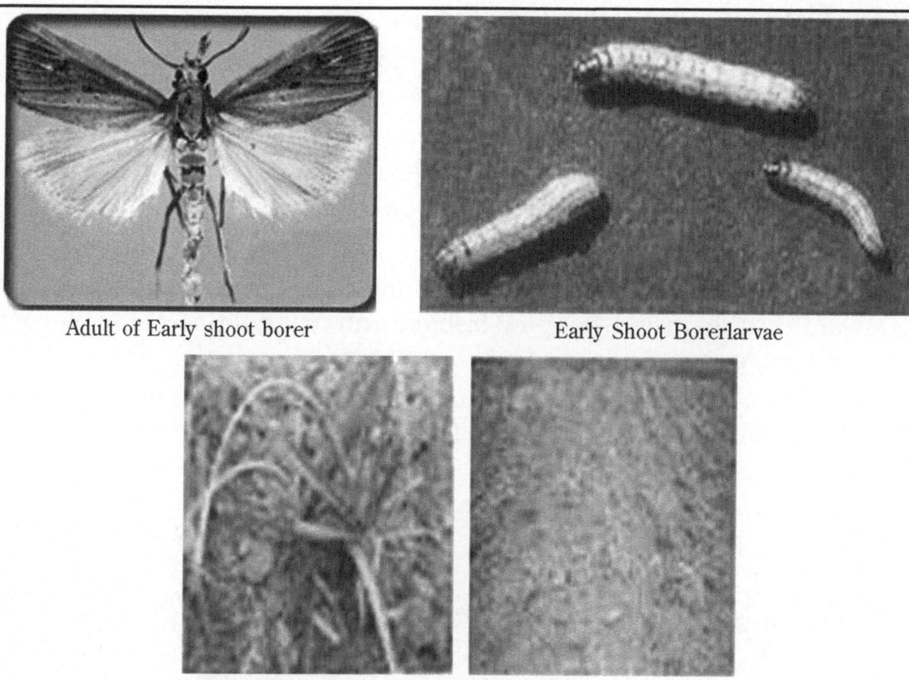

Adult of Early shoot borer — Early Shoot Borerlarvae

Dead Heart — Early Shoot Borer affected field

Fig. 8.1: **Showing different stages of *Early Shoot Borer* in sugarcane**

Management strategies

Following control measure should be adopted:

(i) Light earthing up of the tillers at the early stages of the crop (month old) during May and June reduces the incidence. A second earthing a month later reduces the borer attack considerably.

(ii) Mulching with cane trash at the early stages also has been reported to reduce the incidence and help in conserving moisture.

(iii) Cutting the affected tillers as close to the ground as possible and destroying them.

(iv) Soil application of granules of cartap hydrochloride at 1 kg a.i./ha at planting followed by another application on 45th day for late planted crop.

(v) Cartap hydrochloride 4G, sevidol 8G and chlorpyriphos 10G at 1 kg a.i./ha as whorl application at 35th and 65th day are also found effective.

(vi) Inundative releases of the egg parasitoid *Trichogramma chilonis* @ 50,000/ ha from first month of planting at 7-10 days interval till one month prior to harvest.

(vii) At 30th, 45th and 60th day of crop growth spray granulosis virus of *Chilo infuscatellus* (10^{-7}-10^{-8} inclusion bodies/ml) at 500 l/ha.

(viii) Release of 125 gravid females of *Sturmiopsis inferens* (Tachinidae) per ha at 45th day of crop growth.

Internode Borer (Chilo Saccharifagus Indicus)

- Damages the crop soon after internode formation and its activity continues till hatvest.
- Lodging, high dosage of nitrogen, waterlogged condition and presence of water shoots favour buildup of pest.
- Fresh borer attack is mostly found in the top five immature internodes (Fig. 8.2).
- Caterpillars bore at the nodal region and enter the stem and tunnel upwards in a characteristic spiral fashion. Entrance hole is usually plugged with excreta.
- Larvae feed and multiply in water shoots. One larvae found in a single cane damages 1-3 internodes. The length and girth of the infected internodes get reduced.

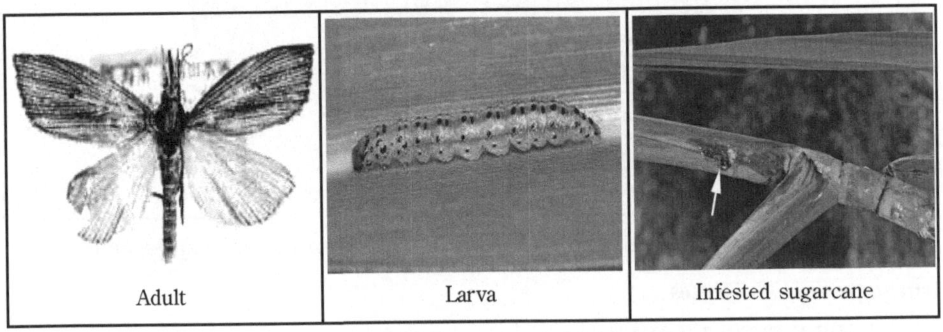

Fig. 8.2: **Showing different stages of Internode Borer in sugarcane**

Management strategies

Subsequent control measure should be adopted:

(i) Inundative release of the egg parasitoid *Trichogramma chilonis* @ 50,000 parasitoid/ha/week from the 4th up to 11th month after planting affords protection.

(ii) Use of resistant varieties are CO 285, 453, 513, 617, 853, 915, 1007, 1287, 6806 and COJ 46.

Top Borer (Scirpophaga Excerptalis)

- Water logging favours moth attack.
- Larva first tunnels into the midrib of the leaves and causes a white streak which later turns reddish brown usually in the second to fifth leaf from the top. As a result of biting across the spindle, a number of shot holes are formed in the leaf. As larva nibbles into the central core of the cane a portion of the internal tissue is eaten resulting in dead heart formation (Conlong 1994a, Chaudhry and Ansari 1988).

- Dead heart when formed is reddish brown, appears charred, and cannot be easily pulled out. In tillering phase of the crop, the attacked shoots die, side shoots (tillers) develop producing a bunchy top appearance. In the grand growth period, the crop growth is arrested, and the crown with dead heart dries and may be blown off leaving the stump (Fig. 8.3).
- Severe yield loss and quality deterioration occurs due to top borer. Depending upon the incidence level yield loss may be up to 20-30 per cent.

Fig. 8.3: **Showing different stages of *Top Borer* in sugarcane**

Management strategies

Following control measure should be adopted:

(i) The egg masses and also the infested portions of plants may be collected and destroyed during the brood emergence period.

(ii) Release of the ichneumonid parasitoid *Gambroides javensis* Rohw, has been found to be promising in Tamil Nadu.

(iii) Variety Co 419 is comparatively resistant to this borer. Other resistant varieties are CoS 767, CoJ 67 and Co 1158.

(iv) Soil application of carbofuran at 2 kg a.i. /ha or phorate at 1 kg a.i./ha for the third brood during first week of July is recommended.

Scale Insect (Melanaspis Glomerata)

- Water logging, high temperature and humidity favour buildup of scale insect population. Rainwater and high wind velocity facilitate dispersal of the pest. It spreads to new areas through seed material. Men and animals passing through the infested fields also lead to spread of the pest to the adjoining areas.
- Scales usually establish on internodes covered with leaf sheath. The leaves of infested canes show signs of tip drying and unhealthy pale green colour and with continued infestation turn yellow. Desapping leads to non-opening of leaves also, which also turn yellow and finally dry out. Nodal region is more infested than internodal region (Fig. 8.4).

Infested sugarcane from scale insect

Adults become black or brown circular scales and cover the nodal region forming a thick encrustation

Fig. 8.4: **Showing infested stages of sugarcane from scale insect**

- Infested crop losses its vigour, canes shrivel, growth is stunted and the internodal length is reduced drastically. Ultimately cane dries up. Such canes when slit open appear brownish red. Thus yield and quality suffer. The yield loss could range from negligible to total crop failure.

Management strategies

Subsequent control measure should be adopted:

(i) Selection of pests free setts.

(ii) Sett treatment with acephate 75 SP @ 1g/lt, Chlorpyriphos 50SC in 100 lit of water.

(iii) Remove lower most 2-3 dry leaves and spray crop with Chlorpyriphos 20 EC @ 5 lit in 1000 lit water/ha.

Leaf hopper (Pyrilla purpusilla Walker)

- Pyrilla is the most destructive foliage-sucking pest of sugarcane. The loss in cane yield due to pyrilla have been estimated to be around 28 per cent with about 1.6 per cent unit loss in sugar (Asre *et al.* 1983).
- Heavy rainfall followed by 75-80 per cent humidity, intermittent drought periods, high temperature (26-30°C) and wind movement favour rapid buildup of pyrilla. Other factors favouring pyrilla buildup are dense and luxuriant crop, excess nitrogen application, water logging, lodging of cane and varieties with broad and succulent leaves (Fig. 8.5).
- Adults and the nymps suck leaf sap from the under surface of the lower leaves. When the infestation is heavy, leaves turn yellowish white and wither away. Due to continuous desapping by large number of hoppers top leaves in the affected canes dry up and lateral buds germinate.

- The hoppers exude a sweet sticky fluid known as honeydew, which promotes quick and luxuriant growth of the fungus, capanodium species and as a result the leaves are completely covered by the sooty mould. This affects photosynthesis.

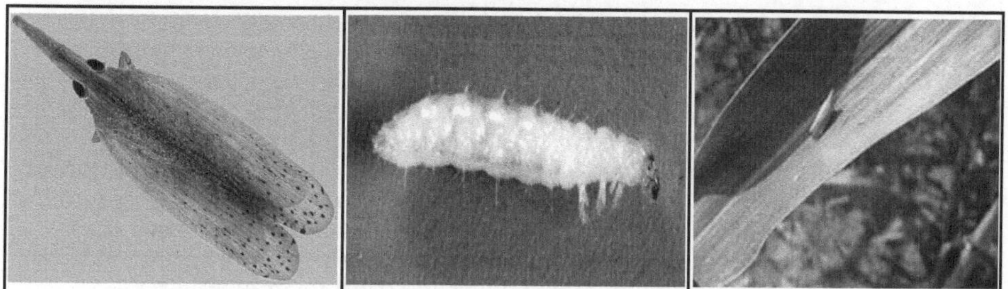

Adult of pyrilla | Larva | Pyrilla on sugarcane

Fig. 8.5: **Showing different stages of Leaf hopper**

Management strategies

Successive control measure should be adopted:

(i) Release of the lepidopteran ectoparasitoid *Epiricania melanoleuca* @ 4000-5000 cocoons or @ 4-6 lakh eggs/ha checks its multiplication.

(ii) Release of spray of Metarhizium anisopliae @ 10^{-6}-10^{-7}spores/ml is quite effective.

Termite (Odentomes obesus)

- Termites attack causes severe damage to sugarcane crop.
- It is polyphagous and found throughout the world. More serious under prolonged drought conditions and in light textured soils *viz;* sandy and sandy loam soils.
- The termites attack setts, shoots, canes and also stubbles (Fig. 8.6).
- The termites gain entry through the cut ends or through buds of the setts and feed on the soft tissue. The tunnel excavated is filled with the soil. This affects germination and thus the initial crop stand and ultimately the cane yield. The germination failure could be up to 60 per cent.
- In the stalks the termites feed on the inner tissues leaving the rind intact. The cavity formed is filled up with moist soil, having galleries, in which, they move about. The affected canes die.

Management strategies

Termites attack the planted sugarcane setts, usually from cut ends or eye buds but in severe cases internode as well. After germination, roots are attacked, eating all their contents and filling galleries with soil, finally leaves dry up and plants die. The damage can be contained by treating the setts with Markar or Fax Gras under:

Termite in sugarcane field

The trunk of the sugarcane turns red in the initial stages of the termite attack

Fig. 8.6: **Showing infested sugarcane from termite attack**

(i) *At the time of sowing:* Mix 10 kg of 'Fax GR' in 15-20 kg of dry sand and broadcast uniformly in one acre over cane setts in furrows. After this, cover the sugarcane setts with soil and given light irrigation.

(ii) *In standing crop:* Mix 8 kg Fax-GR in the 15-20 kg dry sand or in manure and broadcast it in one acre area uniformly and then apply light irrigation.

Sugarcane Woolly aphid, Ceratovacuna lanigera Zehntner

- Nymphs and adults are found on the lower surface of the sugarcane leaves and suck the cell sap and excrete 'honey dew' which is dropped on the upper surface of the lower leaves (Arakaki 1992, Chakrabarti *et al.* 1972, Gupta and Goswami 1995, Haung *et al.* 1995, Tripathi 1986).
- Honey dew encourages the growth of the fungus *Capnodium* spp., which results in black coating called 'sooty mould' on the upper surface of leaves affecting photosynthesis (Fig. 8.7).
- Due to sap sucking, yellowish white spots develop on the leaves leading to drying of leaf edges and complete drying of leaves. Severe infestation causes mottling of leaves, stunted growth, and loss in sugarcane yield and sugar recovery. Losses up to 26 per cent in sugarcane yield and 24 per cent in sugar content have been reported (Gupta and Goswami 1995, Mote *et al.* 2003).

Management strategies

Subsequent control measure should be adopted:

(i) Paired or wider row planting of sugarcane.

(ii) Release of the natural enemies *Dipha aphidivora* Meyr. or *Micromus igorotus* in shade net cages (5m × 5m) @ 50/cage and allow them to develop and disperse by removing the cages.

(iii) Release of *D. aphidivora* larvae @ 1000/ha and *M. igorotus* larvae @ 2500/ha.

(iv) Need based application of metasystox 0.0375 per cent or dimethoate 0.045 per cent in case of severe infestation without the presence of natural enemies.

Nymphs and adult of woolly aphid | Infested sugarcane from woolly aphid | 3rd and 4th instar nymphs are covered with white woolly secretion

Fig. 8.7: **Showing infested sugarcane from woolly aphid**

Whitefly (Aleurolobus Barodensis Mask)

- Water logging and nitrogen starvation cause severe out break of whiteflies. Summer droughts and dry spells during monsoon season also favour buildup of this pest.
- Varieties with broad and long leaves are more susceptible to this pest.
- The nymphs of white flies suck the sap from the under surface of leaves which turn yellow and pinkish in severe cases and gradually dry up (Fig. 8.8).
- Heavy infested leaves are covered by the sooty mould caused by the fungus, which adversely affects photosynthesis. The whitefly infestation retards cane growth and reduces sugar content.

Adult of whitefly | Symptom of Whitefly

Fig. 8.8: **Showing infested sugarcane from whitefly**

Management strategies

Following control measure should be adopted:

(i) Discourage ratooning in low lying areas and avoid water logging. Remove lower leaves containing pupae periodically.

(ii) Spray imidacloprid 0.01 per cent or acetamiprid @ 0.01 per cent after removing infested lower leaves. At least two or more sprays will be required at fortnightly intervals.

Major Diseases of Sugarcane

Red Rot (Colletotrichum Falcatum)

- Red rot is caused by a fungus Colletotrichum *Falcatum*. In India red rot is mainly a disease of the standing stalk. It is the most dreaded disease of sugarcane and for several years has been posing a serious threat to sugarcane growers and the sugar industry (Alexander 1982, 1986).
- Yellowing and drying of leaves from margin to midrib, drying of the entire top including the crown, loss of natural colour and considerable shrinkage of the stalk, appearance of reddish lesions on the rind are some of the external symptoms of red rot disease (Fig. 8.9).
- Most characteristic and diagnostic symptom of the disease is the presence of reddish discoloured patches or lesions interspersed with white horizontal patches on the internal tissue. As the diseases progresses the internal tissues become dark in colour and dry resulting in longitudinal pith cavities (Alexander and Rao 1972, Alexander *et al.* 1976, 1993).

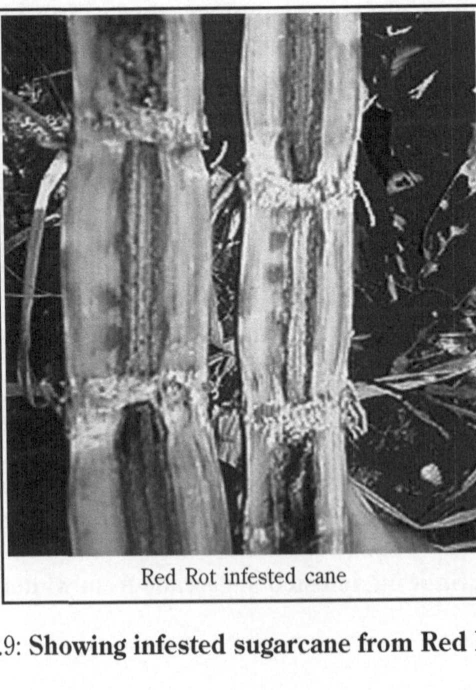

Red Rot infested cane

Fig. 8.9: **Showing infested sugarcane from Red Rot disease**

Ratoon Stunting Disease

- Ratoon stunting disease was first reported in 1956 in India and built up to alarming proportions in varieties such as: Co419, which was ultimately withdrawn from cultivation in Karnataka.
- Ratoon stunting disease has been considered as the most important cause for sugarcane varietal degeneration (Damann and Hollier 1991).
- Primary spread of the disease is through infected setts.
- Also spreads through harvesting implements contaminated with the juice of diseased canes.
- Expression of disease is more under adverse conditions.
- Progressive yield decline takes place due to the disease. Ratoon crop suffers more damage due to RSD than the plant crop (Fig. 8.10).
- Disease is known to reduce germination and yield.
- Most characteristic symptom of the infected stalks is the presence of pin head like orange coloured dots of bacteria on the internal soft tissue in the nodal region.

Ratoon Stunting Disease

Fig. 8.10: **Showing infested sugarcane from Ratoon Stunting Disease**

Smut (Ustilago Scitaminea)

- Smut disease is incited by *Ustilago scitaminea* Syd. Smut disease is endemic in most parts of the sugarcane growing tracts and more prevalent in the tropical areas. The disease is severe in neglected ratoons. Infections build up to higher levels in fatoons if the disease in the plant crop is neglected (Padmanaban 1984, Saxena and Singh 1966).

- Primary spread of the disease is through infected setts and the secondary spread is through wind borne teliospore.
- Stunting of infected stools, profuse sprouting of lateral shoots *i.e.*, tillers, reduction in internodal length, formation of thin stalks and narrow erect leaves are certain symptoms of smut (Fig. 8.11).
- Characteristic symptom is the production of long whip like structure from the terminal bud of the stalk, which is black in colour covered by thin silvery membrane. This silvery membrane ruptures releasing millions of reproductive spores of smut fungus, which are present in the form of powdery mass.
- Losses due to smut in sugarcane depend on various factors *viz*; primary or secondary infection, plant or ratoon crop that is affected and early or late infection and have been reported to range from 30-40 per cent in plant crops and even up to 70 per cent in ratoons. Sucrose content of infected cane is reduced to 3-7 per cent.

Smut Disease

Fig. 8.11: **Showing infested sugarcane from Smut disease**

Wilt (Cephalosporium Sacchari)

- Wilt disease has been reported to be a complex disease involving *Cephalosporium sacchari* Butler and *Fusarium moniliforme*.
- In wilt the affected canes simply dry out and do not break easily.
- Disease spreads through infected setts. The fungi gain entry mainly through injuries. Biotic stresses like: nematode, root borer, termite, scales, mealy bugs etc., and abiotic stresses like: drought, water logging etc., predispose the plants for wilt infection (Sharma, 1976, Singh and Singh 1974).

- Moisture stress coupled with high temperature and low humidity reduces plant resistance to wilt (Fig. 8.12).
- Typical wilt symptoms appear during monsoon and post monsoon periods.
- Affected plant appears wilted and conspicuously stunted. The crown leaves turn yellow, loose turgor and eventually withers.
- Wilt-affected canes loose their normal colour and are light in weight. The most characteristic symptom during the early stage of infection is the presence of diffused reddish brown patches on the internal tissue. Later canes become light and hallow and shrink.
- Disease reduces germination and in severe cases total cane yield losses occur due to drying up of shoots and wilting of the stalks.

Wilt infested crop of sugarcane | Healthy crop of sugarcane

Fig. 8.12: **Showing infested sugarcane from wilt and healthy crop**

Grassy Shoot Disease (Phytoplasma)

- Grassy shoot disease is caused by mycoplasma-like organisms. In India the disease was first observed in 1919 (Vasudeva 1955). It has spread to all the sugar growing areas of this country (Nas are *et al.* 2007, Samaddar and Varma 1977).
- Primary transmission of disease is through disease infected setts.
- Profuse tillering with narrow chlorotic leaves giving a grass like appearance is characteristic symptom of GSD incidence (Fig. 8.13).
- Very few tillers of GSD infected plants develop into canes, which are thin and produce white shoots from the side buds.

Grassy Shoot Disease

Fig. 8.13: **Showing infested sugarcane from Grassy Shoot disease**

Leaf Scald (Xanthomonas Albileneans)

- Leaf scald is a bacterial disease, which was first observed in India in 1962. This disease is a serious problem in varieties such as: B070, C0419, Co 1148, C07304 and CoS659.
- Disease is favoured by wet seasons, water stress due to drought, water logging and low temperatures.
- Disease symptoms appear in two phases, the chronic and acute phases (Davis 1992, Dean and Davis 1990, Rott *et al.* 1995).
- In the chronic phase, 'white pencil line' extending entire length of lamina reaching the margin of young leaves and stripes diffuse later resulting in leaf etiolation (Hoy and Grisham 1994, lrey 1987, Raid *et al.* 1989). Drying from tip onwards presents a scalded appearance and hence the name. Different degrees of chlorosis from total albinism to interveinal chlorosis in young leaves during summer, germination of buds in acropetal manner with bushy appearance in standing cane, cut open stalks showing dark red vascular strands, prominent streaks at node invariably in the side shoots, are other prominent symptoms of chronic phase (Fig. 8.14).
- In the acute phase the symptoms appear suddenly and die without any major leaf symptoms. The masking of symptoms is more common during monsoon and symptoms may appear suddenly any time during crop growth.

Leaf scald infested sugarcane

Fig. 8.14: **Showing Leaf scald disease in sugarcane**

Yellow Leaf Spot (Cercospora Koepkei)

- Prolonged rain with intermittent sunshine, waterlogged conditions and higher nitrogen doses are congenial for disease development.
- Warm humid weather favours rapid and abundant production of conidia by the pathogen and sopread of the disease.
- Characteristic symptoms are presence of small, yellow coloured, irregularly shaped spots over the leaf surface. Density of spots is minimum in the lower surface, moderate in the middle and maximum towards the tip of the leaf. Spots coalesce at late stages and cause drying of leaves. Badly affected foliage looks reddish-brown when viewed from a distance (Fig. 8.15).

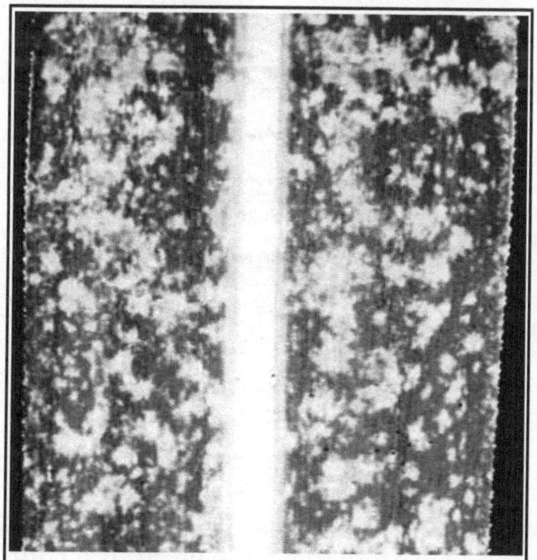

Yellow Leaf Spot on sugarcane

Fig. 8.15: **Showing Yellow Leaf Spot on sugarcane**

Eye spot (Helminthosporium sacchari)

- Usually a crop of 6-7 months is more susceptible to the disease.
- Fungus penetrates the host tissue either through stomota, bulliform cells or directly through the cuticle.
- Cloudy weather, high humidity with drizzle coupled with low night temperatures, wetting of leaves either through precipitation or dew greatly enhance disease development.
- Likewise water logging, high fertility status and excess nitrogen fertilization also favour the spread of the disease (Fig. 8.16).
- Lesions first appear as small water soaked spots, darker than the surrounding tissues. The spot becomes more elongated, resembling the shape of an â€˜eye' and turns straw coloured within a few days. Finally the central portion becomes reddish brown surrounded by straw coloured tissues. Then reddish brown streaks of â€˜runners' develop extending from the lesions towards the leaf tip along the veins. Later the spots and streaks coalesce to form large patches and causes drying of leaves.

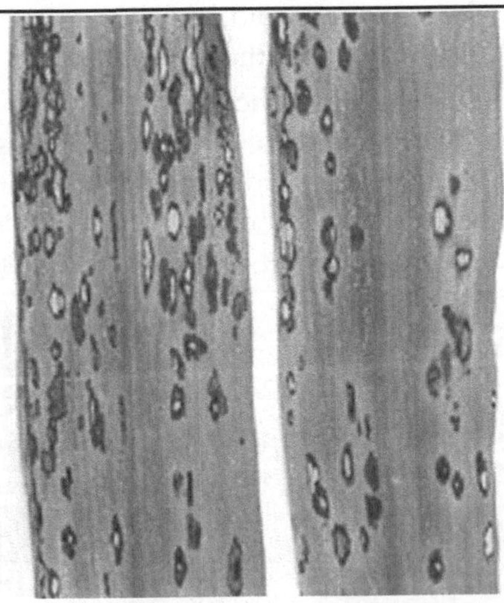

Eye spot on sugarcane

Fig. 8.16: **Showing yellow eye spots on sugarcane**

Conclusion

Sugarcane is a major commercial crop grown in tropical and subtropical regions of the country. During the last 100 years, the country has witnessed epidemics of various diseases like: red rot, smut, wilt, rust, leaf scald and yellow leaf (YLD). The damage caused to sugarcane during each epidemic would vary depend upon the nature of disease and spread of the affected varieties. Many sugarcane varieties were replaced due to their breakdown to a new disease or to a new pathogenic strain. Still, red rot remains to be the major disease of sugarcane in the country and wilt and smut are the other major diseases seriously affecting cane production in India. Use of disease resistant varieties along with healthy seed nursery programmes would form the basis to successfully manage the diseases in sugarcane. Due to long duration of sugarcane, crop attracts number of insect-pests . Damage caused by insects during germination and tillering caused yield reduction. Whereas pest attack during grand growth and ripening mars juice quality and sugar yield. In order to save the crop from insect pests' diverse integrated pest management strategy should be adopted including: predators, resistant genotypes, culture practices and finally insecticides.

REFERENCES

Alexander, K.C., Padmanaban, P., Mohanraj, D., Rao, M.M. and Viswanathan, R. (1993). Characterisation of Major Variants of Sugarcane Pathogens. Annual Report 0992-93. Sugarcane Breeding Institute, Coimbatore, India, 57-58.

Alexander, K.C. (1986). Diseases of Sugareane and their Management. *Indian Journal of Mycology Plant Pathology,* 16, 16-29.

Alexander, KC. (1982). Sugarcane Disease Management - Latest Trends in Evolving Varieties Resistant to Diseases. Sugar News, Madras, India. August, 35/82.

Alexander, K.C., Kandaswamy, P.A., Ramana Rao, T.C., Mohanraj, D. and Rao, M.M. (1976). Breeding for Horizontal Resistance to Red Rol. Annual Report (1976-77). Sugarcane Breeding Institute. Coimbatore, India.

Alexander, KC. and Rao, M.M. (1972). Comparative Evaluation of Genotypes in the Different Centres in India for Red rot and Smut. Proceedings of the Diamond Jubilee Symposium. Sugarcane Breeding Institute, Coimbatore, India.

Arakaki, N., (1992). Seasonal Occurrence of the Sugarcane Woolly Aphid, *Ceratovacuna lanigera* Zehntner (Homoptera: Aphididae), and its Predators in Sugarcane Fields of Okinawa Island. *Appl. Entomol. Zool.,* 27: 99-105.

Asre, R., Gupta, P.K. and Pawar, A.D. (1983). Control of Sugarcane Pyrilla by its Natural Enemies. *Indian Farming* 33,37-38.

Chakrabarti, S., Ghosh. A.K. and Raychaudhuri, D.N., (1972). A New Genus, A New Species and Further Records of Aphids (Homoptera: Aphididae) from the Kumaon Hills, Northwest Himalaya, India. Orient. Insects, 6: 387-400.

Chaudhry, N.A., and Ansari, M.A. (1988). Insect Pests of Sugar Cane in Pakistan. Progressive Farming, 8(4): 10-18.

Conlong, D.E. (1994a). Biological Control in Sugarcane. In: Proceedings of the Third International Conference on Tropical Entomology (ed R.K. Saini), pp. 73-101. ICIPE Science Press, Nairobi, Kenya.

Damann. K.E. and Hollier, C.A. (1991). Distribution and Incidence of Ratoon Stunting Disease in Louisiana Sugarcane. *Plant Disease,* 75. 568-571.

Davis. M.J. (1992). Increased Incidence of Leaf Scald Disease in Florida Associated with a Genetic Variant of Xanthomonas Albilineans. Sugar y Azucar, 87,34.

Dean. J.L. and Davis, MJ. (1990). Losses Caused by Ratoon Stunting Disease of Sugarcane in Florida. *Journal of the American Society Sugar Cane Technologists.* 10, 66-72.

Duke, N.H. and Eastwood D. (1997). Production Losses in Sugarcane Attached by the Giant Borer Castniomera licus (Drury) Lepidoptera: Castniidae in Guyana. Proceedings of the West Indies Sugar Technologists Association, 26: 169-176.

Gupta, M.K. and Goswami, P.K. (1995). Incidence of Sugarcane Woolly Aphid and its Effect on Yield Attributes and Juice Quality. Indian Sugar, 44: 883-885.

Haung, Y.K., Li, W.F. and Huang, Y.K., (1995). Effects of Isocarbophos on *Ceratovacuna lanigera* Zehntner. Pestic. - China, 34: 8-39.

Hoy, lW. and Grisham, M.P. (1994). Sugarcane Leaf Scald Distribution, Symptomatology, and Effect on Yield in Louisiana. *Plant Disease,* 78.1083-1087.

lrey, M.S. (1987). Effect of the Environment on Sugarcane Rust Epidemics in Florida. *Journal of the American Society of Sugar Cane Technologists,* 7, 30-35.

Khanzada, A.G. (1993). Pest Management in Sugarcane: An un-abridged Review. *Pakistan Sugar Journal.* 7(2): 11-18.

Mote, U.N. and Puri, S.N. 10 June (2003). Present Status of Sugarcane Woolly Aphid, *Ceratovacuna lanigera* Zehntner, A New Pest Problem on Sugarcane in Maharashtra. Paper presented at Brain Storming Session on Sugarcane Woolly Aphid.

Nasare, K., Yadav, Amit., Singh, A.K., Shivasharanappa, K.B., Nerkar, Y.S., and Reddy, V.S. (2007). Molecular and Symptom Analysis Reveal the Presence of New phytoplasmas Associated with Sugarcane Grassy Shoot Disease in India. *Plant Disease.* 91:1413-1418.

Padmanabhan, M.D., John, A.H., Raja, A., Natarajan, S. and Rajashekaran, S. (1992). Bioefficacy of Endosulfan for the Control of Shoot borer of Sugarcane, Chilo Infuscateleus Snellen, Bharatiya Sugar, 21: 61-64.

Padmanaban, P. (1984). Studies on smut Disease of Sugarcane caused by Ustilago scitaminea Syd. PhD thesis, Tarnil Nadu Agricultural University, Coimbatore, India, 157.

Raid, R.N., Anderson, D.L. and Coale, F.J. (1989). Yield Comparison of CP 72-121 0 and CP 78-1247 and its Relationship to Sugarcane Rust. Belle Glade EREC Res. Report EV-1989(3), 22-26.

Rott, P., Soupa, D., BruneI, Y., Feldmann. P. and Lelourmy, P. (1995). Leaf Scald (Xanth()monas albilineans) Incidence and Its Effect on yield in Seven Sugarcane Cultivars in Guadeloupe. *Plant Pathology* (in press).

Sharma, M.N. (1976). Wilt Disease of Sugarcane. Sugarcane Pathologists Newsletter, 15116, 30.

Samaddar, K., Singh, K. and Varma, A. (1977). Studies on the Vectors of Grassy Shoot Disease of Sugarcane. Annual Report, ISSR, Lucknow, India, 108.

Saxena, KM, S. and Singh, K. (1966). The Mating Pattern in Ustilago scitaminea. *Indian Phytopathology,* 19,286-289.

Singh, K. and Singh, R.P. (1974). Involvement of Acremonium sp. in wilt Syndrome of Sugarcane. Sugarcane Pathologists Newsletter, 12,24-25.

Tripathi, G.M., (1986). Record of Parasite and Predator Complex of Sugarcane Woolly Aphid, *Ceratovacuna lanigera* Zehntner in Nagaland. Indian Sugar, 44: 883-885.

Vasudeva, R.S. (1955). Stunting of Sugarcane. Commonwealth Phytopathology Newsletter, I, 11.

Williams, J.R. (1983). The Sugarcane Stem Borer (*Chilo sacchariphagus*) in Mauritius. Revue Agricole et Sucriere dei'lleMaurice, 62, 5-23.

Index

****